**PRACTICE
MAKES
PERFECT**

German
Vocabulary

PRACTICE MAKES PERFECT

German Vocabulary

Ed Swick

New York   Chicago   San Francisco   Lisbon   London   Madrid   Mexico City
Milan   New Delhi   San Juan   Seoul   Singapore   Sydney   Toronto

Copyright © 2007 by Ed Swick. All rights reserved. Printed in the United States of America. Except as permitted under the United States Copyright Act of 1976, no part of this publication may be reproduced or distributed in any form or by any means, or stored in a database or retrieval system, without the prior written permission of the publisher.

4 5 6 7 8 9 10 11 12 13 14 15 16 17 18 19 20 21 22 23 24 25 26 27 28 29   QWD/QWD   0 9

ISBN-13: 978-0-07-148285-1
ISBN-10:   0-07-148285-7
Library of Congress Control Number: 2006931665

Interior design by Village Typographers, Inc.

McGraw-Hill books are available at special quantity discounts to use as premiums and sales promotions, or for use in corporate training programs. For more information, please write to the Director of Special Sales, Professional Publishing, McGraw-Hill, Two Penn Plaza, New York, NY 10121-2298. Or contact your local bookstore.

This book is printed on acid-free paper.

Contents

Preface

Building a broad vocabulary in a second language is an important part of language learning. The richer your vocabulary is, the more skilled you become in speaking and writing your new language. Learning German is certainly no exception to this idea.

But vocabulary development and enrichment do not entail merely the memorization of word lists. Since most people gain more from studying phrases and sentences that illustrate the specific use of a word, this book provides examples that place new words in a practical context. Moreover, each word list is usually composed of items that can be "plugged into" a useful pattern sentence that is provided. For example, the nouns *shirt*, *blouse*, *pants*, and *skirt* are useful words to know. But just memorizing that list is not as useful as applying the words to practical sentences:

> Tom hates ironing *cotton shirts*.
> Mary hates ironing *silk blouses*.
> I hate ironing *pants*.
> Do you hate ironing *pleated skirts*?

Although grammar is not stressed in this book, on occasion a brief grammatical explanation is given to describe more precisely how a particular word or phrase should be used: for example, how Germans say *to like*.

As much as possible, words are illustrated in a form that shows a link or commonality among the provided words. Also, the chapters describe words that combine with others to form new words or that are derived from a base word. This is a significant concept in German, which uses many types of words as prefixes for new words:

die Sprache	*language*
die Sprachenschule	*language school*
ihre englischen Sprachkenntnisse	*her knowledge of English*
die Sprachlehre	*grammar book*
sprachlich	*linguistic*

There are twenty chapters on a variety of traditional and contemporary topics. Each one is a building block for your new German vocabulary storehouse. In each chapter are exercises that help bring your new vocabulary to life. The questions not only are general ones that anyone can answer but also involve your personal experience. In either case, you have the opportunity to put your new words to practical use.

At the end of each chapter are writing exercises that give you even more practice with the new material. If new verbs are involved, you are asked to manipulate the new verbs in various tenses. Other exercises ask you to provide an appropriate completion for a sentence. Finally, you are given a list of multiple-choice exercises that help you reinforce your new vocabulary. An answer key is located at the end of the book.

Acknowledgment

With much gratitude to Stefan Feyen for all his help and suggestions.

Alles Gute!

Family and friends

Die Familie

The German extended family consists of a variety of people, both young and old, just like any other family. Naturally, the basic family unit is made up of parents and their children. But beyond that small circle is a large group of relatives who affect family life to some degree: the extended family. Let's look at the German vocabulary that describes a typical family. First, we'll meet the oldest members of the family:

die Urgroßeltern	*great-grandparents*
der Urgroßvater	*great-grandfather*
die Urgroßmutter	*great-grandmother*
die Großeltern	*grandparents*
der Großvater	*grandfather*
die Großmutter	*grandmother*
der Schwiegervater	*father-in-law*
die Schwiegermutter	*mother-in-law*
der Senior	*senior citizen (male)*
die Seniorin	*senior citizen (female)*

Sometimes the grandparents are called by more affectionate names:

der Opa	*grandpa*
die Oma	*grandma*

The word **groß** is also used as a prefix for other members of the family who are more than a generation apart:

der Großonkel	*great-uncle*
die Großtante	*great-aunt*
der Großneffe	*great-nephew*
die Großnichte	*great-niece*
der Großenkel	*great-grandson*
die Großenkelin	*great-granddaughter*

Parents and their children are the hub of family life. They each have a specific name:

die Eltern	*parents*
der Vater	*father*
die Mutter	*mother*

Just like the grandparents, sometimes the parents are called by more affectionate names:

der Vati	daddy
die Mutti	mommy
der Papa	dad
die Mama	mom

The children have different names depending on their relationship to other members of the family:

das Kind	child
das Baby	baby
der Sohn	son
die Tochter	daughter
die Geschwister	brothers and sisters, siblings
der Bruder	brother
die Schwester	sister
der Schwiegersohn	son-in-law
die Schwiegertochter	daughter-in-law
der Enkel	grandson
die Enkelin	granddaughter

The word **Gebrüder** is a collective noun meaning *brothers*. It is no longer used to talk about a group of brothers in general. But it still functions in company names:

| Die Gebrüder Keller | *The Keller Brothers* |

When two people combine their families into one, the word **Stief** is used as a prefix:

der Stiefvater	stepfather
die Stiefmutter	stepmother
die Stiefkinder	stepchildren
der Stiefsohn	stepson
die Stieftochter	stepdaughter
die Stiefgeschwister	stepbrothers and sisters
der Stiefbruder	stepbrother
die Stiefschwester	stepsister

The families of the brothers and sisters of one's parents make up another segment of the family structure:

die Verwandten	relatives
der Onkel	uncle
die Tante	aunt
der Schwager	brother-in-law
die Schwägerin	sister-in-law
der Neffe	nephew
die Nichte	niece
der Vetter, der Cousin	cousin (male)
die Kusine, die Cousine	cousin (female)

Answer the following questions, based on your family if possible. Sample answers are provided in the answer key.

1. Wer ist neunundachtzig Jahre alt? _____

2. Wie ist der Mann Ihrer Tante mit Ihnen verwandt? _____

3. Wer sind Ihre Geschwister? _____

4. Wie ist die Tochter Ihrer Stiefmutter mit Ihnen verwandt? _____

   _____

5. Welche von Ihren Verwandten wohnen weit weg von Ihnen? _____

   _____

Let's look at how these family names can be used in some sentences:

Kennen Sie meinen Großvater?	*Do you know my grandfather?*
Kennen Sie meine Mutter?	*Do you know my mother?*
Kennen Sie meinen Schwager?	*Do you know my brother-in-law?*
Kennen Sie meine Nichte?	*Do you know my niece?*
Seine Eltern wohnen jetzt in Berlin.	*His parents live in Berlin now.*
Seine Geschwister wohnen jetzt in Berlin.	*His siblings live in Berlin now.*
Sein Onkel wohnt jetzt in Berlin.	*His uncle lives in Berlin now.*
Seine Schwester wohnt jetzt in Berlin.	*His sister lives in Berlin now.*
Wie alt ist ihr Sohn?	*How old is her son?*
Wie alt sind ihre Kinder?	*How old are her children?*
Wie alt ist ihr Neffe?	*How old is her nephew?*
Wie alt ist ihre Schwägerin?	*How old is her sister-in-law?*

A variety of adjectives can be used to describe family members. Here are several useful antonyms:

jung	*young*
alt	*old*
schön *or* hübsch	*pretty, nice* or *handsome, beautiful*
hässlich	*ugly*
groß	*big*
klein	*little*
dumm	*stupid*
klug	*smart*
gesund	*healthy, well*
krank	*sick*

The adjectives for *young* and *old* are often used in the comparative or superlative to show the relationship of age between siblings or relatives:

mein jüngerer Bruder	*my younger brother*
meine jüngste Schwester	*my youngest sister*
ihr älterer Onkel	*her older uncle*
ihre älteste Tante	*her oldest aunt*

Put an X in the blanks where an adjective and a person used together make sense.

	Vater	Tochter	Baby	Großmutter	Urgroßvater
1. alt	_____	_____	_____	_____	_____
2. am ältesten	_____	_____	_____	_____	_____
3. jung	_____	_____	_____	_____	_____
4. am jüngsten	_____	_____	_____	_____	_____
5. klein	_____	_____	_____	_____	_____

Let's look at how the adjectives can be used in some sentences:

Ist sein Bruder dumm oder klug?	*Is his brother stupid or smart?*
Ist sein Bruder groß oder klein?	*Is his brother big or little?*
Ist sein Bruder gesund oder krank?	*Is his brother healthy or sick?*
Ist sein Bruder jung oder alt?	*Is his brother young or old?*
Meine Nichte war sehr schön.	*My niece was very pretty.*
Meine Nichte war sehr jung.	*My niece was very young.*
Meine Nichte war sehr hübsch.	*My niece was very beautiful.*
Meine Nichte war sehr krank.	*My niece was very sick.*
Seine älteste Schwester arbeitet in Bonn.	*His oldest sister works in Bonn.*
Seine jüngere Schwester arbeitet in Bonn.	*His younger sister works in Bonn.*
Seine kluge Schwester arbeitet in Bonn.	*His smart sister works in Bonn.*
Seine schöne Schwester arbeitet in Bonn.	*His pretty sister works in Bonn.*

Answer the following questions, based on your family if possible. Sample answers are provided in the answer key.

1. Wie sieht Ihre Großmutter aus? _____

2. Wo arbeitet Ihr Vater? _____

3. Wer in Ihrer Familie ist krank geworden? _____

4. Wer ist älter? Ihr Vater oder Ihre Mutter? _____

Die Freunde

Friends are an important part of one's life. People share significant moments with friends and rely on friends in times of difficulty. But there are different kinds of friends and different levels of friendship. They can be very close to you, or they can be just acquaintances. German has as many words for these various kinds of friends as English does.

Remember that German has three pronouns that stand for *you*. They are **du**, **ihr**, and **Sie**. Use **du** with family members, children, and close friends, as well as in informal situations. **Ihr** is the plural of **du**. Use **Sie** in formal situations and with adults who are strangers to you. Don't forget that **Sie** is used both with a single person and with two or more persons in a formal situation. These pronouns are the clue that German differentiates close friendships and new acquaintances.

If you have just met someone, you will probably use the pronoun **Sie** with that person. There is a verb to describe this: **siezen** (*to address someone with* **Sie**). Although in English you might refer to a person you met recently as *a friend*, that would not be the case in German. **Freund** is not the appropriate word for someone you just met. Use these words instead:

der Bekannte	*acquaintance (male)*
die Bekannte	*acquaintance (female)*

Use these words with close or longtime friends:

der Freund	*friend (male)*
die Freundin	*friend (female)*

The word **Bekannte** comes from a past participle (of the verb **bekennen**), which like other participles can be used as an adjective. The adjective form is then used as a noun. But because it is an adjective, the influence of **ein** words and **der** words on adjective endings becomes important in its noun usage. Compare the following declensions, one with an **ein** word and one with a **der** word, especially noting the nominative case:

NOMINATIVE	ein Bekannter	der Bekannte
ACCUSATIVE	einen Bekannten	den Bekannten
DATIVE	einem Bekannten	dem Bekannten
GENITIVE	eines Bekannten	des Bekannten

When these different forms for the word *friend* and *acquaintance* are used in sentences, Germans immediately understand what kind of relationship exists between the parties:

Das ist ein Bekannter von mir.	*That's a friend (new acquaintance) of mine.*

It is understood that the speaker probably just met this person or still uses the pronoun **Sie** when speaking to the person. But in the following sentence, the person mentioned clearly is a close friend because the noun **Freund** is used:

Das ist ein Freund von mir.	*That's a friend of mine.*

The word **Freund** indicates that the relationship between the speaker and the *friend* is close and that they probably use the pronoun **du** when addressing one another. The verb used in such a relationship is **duzen** (*to address someone with* **du**). Compare the following sentences:

Mein Chef und ich siezen einander.	*My boss and I address each other with* **Sie**.
Gudrun und ich duzen einander seit drei Jahren.	*Gudrun and I have been addressing each other with* **du** *for three years.*

When you specifically mean that your friend is the person you are dating or is the romantic interest in your life, you also use **Freund** and **Freundin**:

Mein Freund hat einen neuen Wagen gekauft.	*My boyfriend bought a new car.*	
Wohnt deine Freundin noch in Oldenburg?	*Does your girlfriend still live in Oldenburg?*	

Let's take a look at a series of words that describe a variety of friends and acquaintances:

MALE	FEMALE	
der Nachbar	die Nachbarin	*neighbor*
der Kollege	die Kollegin	*colleague, coworker*
der Klassenkamerad	die Klassenkameradin	*classmate*
der Mitarbeiter	die Mitarbeiterin	*associate, coworker*
der Mannschaftskamerad	die Mannschaftskameradin	*teammate*
der Genosse	die Genossin	*associate, party member*
der Wirt	die Wirtin	*landlord, landlady*
der Mieter	die Mieterin	*tenant*
der Mitbewohner	die Mitbewohnerin	*fellow lodger*
der Zimmergenosse	die Zimmergenossin	*roommate*
der Klubkamerad	die Klubkameradin	*fellow member of a club*
der Landsmann	die Landsmännin	*fellow countryman, compatriot*

The following nouns do not have separate forms for males and females:

das Mitglied	*member*
der Mitmensch	*fellow human being*

ÜBUNG
1·4

*Put an X in the blanks that show what relationship you would have with the persons listed on the left. Would you say **du**, **ihr**, or **Sie** to these persons?*

	du	ihr	Sie
1. Tante und Onkel	_____	_____	_____
2. Nachbar	_____	_____	_____
3. Mieter	_____	_____	_____
4. Wirtin	_____	_____	_____
5. Zimmergenosse	_____	_____	_____
6. Neffe	_____	_____	_____
7. Freundin	_____	_____	_____
8. Chef und Klubkamerad	_____	_____	_____
9. Sohn	_____	_____	_____

Answer the following questions, based on your family if possible. Sample answers are provided in the answer key.

1. Wie heißt Ihr bester Freund? _____

2. Wie alt ist Ihre Wirtin? _____

3. In welchem Klub sind Sie Mitglied? _____

4. In welcher Stadt wohnt Ihr Chef? _____

Now let's look at a series of sentences that use some of these new nouns together with the following adjectives:

neu	*new*
schlecht	*bad*
gut	*good*
glücklich	*happy, lucky*
traurig	*sad*
faul	*lazy*
fleißig	*hardworking*

Haben Sie unsere neuen Mitglieder kennen gelernt?	*Did you meet our new members?*
Haben Sie unseren neuen Mitbewohner kennen gelernt?	*Did you meet our new fellow lodger?*
Haben Sie unsere neue Wirtin kennen gelernt?	*Did you meet our new landlady?*
Haben Sie unseren neuen Mannschafts-kameraden kennen gelernt?	*Did you meet our new team member?*
Ihre neue Klassenkameradin ist sehr faul.	*Their new classmate is very lazy.*
Ihr neuer Mieter ist sehr faul.	*Their new tenant is very lazy.*
Ihre neuen Kollegen sind sehr faul.	*Their new colleagues are very lazy.*
Ihr neuer Nachbar ist sehr faul.	*Their new neighbor is very lazy.*
Mein Klassenkamerad ist nicht faul, sondern fleißig.	*My classmate isn't lazy but hardworking.*
Mein Klassenkamerad ist nicht traurig, sondern glücklich.	*My classmate isn't sad but happy.*
Mein Klassenkamerad ist nicht schlecht, sondern gut.	*My classmate isn't bad but good.*

Fill in each blank with the name of the appropriate relative.

EXAMPLE   Der Vater meines Bruder ist mein ___*Vater*___.

1. Mein Bruder und meine Schwester sind meine _____.

2. Die Mutter meiner Mutter ist meine _____.

3. Der Sohn meines Onkels ist meine _____.

4. Die Tochter meines Onkels ist meine _____.

5. Die Mutter meines Großvaters ist meine _____.

6. Meine Schwester ist die _____ meiner Eltern.

7. Der Bruder meiner Frau ist mein _____.

8. Der Vater meines Mannes ist mein _____.

9. Die Tochter meines Mannes und seiner ersten Frau ist meine _____.

10. Die Schwester meines Vaters ist meine _____.

11. Die Tochter meines Sohnes ist meine _____.

12. Der Bruder meiner Mutter ist mein _____.

13. Die Schwester meines Vetters ist meine _____.

14. Die Mutter meines Mannes ist meine _____.

15. Der Sohn meiner Tante ist mein _____.

Fill in each blank with an appropriate antonym.

1. Tante Luise ist nicht alt, sondern _____.

2. Deine Schwester ist nicht hässlich, sondern _____.

3. Unser Neffe ist nicht dumm, sondern _____.

4. Euer Sohn ist nicht groß, sondern _____.

5. Meine Kusine ist nicht faul, sondern _____.

6. Oma ist nicht jung, sondern _____.

7. Ist Onkel Heinz krank oder _____?

8. Ist ihr Schwager hübsch oder _____?

9. Sind deine Eltern traurig oder _____?

10. Ist eure Familie klein oder _____?

Fill in each blank with a word that describes a friend or acquaintance.

EXAMPLE   Erik mietet ein Zimmer. Er ist ein ___*Mieter*___.

1. Martin und ich sind Mitglieder der Fußballmannschaft. Wir sind _____.

2. Frau Bauer hat drei Zimmer zu vermieten. Sie ist eine _____.

3. Ich bin Deutsch. Paul ist Deutsch. Er ist mein _____.

4. Herr Dorf wohnt in der Wohnung neben meiner Wohnung. Er ist mein ____   ____

5. Lisa und ich sind in der zehnten Klasse. Wir sind _____.

6. Angela hat neulich eine Wohnung gemietet. Sie ist die neueste _____ im Wohnhaus.

7. Rainer und ich wohnen in demselben Zimmer im Studentenheim. Rainer ist mein _____.

*Look at each family member or friend in the following list. Indicate how you would most likely address that person by circling **du**, **ihr**, or **Sie**.*

1. der kleine Sohn meiner Kusine	**du**	**ihr**	**Sie**
2. Oma	**du**	**ihr**	**Sie**
3. Vater und Mutter	**du**	**ihr**	**Sie**
4. Onkel Peter	**du**	**ihr**	**Sie**
5. das neue Mitglied eines Klubs	**du**	**ihr**	**Sie**
6. mein Bruder	**du**	**ihr**	**Sie**
7. Ihr Urgroßvater	**du**	**ihr**	**Sie**
8. meine Tochter	**du**	**ihr**	**Sie**
9. Herr Bauer und Frau Bauer	**du**	**ihr**	**Sie**
10. Frau Schneider, meine Wirtin	**du**	**ihr**	**Sie**
11. meine Schwägerin	**du**	**ihr**	**Sie**
12. Herr Keller, der neue Mieter	**du**	**ihr**	**Sie**
13. der Artzt und der Rechtsanwalt	**du**	**ihr**	**Sie**
14. ein Kind	**du**	**ihr**	**Sie**
15. mein Neffe und meine Nichte	**du**	**ihr**	**Sie**

Circle the letter of the word or phrase that best completes each sentence.

1. Mein Bruder ist nicht faul. Er ist sehr _____.
   a. Geschwister   b. fleißig   c. hübsch   d. ein Bekannter

2. Werner Bach ist _____ eines Tennisklubs.
   a. Mitglied   b. Wirtin   c. Zimmergenoss   d. sein Chef

3. Der Sohn meiner _____ ist mein Cousin.
   a. Schwester   b. Kusine   c. Großmutter   d. Tante

4. Er weint, denn er ist _____.
   a. jung   b. traurig   c. glücklich   d. zu Hause

5. Guten Tag, Professor Schneider. _____ noch in Bonn?
   a. Wohnen Sie   b. Kommt sie   c. Arbeitest du   d. Fahrt ihr

6. Warum _____ sie einander?
   a. siezen   b. wohnen   c. arbeiten   d. werden

7. Kinder, wo _____?
   a. seid ihr   b. sind Sie   c. bist du   d. kommen sie

8. Dieser junge Mann ist nicht hässlich, sondern _____.
   a. nett   b. faul   c. glücklich   d. hübsch

9. Andreas ist ein _____ von mir.
   a. Freundin   b. Bekannter   c. Wirt   d. Mitglied

10. Mein Onkel ist _____ als mein Vater.
    a. fleißig   b. jünger   c. am schlechtesten   d. klein

Occupations

Berufe

As men and women enter their career fields, they become known by a term that identifies what they do for a living: a *lawyer*, an *engineer*, a *tailor*, and so on. In English, we avoid identifying a specific gender with a specific occupation. When someone calls a restaurant employee a *server*, we don't know whether that person is male or female. This is true of many English words: a *teacher*, a *doctor*, a *salesperson*, and so on.

But German is different. The makeup of the language makes it necessary to identify the gender of people in their professions. It is quite common to add the suffix **-in** to a masculine noun for a profession in order to identify a female in the same profession. Let's look at a few:

MALES	FEMALES	
der Arbeiter	die Arbeiterin	*laborer, worker*
der Arzt	die Ärztin	*physician*
der Bauer	die Bäuerin	*farmer*
der Briefträger	die Briefträgerin	*mail carrier*
der Bürgermeister	die Bürgermeisterin	*mayor*
der Dolmetscher	die Dolmetscherin	*interpreter*
der Fotograf	die Fotografin	*photographer*
der Gärtner	die Gärtnerin	*gardener*
der Kanzler	die Kanzlerin	*chancellor*
der Lehrer	die Lehrerin	*teacher*
der Makler	die Maklerin	*real estate agent*
der Mechaniker	die Mechanikerin	*mechanic*
der Professor	die Professorin	*professor*
der Richter	die Richterin	*judge*
der Sänger	die Sängerin	*singer*
der Schaffner	die Schaffnerin	*conductor*
der Schauspieler	die Schauspielerin	*actor*
der Taxifahrer	die Taxifahrerin	*taxi driver*
der Verkäufer	die Verkäuferin	*salesperson*

When you ask what someone's occupation is, you say:

Was machen Sie beruflich?   *What is your occupation?*

or

Was sind Sie von Beruf?

You reply:

Ich bin Taxifahrer.	*I'm a taxi driver.*

or

Ich bin Richterin.	*I'm a judge.*

Notice that you don't need an indefinite article (**ein, eine**) in the German response.

Each of these occupations has specific tasks. If you say that "someone is treating a patient," you must be talking about a physician, not an actor. Let's look at the specific actions of each of these professions:

Was tut ein Arbeiter?	*What does a laborer (worker) do?*
Ein Arbeiter arbeitet in einer Fabrik.	*A laborer works in a factory.*
Ein Arbeiter ist ein Handwerker und macht Zimmerhandwerk oder Tischlerhandwerk.	*A worker is a tradesman and does carpentry or builds furniture.*
Was tut eine Ärztin?	*What does a physician do?*
Eine Ärztin behandelt kranke Leute.	*A physician treats sick people.*
Eine Ärztin heilt Menschen von einer Krankheit.	*A physician heals people of a disease.*
Was tut ein Bauer?	*What does a farmer do?*
Ein Bauer pflanzt Gemüse und Getreide.	*A farmer plants vegetables and grain.*
Ein Bauer pflegt das Vieh.	*A farmer tends the livestock.*
Was tut eine Briefträgerin?	*What does a mail carrier do?*
Eine Briefträgerin sortiert die Post.	*A mail carrier sorts the mail.*
Eine Briefträgerin bringt Briefe.	*A mail carrier brings letters.*
Was tut ein Bürgermeister?	*What does a mayor due?*
Ein Bürgermeister leitet die städtische Verwaltung.	*A mayor heads the city administration.*
Ein Bürgermeister vertritt die Einwohner einer Stadt.	*A mayor represents the citizens of a city.*
Was tut eine Dolmetscherin?	*What does an interpreter do?*
Eine Dolmetscherin übersetzt Sprachen.	*An interpreter translates languages.*
Eine Dolmetscherin kann mehr als eine Sprache sprechen.	*An interpreter can speak more than one language.*
Was tut ein Fotograf?	*What does a photographer do?*
Ein Fotograf fotografiert Menschen und Landschaften.	*A photographer photographs people and landscapes.*
Ein Fotograf entwickelt Filme.	*A photographer develops film.*
Was tut eine Gärtnerin?	*What does a gardener do?*
Eine Gärtnerin pflegt einen Garten.	*A gardener tends a garden.*
Eine Gärtnerin pflanzt Blumen.	*A gardener plants flowers.*
Was tut ein Kanzler?	*What does a chancellor do?*
Ein Kanzler vertritt das Land.	*A chancellor represents the country.*
Ein Kanzler trifft sich mit anderen Staatsoberhäuptern.	*A chancellor meets with other heads of state.*
Was tut eine Lehrerin?	*What does a teacher do?*
Eine Lehrerin arbeitet in einer Schule.	*A teacher works in a school.*

Eine Lehrerin lehrt Lesen, Schreiben und Rechnen.	A teacher teaches reading, writing, and arithmetic.
Was tut ein Makler?	What does a real estate agent do?
Ein Makler vermittelt jemandem eine Wohnung.	A real estate agent finds someone an apartment.
Ein Makler verkauft Häuser.	A real estate agent sells houses.
Was tut eine Mechanikerin?	What does a mechanic do?
Eine Mechanikerin arbeitet in einer Werkstatt.	A mechanic works in a repair shop.
Eine Mechanikerin repariert Autos.	A mechanic repairs cars.
Was tut ein Professor?	What does a professor do?
Ein Professor unterrichtet an einer Universität.	A professor teaches at a university.
Ein Professor hält Vorlesungen.	A professor gives lectures.
Was tut eine Richterin?	What does a judge do?
Eine Richterin entscheidet einen Fall.	A judge decides a case.
Eine Richterin verurteilt Verbrecher.	A judge sentences criminals.
Was tut ein Sänger?	What does a singer do?
Ein Sänger singt Lieder.	A singer sings songs.
Ein Sänger begleitet sich auf dem Klavier.	A singer accompanies himself on the piano.
Was tut eine Schaffnerin?	What does a conductor do?
Eine Schaffnerin arbeitet bei der Eisenbahn.	A conductor works for the railroad.
Eine Schaffnerin kontrolliert die Fahrkarten.	A conductor checks the tickets.
Was tut ein Schauspieler?	What does an actor do?
Ein Schauspieler spielt eine Rolle auf der Bühne.	An actor plays a role on the stage.
Ein Schauspieler spielt in einem Film mit.	An actor performs in a movie.
Was tut eine Taxifahrerin?	What does a taxi driver do?
Eine Taxifahrerin fährt ein Taxi.	A taxi driver drives a taxi.
Eine Taxifahrerin fährt Fahrgäste zum Flughafen.	A taxi driver drives passengers to the airport.
Was tut ein Verkäufer?	What does a salesperson do?
Ein Verkäufer arbeitet in einem Kaufhaus.	A salesperson works in a department store.
Ein Verkäufer berät Kunden und verkauft verschiedene Sachen.	A salesperson advises customers and sells various things.

ÜBUNG
2·1

Answer the following questions, based on your life if possible. Sample answers are provided in the answer key.

1. Was sind Sie von Beruf? _____

2. Sind Ihre Verwandten Arbeiter oder Bauern? _____

3. Wohnen Sie in einem Haus oder in einer Wohnung? _____

4. Wer kann Ihnen eine neue Wohnung vermitteln? _____

5. Wer kontrolliert die Fahrkarten? _____

An der Arbeit

As people in their various occupations carry out their daily functions, they use a variety of materials and tools. Let's look at some of them:

der Arbeiter, die Arbeiterin
die Schaufel	*shovel*
der Pinsel	*paintbrush*
die Axt	*axe*

der Arzt, die Ärztin
das Thermometer	*thermometer*
das Heilmittel, die Medizin	*medicine*
die Spritze	*injection*

der Bauer, die Bäuerin
der Traktor	*tractor*
die Ernte	*harvest*
der Stall, die Scheune	*barn*

der Briefträger, die Briefträgerin
die Ansichtskarte	*picture postcard*
die Postkarte	*postcard*
das Paket	*package*

der Bürgermeister, die Bürgermeisterin
das Rathaus	*city hall*
das Gesetz	*law*
die Polizei	*police*

der Dolmetscher, die Dolmetscherin
das Wörterbuch	*dictionary*
die Fremdsprache	*foreign language*
die Übersetzung	*translation*

der Fotograf, die Fotografin
der Fotoapparat	*camera*
die Aufnahme	*snapshot*
das Dia	*slide*

der Gärtner, die Gärtnerin
der Spaten	*spade*
die Samen	*seeds*
das Blumenbeet	*flower bed*

der Kanzler, die Kanzlerin
das Grundgesetz	*constitution*
die Regierung	*government*
die Wahl	*election*

der Lehrer, die Lehrerin
das Lehrbuch	*textbook*
die Prüfung	*test*
das Klassenzimmer	*classroom*

der Makler, die Maklerin
das Mietshaus	*apartment building*
die Hypothek	*mortgage*
die Anzahlung	*down payment*

der Mechaniker, die Mechanikerin
der Hammer	*hammer*
der Schraubenzieher	*screwdriver*
die Zange	*pliers*

der Professor, die Professorin
der Hörsaal	*lecture hall, auditorium*
die Forschung	*research*
das Examen	*exam*

der Richter, die Richterin
das Gericht	*court*
der Angeklagte	*defendant*
das Urteil	*judgment*

der Sänger, die Sängerin
die Musik	*music*
die Stimme	*voice*
das Konzert	*concert*

der Schaffner, die Schaffnerin
die Straßenbahn	*streetcar*
die U-Bahn	*subway*
die Haltestelle	*stop*

der Schauspieler, die Schauspielerin
das Theater	*theater*
die Vorstellung	*performance*
der Beifall	*applause*

der Taxifahrer, die Taxifahrerin
der Verkehr	*traffic*
die Adresse, die Anschrift	*address*
das Trinkgeld	*tip*

der Verkäufer, die Verkäuferin
der Ausverkauf	*sale*
die Quittung	*receipt*
die Registrierkasse	*cash register*

ÜBUNG
2·2

Place an X in the blanks that identify the persons who would use the tools and items listed on the left.

	Arzt	Bauer	Fotograf	Lehrer	Mechaniker	Sänger
1. Prüfung	_____	_____	_____	_____	_____	_____
2. Aufnahme	_____	_____	_____	_____	_____	_____
3. Musik	_____	_____	_____	_____	_____	_____
4. Hammer	_____	_____	_____	_____	_____	_____
5. Zange	_____	_____	_____	_____	_____	_____
6. Spritze	_____	_____	_____	_____	_____	_____
7. Forschung	_____	_____	_____	_____	_____	_____
8. Ernte	_____	_____	_____	_____	_____	_____

Answer the following questions, based on your life if possible. Sample answers are provided in the answer key.

1. Haben Sie in einem großen Kaufhaus gearbeitet? _____

2. Haben Sie einen Freund, der Schauspieler ist?_____

3. Was für Werkzeug benutzt ein Mechaniker?_____

In each blank provided, write the female form of each occupation.

1. der Sekretär (*secretary*) _____

2. der Präsident (*president*) _____

3. der Beamte (*official*) _____

4. der Direktor (*director*) _____

5. der Leiter (*leader*) _____

In each blank provided, write the male form of each occupation.

6. die Dirigentin (*conductor*) _____

7. die Chirurgin (*surgeon*) _____

8. die Pflegerin (*nurse*) _____

9. die Köchin (*cook*) _____

10. die Läuferin (*runner*) _____

Fill in each blank with the appropriate occupation, using the correct gender.

1. Ein _____ behandelt kranke Leute.

2. Eine _____ singt im Chor.

3. Der _____ und seine Frau pflegen das Vieh.

4. Die _____ leitet die städtische Verwaltung.

5. Eine _____ wird sich mit anderen Staatsoberhäuptern treffen.

6. Der _____ bringt uns Briefe.

7. Die _____ wird die Farbfilme entwickeln lassen.

8. Der _____ fuhr den Fahrgast zum Stadtzentrum.

9. Die _____ muss einen komplizierten Fall entscheiden.

10. Der _____ vermittelte Herrn Bauer eine neue Wohnung.

11. Dieser _____ ist ein Handwerker.

12. Der _____ kann den alten VW nicht reparieren.

13. Die _____ hat unsere Fahrkarten schon kontrolliert.

14. Ihre _____ kann vier Sprachen sprechen.

15. Ein junger _____ spielt die Rolle des Faust.

Answer each question with the appropriate occupation, male or female.

1. Wer hat dir die Quittung gegeben? _____

2. Wer hält eine Vorlesung im großen Hörsaal? _____

3. Wer vertritt die Einwohner dieser Stadt? _____

4. Wer arbeitet mit einer Schaufel? _____

5. Wer gibt dem Kranken eine Spritze? _____

6. Wer bringt die Ernte in die Scheune? _____

7. Wer hat uns das Paket gebracht? _____

8. Wer hört lauten Beifall im Theater? _____

9. Wer hat die Anzahlung für das neue Haus angenommen? _____

10. Wer hat das Getreide gepflanzt? _____

11. Wer braucht einen größeren Schraubenzieher? _____

12. Wer gibt dem Patienten das Heilmittel? _____

13. Wer arbeitet im Gericht? _____

14. Wer bereitet eine Prüfung vor? _____

15. Wer arbeitet im Rathaus? _____

Circle the letter of the word or phrase that best completes each sentence.

1. Er hat uns eine große Wohnung in der Stadt _____.
   a. verloren   b. vermittelt   c. gebracht   d. gesehen

2. Der Bauer muss _____ pflegen.
   a. das Vieh   b. vom Feld   c. in der Scheune   d. Gärtnerin

3. Die Pflegerin hat mir eine _____ gegeben.
   a. Getreide   b. Hammer   c. Registrierkasse   d. Spritze

4. _____ wachsen weiße Nelken und rote Rosen.
   a. Der Gärtner   b. Im Blumenbeet   c. Die Bäuerin   d. Vom Stall

5. Wir haben sehr lange an der _____ gewartet.
   a. Schaffnerin   b. Haltestelle   c. Kaufhaus   d. Mietshaus

6. Der Kanzler muss das _____ schützen.
   a. Bürgermeisterin   b. Ernte   c. Polizei   d. Grundgesetz

7. Die letzte _____ des Films war am Freitag.
   a. Vorstellung   b. Rolle   c. Schauspieler   d. Theater

8. Viele Studenten waren schon im _____.
   a. Universität   b. Scheune   c. Eisenbahn   d. Hörsaal

9. Durch seine _____ ist der Professor berühmt geworden.
   a. Gesetz   b. Forschung   c. Spaten   d. Angeklagte

10. Der Lehrer findet die alten _____ im Schrank.
    a. Lehrbücher   b. Professorin   c. Zange   d. Fahrgast

11. Der Schaffner vergisst meine Fahrkarte zu _____.
    a. arbeiten   b. begleiten   c. entscheiden   d. kontrollieren

12. Frau Schneider hat den Kunden gut _____.
    a. repariert   b. verkauft   c. beraten   d. gekauft

13. Sie hat in einem neuen Film _____.
    a. aufgeführt   b. gesehen   c. gepflegt   d. gefahren

14. Der Richter hat ihren Fall schon _____.
    a. vertritt   b. entschieden   c. geführt   d. begleitet

15. Der Kanzler hat sich mit dem Präsidenten _____.
    a. verurteilt   b. aufgeführt   c. getroffen   d. repariert

Around the house

A German apartment or house has the same kinds of rooms as found in other European or American homes. Some living spaces can be described in the following ways:

eine geräumige Wohnung	*a roomy apartment*
ein zweigeschossiges Haus	*a two-story house*

Das Zimmer

Was für Zimmer habt ihr in eurem neuen Haus?	*What kind of rooms do you have in your new house?*
der Flur	*hallway*
das Wohnzimmer	*living room*
das Esszimmer	*dining room*
das Schlafzimmer	*bedroom*
die Küche	*kitchen*
das Badezimmer	*bathroom*
der Keller	*cellar, basement*
die Dachkammer	*attic*
die Toilette	*toilet*
das WC	*toilet (water closet)*
das Klo	*toilet, john*

Note that **das Badezimmer** is a room for bathing or showering. **Die Toilette** is the room that has a toilet. In public places, you cannot ask for **das Badezimmer** if you are looking for the restroom. Ask for **die Toilette** or **das WC**.

Die Möbel

Was für Möbel stehen im Flur?	*What kind of furniture is there in the hallway?*
Im Flur gibt es nur eine Garderobe.	*There's only a coatrack in the hallway.*
Was für Möbel stehen im Wohnzimmer?	*What kind of furniture is there in the living room?*
Im Wohnzimmer haben wir ...	*In the living room we have . . .*
... ein Sofa.	*. . . a sofa.*
... einen Sessel.	*. . . an armchair.*
... einen kleinen Tisch.	*. . . a small table.*
... zwei Stühle.	*. . . two chairs.*
... einen Fernsehapparat.	*. . . a TV.*

... ein Klavier.	. . . a piano.
... eine Stehlampe.	. . . a floor lamp.

Was für Möbel stehen im Esszimmer?

What kind of furniture is there in the dining room?

Im Esszimmer ...
... steht ein langer Esstisch.
... stehen sechs Stühle.
... steht ein Büffet.
... steht ein Aquarium.
... hängt ein Kronleuchter.

In the dining room . . .
. . . there is a long dining table.
. . . there are six chairs.
. . . there is a sideboard.
. . . there is an aquarium.
. . . there is a chandelier.

Was für Möbel habt ihr im Schlafzimmer?

What kind of furniture do you have in the bedroom?

Im Schlafzimmer haben wir ...
... zwei Betten.
... einen Kleiderschrank.
... einen Schreibtisch.
... einen Stuhl.
... zwei Lampen.

In the bedroom we have . . .
. . . two beds.
. . . a wardrobe.
. . . a desk.
. . . a chair.
. . . two lamps.

Was für Möbel habt ihr in der Küche?

What kind of furniture do you have in the kitchen?

In der Küche haben wir ...
... einen Kühlschrank.
... einen Herd.
... ein Waschbecken.

In the kitchen we have . . .
. . . a refrigerator.
. . . a stove.
. . . a sink.

Was gibt es im Badezimmer?
Im Badezimmer gibt es ...
... eine Badewanne.
... eine Dusche.
... ein Waschbecken.

What is there in the bathroom?
In the bathroom there is . . .
. . . a bathtub.
. . . a shower.
. . . a sink.

Was habt ihr im Keller?
Im Keller haben wir ...
... die Waschmaschine.
... den Trockner.
... die Heizung.

What do you have in the cellar?
In the cellar we have . . .
. . . the washing machine.
. . . the dryer.
. . . the heating system.

Was gibt es in der Dachkammer?
In der Dachkammer gibt es ...
... einen Schrankkoffer.
... drei Koffer.
... einen alten Bücherschrank.

What is there in the attic?
In the attic there . . .
. . . is a travel trunk.
. . . are three suitcases.
. . . is an old bookcase.

In der Toilette gibt es eine Toilette.
Das WC ist hier links.
Wo ist das Klo?
Das Klo ist um die Ecke.

In the bathroom there's a toilet.
The restroom is here on the left.
Where's the john?
The john is around the corner.

Answer the following questions, based on your home if possible. Sample answers are provided in the answer key.

1. Wie viele Schlafzimmer haben Sie in Ihrem Haus? _____

2. Was gibt es in Ihrem Keller? _____

3. In welchem Zimmer ist der Bücherschrank? _____

4. Wie viele Stühle haben Sie im Esszimmer? _____

5. Haben Sie eine Badewanne und eine Dusche im Badezimmer? _____

_____

Place an X in the blanks that identify the rooms where you would find the furniture listed on the left.

	Badezimmer	Wohnzimmer	Küche	Schlafzimmer	Keller
1. Doppelbett	_____	_____	_____	_____	_____
2. Sessel	_____	_____	_____	_____	_____
3. WC	_____	_____	_____	_____	_____
4. Herd	_____	_____	_____	_____	_____
5. Dusche	_____	_____	_____	_____	_____
6. Badewanne	_____	_____	_____	_____	_____
7. Stehlampe	_____	_____	_____	_____	_____
8. Kleiderschrank	_____	_____	_____	_____	_____
9. Heizung	_____	_____	_____	_____	_____
10. Schreibtisch	_____	_____	_____	_____	_____

In each of the rooms of an apartment or house, people carry out specific functions. If someone is making breakfast, it surely must be in the kitchen and not in the bedroom or any other room. Let's look at some of the actions that take place in each room:

Aufhängen

Im Flur hängt man seinen Mantel an der Gardcrobe auf.

In the hallway you hang up your coat on the coatrack.

Empfangen, fernsehen

Im Wohnzimmer empfängt die Familie Gäste.

The family receives guests in the living room.

Im Wohnzimmer sehen die Kinder fern.

The children watch TV in the living room.

Sammeln, feiern

Im Esszimmer sammelt sich die Familie zum Abendessen.	*The family gathers in the dining room for dinner.*
Im Esszimmer feiert die Familie einen Geburtstag.	*The family celebrates a birthday in the dining room.*

Schlafen, ein Nickerchen machen

Im Schlafzimmer schlafen die beiden Brüder.	*The two brothers sleep in the bedroom.*
Im Schlafzimmer macht unser Vater ein Nickerchen.	*Our father takes a nap in the bedroom.*

Frühstücken, vorbereiten, kochen

In der Küche frühstückt die Familie.	*The family has breakfast in the kitchen.*
In der Küche bereitet man das Essen vor.	*You prepare food in the kitchen.*
In der Küche kocht man.	*You cook in the kitchen.*

Baden, unter die Dusche gehen, waschen

Im Badezimmer badet man.	*You bathe in the bathroom.*
Im Badezimmer geht man unter die Dusche.	*You take a shower in the bathroom.*
Im Badezimmer wäscht man sich das Gesicht und die Hände.	*You wash your face and hands in the bathroom.*

Waschen, trocknen

Im Keller wäscht man die Wäsche in der Waschmaschine.	*You wash clothes in the washing machine in the basement.*
Im Keller kann man die Wäsche trocknen.	*You can dry the clothes in the basement.*

Aufbewahren

In der Dachkammer kann man alte Kleidung und Möbel aufbewahren.	*You can store old clothing and furniture in the attic.*

ÜBUNG
3·3

Answer the following questions, based on your home if possible. Sample answers are provided in the answer key.

1. Wo bewahren Sie Ihre Bücher auf? _____

2. Wo hängen Sie Ihre Jacke und Ihren Hut auf? _____

3. In welchem Zimmer frühstückt Ihre Familie? _____

4. In welchem Zimmer sieht Ihre Familie fern? _____

5. In welchem Zimmer kann man ein Nickerchen machen? _____

_____

For each item or piece of furniture on the left, write in the blank the name of the room where you would find it: **der Flur, das Wohnzimmer, das Esszimmer, das Schlafzimmer, die Küche, das Badezimmer, der Keller,** *and* **die Dachkammer.**

1. das Doppelbett _____

2. der Fernsehapparat _____

3. der Herd _____

4. der Esstisch _____

5. die Garderobe _____

6. das Sofa _____

7. der Sessel _____

8. die Stehlampe _____

9. der Kühlschrank _____

10. die Waschmaschine _____

11. der Kronleuchter _____

12. der Kleiderschrank _____

13. der Schrankkoffer _____

14. das Büffet _____

15. der Schreibtisch _____

16. die Heizung _____

17. die Dusche _____

18. der Trockner _____

19. das Waschbecken _____

20. ein alter Koffer _____

Rewrite each of the following sentences in the past, present perfect, and future tenses.

EXAMPLE   Er wohnt in Stuttgart.

PAST   *Er wohnte in Stuttgart.*

PRESENT PERFECT *Er hat in Stuttgart gewohnt.*

FUTURE   *Er wird in Stuttgart wohnen.*

1. Wo kann man seinen Regenmantel aufhängen?

   PAST   _____

   PRESENT PERFECT _____

   FUTURE   _____

2. Wir frühstücken jeden Morgen in der Küche.

   PAST   _____

   PRESENT PERFECT _____

   FUTURE   _____

3. Wir empfangen Gäste in diesem großen Zimmer.

   PAST   _____

   PRESENT PERFECT _____

   FUTURE   _____

4. Muss Ihr Sohn auch kochen?

   PAST   _____

   PRESENT PERFECT _____

   FUTURE   _____

5. Mein Vater hilft meiner Mutter die Wäsche trocknen.

   PAST   _____

   PRESENT PERFECT _____

   FUTURE   _____

6. Wer geht unter die Dusche?

   PAST   _____

   PRESENT PERFECT _____

   FUTURE   _____

7. Im Wohnzimmer feiern wir Weihnachten.

PAST   _____

PRESENT PERFECT   _____

FUTURE   _____

8. Die Kinder waschen sich die Hände.

PAST   _____

PRESENT PERFECT   _____

FUTURE   _____

Fill in the blanks with the appropriate words.

1. Die neuen Kleider und Röcke sind im _____.

2. Hängt mein Regenmantel an der _____?

3. Erik steht am _____ und wäscht sich das Gesicht.

4. Sie bewahren alte Möbel in der _____ auf.

5. Es ist dunkel im Wohnzimmer. Wo ist eine _____?

6. Jeden Abend sammeln sie sich im _____.

7. Ist das Wasser nicht kalt? Du sitzt schon eine halbe Stunde in der _____.

8. Angela setzt sich an den _____ und fängt an zu schreiben.

9. Ich mag kaltes Bier. Sind die Flaschen im _____?

10. Meine Tante sitzt am _____ und spielt ein altes Lied.

11. Wer hat diese Suppe _____? Sie ist kalt!

12. Jedes Kind hat sein eigenes _____.

13. Die Fische im _____ sind tot!

14. Diese Wohnung ist groß. Sie ist sehr _____.

15. Wir können nicht kochen! Der _____ ist kaputt!

Circle the letter of the word or phrase that best completes each sentence.

1. Die _____ sammeln sich im Wohnzimmer.
   a. Stehlampe   b. Gäste   c. Möbel   d. Familie

2. Maria singt und begleitet sich auf dem _____.
   a. Stuhl   b. Küche   c. Badewanne   d. Klavier

3. Wir _____ um 8 Uhr.
   a. aufhängen   b. frühstücken   c. bewahren auf   d. trocknen

4. _____ du wieder fern? Du solltest ein Buch lesen.
   a. Feierst   b. Kochst   c. Siehst   d. Gehst

5. Hier ist ein _____. Bitte setzen Sie sich!
   a. Tisch   b. Stuhl   c. Dusche   d. Herd

6. Jeden Morgen gehe ich unter die _____.
   a. Küche   b. alten Lehrbücher c. Dusche   d. Waschbecken

7. Ich habe _____ in meinem Schlafzimmer.
   a. eine Küche   b. die Badewanne   c. einen Schreibtisch d. der Herd

8. Ich hänge meinen Regenmantel _____ auf.
   a. unter dem   b. an der Garderobe c. schlechtes Wetter d. am
      Esstisch   Waschbecken

9. Ist der neue _____ im Keller?
   a. Geschwister   b. Schlafzimmer   c. Doppelbett   d. Trockner

10. Die ganze Familie _____ in der Küche.
    a. treffen   b. sammelte sich   c. bewahrte auf   d. empfangen

11. Unter dem Bild steht ein _____.
    a. altes Klavier   b. großes Wohnzimmer c. neue Waschmaschine d. kleinen Herd

12. Der alte Bücherschrank ist _____.
    a. in der   b. an der Gardrobe   c. unter der Dusche d. im
       Kühlschrank   Dachkammer

13. Kann Ihr Mann wirklich _____?
    a. wäscht sich   b. kochen   c. sammelt sich   d. aufhängen

14. Was für _____ gibt es im Wohnzimmer?
    a. Möbel   b. Kühlschrank   c. Stehlampe   d. das Sofa

15. Ist die Garderobe _____?
    a. aufgehängt   b. in der   c. ein Waschbecken   d. im Flur
                            Waschmaschine

Animals

For millennia, human beings have interacted with animals. Sometimes those interactions were predatory—with either the human or the animal being predator or prey.

das Raubtier	*predator*
die Beute	*prey*

As humans and animals began to trust one another, and as they discovered a mutual benefit in serving one another, animals were invited into human homes and became part of the family group. These *domesticated animals* warned the family of intruders, helped protect the family from invaders, and often became an important element of the hunt.

Today, many families reside with pets that are often treated like humans and are truly members of the family.

Die Haustiere

Some of the most common **Haustiere** (*pets*) are as follows:

der Hund	*dog*
die Hündin	*female dog*
das Hündchen	*puppy*
der Kater	*tomcat*
die Katze	*cat*
das Kätzchen	*kitten*
das Kaninchen	*rabbit*
die Maus	*mouse*
die Ratte	*rat*
der Hamster	*hamster*
der Igel	*hedgehog*
die Schlange	*snake*
der Kanarienvogel	*canary*
der Papagei	*parrot*

Pets come in all kinds of sizes, shapes, and colors. Let's describe some of them:

Wie groß ist Ihr Hund?	*How big is your dog?*
Mein Schäferhund ist sehr groß und wiegt 30 Kilo.	*My German shepherd is very big and weighs 30 kilograms.*
Mein Dackel ist klein und wiegt 6 Kilo.	*My dachshund is small and weighs 6 kilograms.*

Wie groß ist Ihre Katze?	*How big is your cat?*
Meine Perserkatze ist sehr klein und wiegt nur 4 Kilo.	*My Persian cat is very little and weighs only 4 kilograms.*
Meine Tigerkatze ist ziemlich klein und wiegt 5 Kilo.	*My tabby cat is rather small and weighs 5 kilograms.*
Sind Hamster dick oder dünn?	*Are hamsters fat or thin?*
Hamster sind dick.	*Hamsters are fat.*
Haben Igel ein dunkles oder ein helles Fell?	*Do hedgehogs have dark or light fur?*
Igel haben ein dunkles Fell.	*Hedgehogs have dark fur.*
Sind Schlangen lang oder kurz?	*Are snakes long or short?*
Schlangen sind lang.	*Snakes are long.*
Welche Farbe hat Ihr Kaninchen?	*What color is your rabbit?*
Mein Kaninchen ist weiß.	*My rabbit is white.*
Welche Farbe hat Ihre Maus?	*What color is your mouse?*
Meine Maus ist grau.	*My mouse is gray.*
Welche Farbe hat Ihre Ratte?	*What color is your rat?*
Meine Ratte ist schwarz.	*My rat is black.*
Welche Farbe hat Ihr Kanarienvogel?	*What color is your canary?*
Mein Kanarienvogel ist gelb.	*My canary is yellow.*
Welche Farbe hat Ihr Papagei?	*What color is your parrot?*
Mein Papagei ist grün und rot.	*My parrot is green and red.*
Welches Haustier ist braun?	*What pet is brown?*
Hunde sind braun.	*Dogs are brown.*

ÜBUNG
4·1

Place an X in the blanks that tell what color(s) the pets listed on the left can be.

	braun	gelb	grau	grün	rot	schwarz
1. Hund	_____	_____	_____	_____	_____	_____
2. Katze	_____	_____	_____	_____	_____	_____
3. Kaninchen	_____	_____	_____	_____	_____	_____
4. Maus	_____	_____	_____	_____	_____	_____
5. Ratte	_____	_____	_____	_____	_____	_____
6. Igel	_____	_____	_____	_____	_____	_____
7. Schlange	_____	_____	_____	_____	_____	_____
8. Kanarienvogel	_____	_____	_____	_____	_____	_____
9. Papagei	_____	_____	_____	_____	_____	_____

The German question that asks *what color* an animal is occurs in a slightly different form from the answer. Look at the following sentences:

Welche Farbe **hat** Ihre Katze?	*What color **is** your cat?*
Meine Katze **ist** Schwarz.	*My cat **is** black.*

Answer the following questions. Sample answers are provided in the answer key.

1. Welche Farbe hat ein Igel? _____

2. Welches Haustier ist sehr lang und grün? _____

3. Ist ein Hündchen groß oder klein? _____

4. Welches Haustier kann singen? _____

5. Welches Haustier kann sprechen? _____

Not all domesticated animals live with a family. Farm animals are domesticated, but they live separately from the family. Humans rely on such animals for many of the products they produce or for the work they can carry out.

Das Nutzvieh

Some of the important **Nutzvieh** (*farm animals*) follow:

das Pferd	*horse*
die Kuh	*cow*
der Esel	*donkey*
das Schwein	*pig*
das Schaf	*sheep*
die Ziege	*goat*
die Ente	*duck*
die Henne	*hen*
die Gans	*goose*
das Huhn	*chicken*

These animals can be found on **der Bauernhof** (*farm*). A small farm is called **der kleine landwirtschaftliche Betrieb** (or **der kleine bäuerliche Betrieb**). Although the phrase is long, it is used quite often.

An American *barn* is a place where animals are housed, grain or hay is stored, and farm equipment tools are kept. German tends to be more specific.

die Scheune	*barn (for grain or hay)*
der Stall	*stable (for housing animals)*
der Schuppen	*shed (for storing tools and equipment)*

The word **Stall** can be combined with animal names to define a specific kind of shelter:

der Hühnerstall	*henhouse, chicken coop*
der Kuhstall	*cow barn, cowshed*
der Pferdestall	*horse barn*

der Schweinestall	*pigsty*
der Viehstall	*cowshed, cattle barn*

The farmer who tends the animals is **der Bauer** or **der Landwirt**. His wife is **die Bäuerin** or **die Landwirtin**. Naturally, they live in **das Bauernhaus** (*farmhouse*). Let's look at some useful phrases that describe life on a farm:

Der Bauer füttert die Pferde.	*The farmer feeds the horses.*
Die Bäuerin füttert die Hühner.	*The farmer's wife feeds the chickens.*
Der Bauer milkt die Kühe.	*The farmer milks the cows.*
Die Bauern arbeiten auf dem Feld.	*The farmers are working in the field.*
Das Vieh wird von dem Landwirt gezüchtet.	*The cattle are bred by the farmer.*
Die Schweine werden von der Landwirtin gefüttert.	*The pigs are fed by the farmer's wife.*
Die Kühe sind jetzt auf der Weide.	*The cows are out in the pasture now.*
Hinter der Scheune ist ein Teich für die Enten und Gänse.	*There's a shed behind the barn for the ducks and geese.*
Hinter dem Bauernhaus ist ein Stall für die Ziegen und Schafe.	*There's a shed behind the farmhouse for the goats and sheep.*
Ein junger Schäfer hütet die Schafe.	*A young shepherd tends the sheep.*
Der Bauer hütet das Vieh.	*The farmer tends the cattle.*
Die Hennen legen jeden Tag ein Ei.	*The hens lay one egg a day.*

The verb **melken** (*to milk*) has an irregular conjugation. Take note of its forms in the following tenses, which are provided in the third-person singular:

PRESENT	er milkt
PAST	er molk
PRESENT PERFECT	er hat gemolken
FUTURE	er wird melken

ÜBUNG
4·3

Answer the following questions. Sample answers are provided in the answer key.

1. In was für einem Haus wohnt der Bauer? _____

2. Welche Farbe hat die Scheune? _____

3. Ist ein Esel größer als ein Pferd? _____

4. Von wem wird das Vieh gezüchtet? _____

5. Wer milkt die Kühe? _____

6. Wer füttert die Enten und Gänse? _____

7. Welche Tiere sind auf der Weide? _____

8. Welche Tiere schwimmen im Teich? _____

9. Was macht der Schäfer? _____

10. Wer hütet die Hühner? _____

The noun **der Bauer** has a special declension like the one for **der Held** (*hero*) or **der Soldat** (*soldier*) and certain other German words:

NOMINATIVE	der Bauer	der Held	der Soldat
ACCUSATIVE	den Bauern	den Helden	den Soldaten
DATIVE	dem Bauern	dem Helden	dem Soldaten
GENITIVE	des Bauern	des Helden	des Soldaten

Wilde Tiere

Wild animals live everywhere in the world and can be found in lakes and oceans, deserts, mountains, forests, and jungles. Their varieties are numerous, but here are a few familiar examples:

Diese wilden Tiere leben im Wald, im Dschungel oder in der Wüste.

These wild animals live in the forest, the jungle, or the desert.

das Kamel	*camel*
das Reh	*deer, doe*
der Affe	*ape, monkey*
der Bär	*bear*
der Elefant	*elephant*
der Hirsch	*deer, stag*
der Löwe	*lion*
der Tiger	*tiger*
der Wolf	*wolf*
die Löwin	*lioness*

Diese wilden Tiere leben in Seen oder im Ozean.

These wild animals live in lakes or the ocean.

das Krokodil	*crocodile*
der Fisch	*fish*
der Frosch	*frog*
der Haifisch	*shark*
der Seehund	*seal*
der Wal	*whale*
die Schildkröte	*turtle*
die Schnecke	*snail*

Diese Insekten leben überall auf der Erde.

These insects live everywhere on the earth.

das Insekt	*insect*
der Käfer	*beetle*
der Schmetterling	*butterfly*
die Ameise	*ant*
die Biene	*bee*
die Fliege	*fly*
die Motte	*moth*
die Mücke	*gnat, mosquito*
die Schabe	*cockroach*
die Spinne	*spider*

Let's look at some sentences with adjectives useful for describing wild animals:

Affen und Bären sind warmblütige Tiere.	*Apes and bears are warm-blooded animals.*
Ist ein Frosch ein warmblütiges Tier?	*Is a frog a warm-blooded animal?*
Nein, ein Frosh ist ein kaltblütiges Tier.	*No, a frog is a cold-blooded animal.*
Ein Krokodil ist auch ein kaltblütiges Tier.	*A crocodile is also a cold-blooded animal.*
Viele wilde Tiere sind gefährlich.	*Many wild animals are dangerous.*
Tiger und Löwen sind gefährlich.	*Tigers and lions are dangerous.*
Viele wilde Tiere sind harmlos.	*Many wild animals are harmless.*
Ein Schmetterling ist harmlos.	*A butterfly is harmless.*
Einige Tiere und Insekten sind giftig.	*Some animals and insects are poisonous.*
Einige Schlangen sind giftig.	*Some snakes are poisonous.*
Eine Klapperschlange ist giftig.	*A rattlesnake is poisonous.*
Eine Spinne kann giftig sein.	*A spider can be poisonous.*

ÜBUNG 4·4

Place an X in the blanks under the words that can describe the animals listed on the left.

	Haustier	Nutzvieh	wild	harmlos	gefährlich	giftig
1. Schmetterling	_____	_____	_____	_____	_____	_____
2. Schaf	_____	_____	_____	_____	_____	_____
3. Bär	_____	_____	_____	_____	_____	_____
4. Kätzchen	_____	_____	_____	_____	_____	_____
5. Kamel	_____	_____	_____	_____	_____	_____
6. Wal	_____	_____	_____	_____	_____	_____
7. Reh	_____	_____	_____	_____	_____	_____
8. Spinne	_____	_____	_____	_____	_____	_____
9. Henne	_____	_____	_____	_____	_____	_____

ÜBUNG 4·5

Fill in each blank with an appropriate missing word.

1. Im Schweinestall schlafen die _____.

2. Der _____ füttert die Pferde.

3. Der _____ hütet die Schafe.

4. Auf der Weide sehen wir viele _____.

5. Ein _____ ist kleiner als ein Pferd.

6. Jeden Morgen _____ die Bäuerin die Kühe.

7. Das _____ lebt in der Wüste.

8. Frösche sind _____ Tiere.

9. Ist ein Wolf _____ oder gefährlich?

10. Der _____ hat schöne Flügel.

11. Vorsicht! Klapperschlangen sind _____.

12. Der _____ ist das größte Tier im Ozean.

13. Unsere _____ legen keine Eier.

14. Ein _____ kann sprechen.

15. Eine Fliege ist ein _____.

ÜBUNG
4·6

Rewrite each of the following sentences in the past, present perfect, and future tenses.

1. Der Schäfer hütet die Schafe.

   PAST _____

   PRESENT PERFECT _____

   FUTURE _____

2. Einige Spinnen sind gefährlich.

   PAST _____

   PRESENT PERFECT _____

   FUTURE _____

3. Die Hennen legen wenige Eier.

   PAST _____

   PRESENT PERFECT _____

   FUTURE _____

4. Der Landwirt füttert den Esel.

   PAST _____

   PRESENT PERFECT _____

   FUTURE _____

5. Die Bauern züchten das Vieh.

   PAST _____

   PRESENT PERFECT _____

   FUTURE _____

6. Die Katze wiegt 4 Kilo.

   PAST _____

   PRESENT PERFECT _____

   FUTURE _____

Circle the letter of the word or phrase that best completes each sentence.

1. In den Bergen leben wilde _____.
   a. Wal   b. Biene   c. Elefanten   d. Ziegen

2. Unter dem Tisch schläft ein alter _____.
   a. Hund   b. Stehlampe   c. Schlange   d. Huhn

3. Die _____ arbeiten auf dem Feld.
   a. Bauern   b. Landwirtin   c. Vieh   d. Haustiere

4. Jeden Morgen _____ wir die Kühe.
   a. sprechen   b. melken   c. stehen   d. legen

5. Im Pferdestall lebt auch ein _____.
   a. Ente   b. Affe   c. Esel   d. Ameise

6. Eine _____ ist kein Insekt.
   a. Schildkröte   b. Motte   c. Schmetterling   d. Käfer

7. Ein _____ ist ein kaltblütiges Tier.
   a. Reh   b. Wolf   c. Frosch   d. Kamel

8. Im _____ leben Affen und Tiger.
   a. Dschungel   b. Bauernhof   c. Weide   d. Berg

9. Eine _____ kann nicht fliegen.
   a. Kanarienvogel   b. Ente   c. Motte   d. Schabe

10. _____ leben in der Wüste.
    a. Kamele   b. Schweine   c. Wale   d. Seehunde

11. In diesem Wald leben viele _____.
    a. Bären   b. Landwirte   c. Hennen   d. Eier

12. Die Landwirtin _____ die Hühner.
    a. flog   b. hütete   c. gefunden   d. gelegt

13. Ein _____ ist ein warmblütiges Tier.
    a. Spinne   b. Löwe   c. Frosch   d. Scheune

14. Welche _____ hat dein Kaninchen?
    a. Stall   b. Katze   c. Farbe   d. Ameise

15. Dieser Hund hat ein dunkles _____.
    a. Viehstall   b. Schuppen   c. Feld   d. Fell

16. Sind die Pferde schon auf der _____?
    a. Weide   b. Scheune   c. Bauernhof   d. Ozean

17. Die Enten schwimmen im _____.
    a. Viehstall   b. Teich   c. Fisch   d. Schäfer

18. Vorsicht! Dieses Insekt ist _____.
    a. fliegen   b. harmlos   c. hell   d. giftig

19. In der Wüste leben keine _____.
    a. Seehunde   b. Käfer   c. Kamele   d. Menschen

20. Ein Tiger kann sehr _____ sein.
    a. dunkel   b. gefährlich   c. grün   d. kurz

Fun, recreation, and sports

Germans live in a society in which people have a lot of free time. Just like people in other countries, Germans use their free time in a variety of ways. They call their free time **die Freizeit** and use that word to describe things connected to leisure:

die Freizeitbeschäftigung	*leisure activity, hobby*
die Freizeitkleidung	*leisure wear, casual clothing*
das Freizeithemd	*sports shirt*
der Freizeitpark	*amusement park*

Das Hobby

Many people become engaged in collecting objects that interest them or that are suitable for display or as decorations.

Was ist Ihr Hobby?	*What's your hobby?*
Ich sammle Briefmarken.	*I collect stamps.*
Wir sammeln alte Tassen.	*We collect old cups.*
Mein Bruder sammelt Schallplatten.	*My brother collects phonograph records.*
Unser Vater sammelt alte Uhren.	*Our father collects old clocks.*
Was sammeln Sie?	*What do you collect?*
Ich sammle Münzen aus aller Welt.	*I collect coins from around the world.*

The simple reason for having a collection or any other hobby is *because it's fun*: **Es macht Spaß**. The word **der Spaß** is used in several useful phrases:

Viel Spaß!	*Have a good time!*
Das ist kein Spaß.	*That's no fun.*
Verdirb ihm doch nicht seinen Spaß!	*Don't spoil his fun.*
Sie hatten alle viel Spaß.	*They all had a good time.*
Verlieren macht keinen Spaß.	*Losing is no fun.*

Let's look at some of the fun things people do in their leisure time or as a hobby:

Mein Hobby ist Basteln.	*My hobby is doing crafts.*
Ich bastele an einem alten Auto.	*I tinker around with an old car.*
Ihre Tochter strickt gern.	*Her daughter likes knitting.*
Die Jungen spielen gerne Kartenspiele.	*The boys like playing card games.*
Herr Meyer erzählt gerne Witze.	*Mr. Meyer likes telling jokes.*
Wir gehen oft kegeln.	*We often go bowling.*
Sie wetten gerne.	*They like gambling.*

There are some interesting places to go in your spare time:

Heute gehen wir ...	Today we're going . . .
... in den Zirkus.	. . . to the circus.
... in die Kunsthalle.	. . . to the art museum.
... in die Oper.	. . . to the opera.
... ins Kino.	. . . to the movies.
... ins Museum.	. . . to the museum.
... ins Theater.	. . . to the theater.
... zum Park.	. . . to the park.
... zum Schwimmbad.	. . . to the pool.
... zum Spielplatz.	. . . to the playground.
... zum Sportfeld.	. . . to the sports ground.
... zum Sportplatz.	. . . to the playing field.
... zum Zoo.	. . . to the zoo.
... zur Bibliothek.	. . . to the library.

Here are some useful words for talking about leisure time:

angeln	to fish
jagen	to hunt
wandern	to hike
skateboarden	to go skateboarding
das Drachenfliegen	hang gliding
die Gartenarbeit	gardening
der Gartenbau	horticulture
das Damespiel	checkers
das Schach	chess
das Schachbrett	chessboard
das Skeetschießen	skeet shooting
der Skat	skat (a card game)
die Kunst	art
malen	to paint
der Tanz	dance

ÜBUNG
5·1

Answer the following questions, based on your personal experience if possible. Sample answers are provided in the answer key.

1. Was sammeln Sie? _____

2. Was machen Sie in Ihrer Freizeit? _____

3. Was macht Ihr Freund in seiner Freizeit? _____

4. Mit wem spielen Sie Karten? _____

5. Wer geht gerne kegeln? _____

6. Was spielen die Mädchen? _____

7. Wer geht oft angeln? _____

Die Fitness

German and English use the same word when speaking about *fitness*. Throughout Germany you will find an abundance of athletic and health clubs because people want to be **fit**.

das Fitnesszentrum, das Fitness-Center	*fitness center, gym*
das Fitnesstraining	*fitness training, workout*
der Fitnessraum	*workout room*
der Fitnessguru	*fitness guru, authority on fitness*
fit	*fit, in shape*

Wandern hält fit.	*Hiking keeps you in shape.*
Wir werden ihn fit machen.	*We're going to get him in shape.*
Wie hältst du dich fit?	*How do you stay in shape?*

Here is a list of activities that help keep people in shape:

spazieren gehen	*to go for a walk*
joggen	*to jog*
laufen gehen, laufen	*to run*
rennen	*to run, race*
schwimmen	*to swim*
Rad fahren	*to go bike riding*
snowboarden	*to go snowboarding*
bergsteigen	*to go mountain climbing*
tanzen	*to dance*
trainieren	*to train, work out*
die Muskeln trainieren	*to work out your muscles*
Gewichte heben	*to lift weights*
mit Hanteln trainieren	*to work out with weights*
in die Sauna gehen	*to go into the sauna*

Two special words describe the kinds of weights used in weight training:

die (kurze) Hantel	*dumbbell*
die (lange) Hantel	*barbell*

Der Sport

The word **Sport** is used in the singular and means *athletics* or *sport*. When the English word *sports* is plural, its preferable German translation is **die Sportarten** (*kinds of sports*). Let's look at some example sentences:

Meine Schwester treibt viel Sport.	*My sister plays many sports.*
Welche Sportart spielen Sie?	*What sport do you play (go in for)?*
Ich spiele Federball.	*I play badminton.*
Mein Onkel ist Sportfreund.	*My uncle is a sports fan.*
Ihr Sohn will Sportler werden.	*Her son wants to become an athlete.*
Angela ist eine gute Sportlerin.	*Angela is a good athlete.*

Here are a few more vocabulary words related to athletics:

der Sportgeist	*sportsmanship*
der Sportlehrer, die Sportlehrerin	*physical education (PE) teacher*
die Sportmedizin	*sports medicine*
der Sporttaucher	*skin diver*

der Sportverein	*sports club*
der Sportwagen	*sportscar*

Numerous sports attract thousands of enthusiasts. Here are some very popular sports:

das Autorennen	*car racing*
das Golf	*golf*
das Hockey	*hockey*
das Reiten	*riding*
das Ringen	*wrestling*
das Rollschuhlaufen	*roller-skating*
das Schlittschuhlaufen	*ice-skating*
das Skilaufen	*skiing*
der Langlauf	*cross-country skiing*
das Tennis	*tennis*
das Tischtennis	*Ping-Pong*
das Turnen	*gymnastics*
der Basketball	*basketball*
der Fußball	*soccer*
der Handball	*handball*
der Volleyball	*volleyball*
die Leichtathletik	*track and field*

Many of the preceding nouns also have verb forms. Let's compare how the two forms are used differently:

Erik interessiert sich fürs Turnen.	*Erik is interested in gymnastics.*
Aber er turnt nicht gut.	*But he's not a good gymnast.*
Diese Jungen ringen.	*The boys are in wrestling.*
Karl möchte gegen ihn ringen.	*Karl wants to wrestle against him.*
Reiten macht Spaß.	*Riding is fun.*
Ich reite jeden Morgen.	*I go horseback riding every morning.*
Ich habe Rollschuhlaufen gern.	*I like roller-skating.*
Er läuft oft Rollschuh.	*He often goes roller-skating.*
Hier wird das Schlittschuhlaufen nicht erlaubt.	*Ice-skating isn't allowed here.*
Wo kann man hier Schlittschuh laufen?	*Where can you go ice-skating here?*
Auch die Kinder laufen Ski.	*Even the children go skiing.*
Sie dürfen nicht heute Ski laufen.	*They're not allowed to go skiing today.*

Here are just a few more verbs that come in handy when talking about sports:

boxen	*to box*
Drachen steigen lassen	*to fly a kite*
fangen	*to catch*
werfen	*to throw*
klettern	*to climb*
rudern	*to row*
segeln	*to sail*
surfen	*to surf*
tauchen	*to dive*
siegen	*to win (be victorious)*
gewinnen	*to win (gain)*
verlieren	*to lose*

Answer the following questions, based on your personal experience if possible. Sample answers are provided in the answer key.

1. Welche Sportart treiben Sie? _____

2. Wo kann man klettern? _____

3. Was kann man im Park tun? _____

4. Was machen Sie am Wochenende? _____

5. Was kann man im Winter machen? _____

6. Welche Sportart kann gefährlich sein? _____

7. Wie kann man die Muskeln trainieren? _____

You might hear some of these practical words and phrases during an athletic competition:

der Wettkampf	*competition*
die Mannschaft	*team*
die Meisterschaft	*championship*
der Europapokal	*the Europe Cup*
der Sieger (die Siegerin)	*champion, winner*
der Gegner (die Gegnerin)	*opponent*
der Schiedsrichter (-in)	*judge, referee, official*
vor dem Start	*before the start*
durchs Ziel gehen	*to cross the finish line*
das Tor hüten	*to guard the goal*
der Torwart	*the goalie*
einen Treffer erzielen	*to score a goal*
Der Trainer war zufrieden.	*The coach was satisfied.*
Er stellte einen Rekord auf.	*He set a record.*
Sie gewann eine Medaille.	*She won a medal.*

*Place an X in the blanks that identify when and how the sports listed on the left are played: in the summer or winter (**im Sommer, im Winter**), with a ball (**mit einem Ball**), or in a team (**Mannschaft**).*

	im Sommer	im Winter	mit einem Ball	Mannschaft
1. Basketball	_____	_____	_____	_____
2. Fußball	_____	_____	_____	_____
3. Hockey	_____	_____	_____	_____
4. Langlauf	_____	_____	_____	_____
5. Leichtathletik	_____	_____	_____	_____
6. Radfahren	_____	_____	_____	_____

7. Reiten   _____   _____   _____   _____

8. Schach   _____   _____   _____   _____

9. Schlittschuhlaufen   _____   _____   _____   _____

10. Schwimmen   _____   _____   _____   _____

11. Skilaufen   _____   _____   _____   _____

ÜBUNG
5·4

Rewrite each of the following sentences in the past, present perfect, and future tenses.

1. Meine Kusine sammelt Briefmarken.

   PAST _____

   PRESENT PERFECT _____

   FUTURE _____

2. Er erzählt gerne Witze.

   PAST _____

   PRESENT PERFECT _____

   FUTURE _____

3. Die Jungen gehen rudern.

   PAST _____

   PRESENT PERFECT _____

   FUTURE _____

4. Monika gewinnt eine Medaille.

   PAST _____

   PRESENT PERFECT _____

   FUTURE _____

5. Andreas fängt den Ball nicht.

   PAST _____

   PRESENT PERFECT _____

   FUTURE _____

6. Diese Mädchen treiben viel Sport.

   PAST _____

   PRESENT PERFECT _____

   FUTURE _____

Fill in each blank with an appropriate word.

1. Ich kann nicht _____. Ich habe keine Schlittschuhe.

2. Martin wohnt in den _____ und geht jeden Tag Skilaufen.

3. Wo ist das _____? Ich möchte schwimmen gehen.

4. Er kann nicht _____. Er hat kein Pferd.

5. Ich habe Handball gern. Handball macht _____.

6. Drachenfliegen ist eine _____ Sportart.

7. Der Gewichtheber trainiert mit langen _____.

8. Meine Schwester _____ schneller als mein Bruder.

9. Schwimmen hält _____.

10. Der Läufer hat einen neuen _____ aufgestellt.

11. Sie hat kein Fahrrad. Sie kann nicht _____ gehen.

12. Es gibt keinen Schnee. Wir können nicht _____.

13. Hast du ein Segelboot? Ich möchte heute _____.

14. Mein Sohn spielt Fußball. Er ist _____.

15. Unsere Mannschaft ist sehr schlecht. Wir _____ immer.

Circle the letter of the word or phrase that best completes each sentence.

1. Verdirb ihm doch nicht seinen _____.
   a. Radfahren   b. Surfen   c. Spaß   d. Gegner

2. Sie haben drei Pullover _____.
   a. gestrickt   b. aufgestellt   c. gewandert   d. gewinnen

3. Tante Luise sammelt alte _____.
   a. Tassen   b. Uhr   c. Brief   d. Rekord

4. Die Jungen wollen Schach _____.
   a. spielen   b. rennen   c. surfen   d. sammeln

5. Welche _____ treibst du?
   a. Sportmedizin   b. Sportart   c. Freizeit   d. Freizeithemd

6. Sie werden den kranken Mann _____ machen.
   a. trainieren   b. jagen   c. gern   d. fit

7. Der junge Arzt ist auch guter _____.
   a. Rekord   b. Sportler   c. Fitnessraum   d. Schachbrett

8. Es ist viel zu heiß in der _____.
   a. Sommer   b. Sportfeld   c. Sauna   d. Sportart

9. Die Frau _____ mit kurzen Hanteln.
   a. wanderte   b. trainierte   c. brachte   d. machte

10. Meine Eltern _____ jetzt Golf.
    a. verlieren   b. siegen   c. heben   d. spielen

11. Mein Großvater geht jeden Abend _____.
    a. im Fitness-Center   b. spazieren   c. fit   d. erlauben

12. Mein Bruder kann sehr gut _____.
    a. verlieren   b. ringen   c. gefährlich sein   d. gerne

13. Sie hat einen neuen _____ aufgestellt.
    a. Turnen   b. Snowboarden   c. Rekord   d. Spaß

14. Andrea _____ ihm den Ball zu.
    a. darf   b. trainiert   c. angelt   d. wirft

15. Ihre Gegnerin ist schnell durchs _____ gegangen.
    a. Ziel   b. Sportplatz   c. Freizeitbeschäftigung   d. Sportgeist

Education

Perhaps you are aware that there is no single system of education in the United States. The individual states, not the federal government, are responsible for children's education. Therefore, fifty American educational systems with fifty sets of laws govern education. Fortunately, time has proved that it is wise to have similarities among the various systems, and American children can move from one state to another with a certain amount of continuity.

Das deutsche Schulsystem

There are sixteen federal states (**Bundesländer**) in Germany, and as in the United States, each has the responsibility of educating its citizens. Although there are sixteen varieties of education in Germany, the similarities from **Bundesland** to **Bundesland** are enormous. All sixteen systems share the important goal of identifying the learners' intellectual abilities and channeling them through the educational system to an appropriate adult occupation, ranging from manual laborer to university professor. The following is a diagram of the structure of the German school system:

der Kindergarten
für drei- bis sechsjährige Kinder
nursery school
for 3- to 6-year-olds

die Grundschule
für sechs- bis zehnjährige Kinder
elementary school
for 6- to 10-year-olds

die Hauptschule	die Realschule	das Gymnasium
für alle Schüler	**für bessere Schüler**	**für die besten Schüler**
zehn- bis sechzehnjährige	**zehn- bis sechzehnjährige**	**zehn- bis neunzehnjährige**
main school	*secondary school*	*preparatory school*
for all pupils	*for better pupils*	*for the best pupils*
10 to 16 years old	*10 to 16 years old*	*10 to 19 years old*
hauptsächlich	**fast alle**	**alle Ausbildungsberufe**
handwerkliche	**Ausbildungsberufe**	**Zugang zu**
Ausbildungsberufe	*almost all occupations*	**Universitäten**
primarily trades		*all occupations*
requiring apprenticeship		*admission to universities*

44

In some parts of Germany, **die Gesamtschule** for students in grades five to ten has been developed. It is a comprehensive school for students of varying levels of ability.

Let's look at some vocabulary that is useful in talking about schools and education:

der Schüler, die Schülerin	*pupil, student (noncollege)*
der Gymnasiast, die Gymnasiastin	*student attending a preparatory school*
der Student, die Studentin	*student (college)*
der Lehrer, die Lehrerin	*teacher*
der Studienrat, die Studienrätin	*tenured high school teacher*
der Oberstudienrat, die Oberstudienrätin	*lead teacher, department head*
der Professor, die Professorin	*university professor*
der Lehrling	*apprentice*
lehren	*to teach*
unterrichten	*to instruct*
lernen	*to learn, study at precollege level*
studieren	*to study at the college level*
besuchen	*to attend (school)*
sitzen bleiben	*to repeat a school year*
durchfallen	*to fail, flunk*

It is important to remember that Germans do not use the verb **studieren** in the same way that the English verb *study* is used. The German verb is used exclusively to describe university-level studies and does not describe someone sitting over his or her books and notes preparing for a test. Germans would use **lernen** to describe that kind of preparation.

ÜBUNG
6·1

Answer the following questions. Sample answers are provided in the answer key.

1. Welche Schule besucht Ihr Sohn? _____

2. Welche Schule besucht Ihre Tochter? _____

3. Ist dein Bruder Schüler in einer Hauptschule? _____

4. Was lernt man in der Grundschule? _____

5. Was studiert deine Schwester? _____

6. An welche Universität gehst du? _____

7. Ist Ihr Sohn ein guter Schüler? _____

8. Wo studieren Sie? _____

9. Was studieren Sie? _____

10. Ist Ihre Tochter klug? _____

Note that the verbs **durchfallen** and **sitzen bleiben** require the auxiliary **sein** in the perfect tenses:

PRESENT	er fällt durch	er bleibt sitzen
PAST	er fiel durch	er blieb sitzen
PRESENT PERFECT	er **ist** durchgefallen	er **ist** sitzen geblieben
FUTURE	er wird durchfallen	er wird sitzen bleiben

Now let's look at some useful sentences:

Die Grundschule dauert in allen Bundesländern vier Jahre.	*Elementary school lasts four years in all the federal states.*
Aber die Grundschule dauert in Berlin sechs Jahre.	*But elementary school in Berlin lasts six years.*
Gute Schüler haben gute Noten.	*Good students have good grades.*
Gute Schüler können von der Hauptschule auf die Realschule wechseln.	*Good students can change from the main school to the secondary school.*
Gute Schüler können von der Realschule auf das Gymnasium wechseln.	*Good students can change from the secondary school to the preparatory school.*
Er hat einen Hauptschulabschluss bekommen.	*He received a main school diploma.*
Sie hat einen Realschulabschluss bekommen.	*She received a secondary school diploma.*
Ich will das Abitur bekommen.	*I want to receive a preparatory school diploma.*

A preparatory school diploma is commonly called **das Abitur**. But its official name is **die Allgemeine Hochschulreife**.

Das deutsche Notensystem

Grades are called **Noten** in German, and a general system of grades is used by most schools. Naturally, there are variations of this system. Depending on the grade level, ten numbers or six descriptive words are used to evaluate a student's performance. They are as follows:

NUMBERS	WORDS	
10	sehr gut	*very good*
9		
8	gut	*good*
7	befriedigend	*satisfactory*
6	ausreichend	*fair*
5	mangelhaft	*poor*
4		
3	ungenügend	*unsatisfactory*
2		
1		

The number 10, or **sehr gut**, is the highest grade, and the number 1, or **ungenügend**, is the lowest grade.

A German school has a wide variety of subjects, just as any other school; some of these subjects are as follows:

die Biologie	*biology*
die Chemie	*chemistry*
die Fremdsprache	*foreign language*
die Geographie, Erdkunde	*geography*
die Geschichte	*history*
die Grammatik	*grammar*
die Mathematik	*mathematics*
die Physik	*physics*
die Rechtschreibung	*spelling*
die Religion	*religion*

Here are some useful words when talking about school and education:

der Schulbus	*school bus*
die Schultasche	*schoolbag*
die Schulbank	*school desk*
das Schulbuch	*schoolbook*
der Bleistift	*pencil*
der Radiergummi	*eraser*
der Kuli	*ballpoint pen*
das Papier	*paper*
das Lineal	*ruler*
der Computer	*computer*
die Kreide	*chalk*
die Tafel	*blackboard*
die Landkarte	*map*
die Aufgabe	*assignment*
die Hausarbeit	*homework*
die Prüfung	*test*
das Examen	*examination*
die Note	*grade*
das Fach	*subject*
das Lieblingsfach	*favorite subject*
der Schulentlassene	*graduate*

ÜBUNG
6·2

Answer the following questions. Sample answers are provided in the answer key.

1. Was hast du in deiner Schultasche? _____

2. Ist Chemie schwierig oder leicht? _____

3. Ist Deutsch schwierig oder leicht? _____

4. Willst du ins Kino gehen? _____

5. Bekommst du gute oder schlechte Noten? _____

6. Schreibt die Lehrerin mit dem Bleistift? _____

7. Welches Fach findest du interessant? _____

8. Ist *mangelhaft* eine gute oder eine schlechte Note? _____

9. Ist dein Sohn intelligent? _____

10. Was ist wichtig zu lernen? _____

Nützliche Ausdrücke

Just as English has more than one way to thank someone, German also has a variety of ways to express gratitude:

Danke.	*Thanks.*
Vielen Dank.	*Thanks a lot.*

Danke schön.	*Thank you.*
Besten Dank.	*Thanks so much.*
Schönsten Dank.	*Thanks so very much.*
Ich bedanke mich.	*I thank you.*
Ich möchte mich bei Ihnen bedanken.	*I want to express my thanks to you.*
Seien Sie herzlich bedankt.	*Please accept my sincere gratitude.*

Numerous expressions also exist for bidding someone farewell:

Auf Wiedersehen (*or* Wiedersehen).	*Good-bye.*
Auf Wiederschauen (*or* Wiederschauen).	*Good-bye.*
Auf Wiederhören (*or* Wiederhören).	*Good-bye.* (to someone on the phone)
Tschüs.	*So long.*
Bis später.	*See you later.*
Ciao.	*Ciao.*

And there is more than one way to apologize to someone:

Es tut mir leid (*or* Tut mir leid).	*I'm sorry.*
Verzeihung!	*Sorry.*
Bitte, verzeihen Sie mir!	*Please forgive me.*
Entschuldigung!	*Excuse me.*
Entschuldigen Sie die Störung!	*Sorry to bother you.*
Ich bitte Sie um Entschuldigung.	*Pardon me, please.*
Ich muss mich bei Ihnen entschuldigen.	*I have to apologize to you.*
Ich bedauere es sehr.	*I really regret it.*

ÜBUNG
6·3

Rewrite each of the following sentences in the past, present perfect, and future tenses.

1. Was lernst du in der Schule?

   PAST _____

   PRESENT PERFECT _____

   FUTURE _____

2. Erik studiert Jura.

   PAST _____

   PRESENT PERFECT _____

   FUTURE _____

3. Mein Neffe fällt wieder durch.

   PAST _____

   PRESENT PERFECT _____

   FUTURE _____

4. Die Kinder besuchen eine neue Schule.

   PAST   _____

   PRESENT PERFECT _____

   FUTURE _____

5. Angela muss sitzen bleiben.

   PAST   _____

   PRESENT PERFECT _____

   FUTURE _____

6. Die Hauptschule dauert vier Jahre.

   PAST   _____

   PRESENT PERFECT _____

   FUTURE _____

7. Bekommt ihr nur gute Noten?

   PAST   _____

   PRESENT PERFECT _____

   FUTURE _____

8. Diese Schüler wollen ihre Schule wechseln.

   PAST   _____

   PRESENT PERFECT _____

   FUTURE _____

9. Ich danke ihm für das Geschenk.

   PAST   _____

   PRESENT PERFECT _____

   FUTURE _____

10. Es tut mir leid.

    PAST   _____

    PRESENT PERFECT _____

    FUTURE _____

Fill in each blank with an appropriate word.

1. Nur die besten Schüler besuchen das _____.

2. Meine Schwester ist _____ an der Universität Heidelberg.

3. Englisch ist nicht schwierig, sondern _____.

4. *Ungenügend* ist eine schlechte _____.

5. Ich finde Biologie sehr _____.

6. Der faule Schüler ist leider _____.

7. Ich kann nicht mit einem Bleistift schreiben. Hast du einen _____?

8. Ich möchte mich bei Ihnen _____.

9. _____ ist mein Lieblingsfach.

10. Morgen rufe ich dich wieder an. Auf _____!

11. In der Grundschule lernen die Kinder lesen und _____.

12. Ist Mathematik _____ oder leicht?

13. Die Lehrerin steht an der _____ und schreibt mit Kreide.

14. Entschuldigung! Es tut mir _____.

15. Deutschland hat sechzehn _____.

Circle the letter of the word or phrase that best completes each sentence.

1. Ein Schüler kann von der Hauptschule auf die Realschule _____.
   a. bekommen   b. sitzen bleiben   c. wechseln   d. lernen

2. Mein _____ ist Deutsch.
   a. Lieblingsfach   b. Gymnasium   c. Studienrätin   d. Ausbildungsberuf

3. Erik muss vier Jahre als _____ arbeiten.
   a. Lehrling   b. Professorin   c. Gymnasiast   d. Student

4. Meine Kinder _____ eine Realschule in der Nähe.
   a. bekommen   b. durchfallen   c. kommen   d. besuchen

5. Er hat eine schlechte _____ in Physik bekommen.
   a. Tafel   b. Note   c. Schultasche   d. sehr gut

6. Die Allgemeine Hochschulreife ist das _____.
   a. Schulbuch   b. Prüfung   c. Rechtschreibung   d. Abitur

7. Die Grundschule _____ in Berlin sechs Jahre.
   a. besucht   b. dauert   c. bleibt sitzen   d. fällt durch

8. Drei- bis sechsjährige Kinder gehen zum _____.
   a. Universität   b. Kindergarten   c. Schulentlassene   d. Examen

9. Ich finde Erdkunde _____.
   a. leicht   b. faul   c. ein Ausbildungsberuf   d. die Geographie

10. Wo liegt Polen? Hast du eine _____?
    a. Landkarte   b. Schulbank   c. Lineal   d. Radiergummi

11. Die faulen Schüler werden _____.
    a. besuchen   b. durchfallen   c. wechseln   d. studieren

12. Der große Junge ist _____.
    a. lernen   b. Gymnasiast   c. sitzen bleiben   d. Studienrat

13. Ich bitte Sie um _____.
    a. Realschulabschluss   b. vielen Dank   c. Note   d. Entschuldigung

14. Ich muss nach Hause gehen. _____!
    a. Auf Wiederhören   b. Tschüs   c. Wichtig   d. Schwierig

15. Er ist sehr intelligent. Er ist ein _____.
    a. Schüler   b. Verzeihung   c. Geschichte   d. Genie

Holidays

Like people everywhere, Germans like to celebrate. There are many holidays and traditional commemorations to inspire the mood, to have fun, or to come together as a family to observe a special day.

Der Feiertag

Two German words are the basis for forming other words that deal with celebrations. They are **die Feier** and **das Fest**, which mean *party* or *celebration*. When combined with other words and phrases or when used as a verb or modifier, they become more descriptive. Let's look at a few:

der Feierabend	*evening time (after work)*
der Feiertag	*holiday*
ein gefeierter Sportler	*a celebrated athlete*
ein gesetzlicher Feiertag	*a legal holiday*
ein kirchlicher Feiertag	*a religious holiday*
eine feierliche Stille	*a solemn silence*
feierlich	*ceremonial, solemn*
feiern	*to celebrate*
Schönen Feierabend!	*Have a nice evening.*

Notice that the word **Fest**, like **Feier**, generally has a serious tone:

festlich	*festive, formal*
Festlichkeit	*festiveness*
der Festtag	*holiday, feast day*
der Festakt	*ceremonial act*
das Festessen	*banquet*
das Festkleid	*evening dress*
der Festzug	*procession*
die Festansprache	*formal address*
die Festgabe	*holiday gift*
der Festplatz	*fairground*
in Festbeleuchtung erstrahlen	*to be ablaze with festive lights*

An interesting little German phrase suggests in fun that *there can't be a real party until everyone has arrived*: **Keine Feier ohne Meier.** Literally, the phrase means *No party without Meier.*

The major legal and religious holidays in Germany, as well as special family events, are as follows:

der Dreikönigstag	*Three Kings' Day (January 6)*
der Valentinstag	*Valentine's Day*
das Faschingfest	*Mardi Gras*
Karfreitag	*Good Friday*
das Ostern	*Easter*
das Pfingsten	*Whitsun*
der erste Mai	*May Day*
der Muttertag	*Mother's Day (early May)*
der Vatertag	*Father's Day (late May)*
der Tag der Deutschen Einheit	*German Unity Day (October 3)*
das Oktoberfest	*Octoberfest*
das Halloween	*Halloween*
der Reformationstag	*Reformation Day (October 31)*
Allerheiligen	*All Saints Day (November 1)*
der Buß- und Bettag	*Day of Penance (eleven days before Advent)*
das Weihnachten	*Christmas*
das Silvester	*New Year's Eve*
der Geburtstag	*birthday*
der Hochzeitstag	*wedding day*
das Jubiläum	*anniversary*
das fünfundzwanzigjährige Jubiläum	*twenty-fifth anniversary*
das fünfzigjährige Jubiläum	*fiftieth anniversary*
der Todestag	*day of one's death*

You may have been surprised to see *Halloween* in the preceding list. It is only in the recent past that German children have begun to celebrate Halloween. Costume parties are very popular.

When greeting someone on a holiday, you can use a little generic phrase: **Frohes Fest!** (*Happy holidays!*) But there are also specific greetings for holidays and special occasions to be aware of:

Alles Gute zum Geburtstag.	*Best wishes for your birthday.*
Herzlichen Glückwunsch zum Geburtstag.	*Congratulations on your birthday.*
Dem glücklichen Paar alles Schöne am Hochzeitstag und viel Glück in der Zukunft.	*To the happy couple the best of everything upon your marriage and much luck in the future.*
Ein fröhliches Osterfest!	*Happy Easter!*
Frohe Ostern!	*Happy Easter!*
Fröhliche Weihnachten!	*Merry Christmas!*
Frohe Weihnachten!	*Merry Christmas!*
Fröhliche Weihnachten und ein gesundes neues Jahr!	*Merry Christmas and a healthy New Year!*
Ein gesegnetes Weihnachtsfest und viel Glück im neuen Jahr.	*A blessed Christmas and much luck in the New Year.*
Glückliches neues Jahr!	*Happy New Year!*
Prosit Neujahr!	*Happy New Year! (as a toast)*

Let's look at some sentences that illustrate the use of the names of holidays and celebrations:

Der Fasching ist eine südwestdeutsche Tradition.	*Mardi Gras is a southwestern German tradition.*
Martin will an Fasching ein Kostüm tragen.	*Martin wants to wear a costume for Mardi Gras.*
Viele Studenten gehen auf einen Faschingsball.	*Many students are going to a Mardi Gras dance.*
Ist Neujahr ein Feiertag?	*Is New Year's Day a legal holiday?*

An Silvester gehen sie in die Kirche.	On New Year's Eve they go to church.
Die Eltern haben den Weihnachtsbaum geschmückt.	The parents decorated the Christmas tree.
Am sechsten Dezember bringt der Nikolaus Geschenke.	St. Nicholas brings gifts on the sixth of December.
Der Heiligabend ist am vierundzwanzigsten.	Christmas Eve is on the twenty-fourth.
Die Kinder singen Weihnachtslieder.	The children sing Christmas carols.
Zu Ostern bekommen wir oft Besuch.	We often have guests over Easter.
Der Osterhase bringt den Kindern bunte Eier.	The Easter Bunny brings the children colorful eggs.

Answer the following questions, based on your personal knowledge if possible. Sample answers are provided in the answer key.

1. Wo feiert man den Fasching in den USA? _____

2. Was machen Sie am Feierabend? _____

3. Wer hat eine lange Festansprache gehalten? _____

4. Wann ist Ihr Geburtstag? _____

5. Wann war euer Hochzeitstag? _____

6. Welchen neuen Festtag feiern deutsche Kinder? _____

7. Welcher Feiertag ist am ersten Januar? _____

8. Wer schmückt euren Weihnachtsbaum? _____

9. Wann tragen viele Leute Kostüme? _____

10. Wer bringt den Kindern bunte Eier? _____

Place an X in the blanks that identify what kind of holiday is listed on the left: **gesetzlich** (legal), **kirchlich** (religious), or **persönlich** (personal to people and their family).

	gesetzlich	kirchlich	persönlich
1. Weihnachten	_____	_____	_____
2. Ostern	_____	_____	_____
3. Halloween	_____	_____	_____
4. Hochzeit	_____	_____	_____
5. Jubiläum	_____	_____	_____
6. Tag der Deutschen Einheit	_____	_____	_____

7. Fasching	_____	_____	_____
8. Silvester	_____	_____	_____
9. Geburtstag	_____	_____	_____
10. Muttertag	_____	_____	_____
11. Feierabend	_____	_____	_____

Several useful phrases deal with **die Geburt** (*birth*) and **der Tod** (*death*):

Geburt

gebären	*to bear, give birth to*
das Geburtsdatum	*date of birth*
das Geburtsjahr	*year of birth*
der Geburtsort	*place of birth*
das Geburtshaus	*house where someone was born*
leben	*to live*
wohnen	*to live, reside*
das Geburtstagskind	*birthday boy or girl*
die Geburtstagsüberraschung	*birthday surprise*
die Geburtstagsfeier	*birthday party*
die Geburtstagstorte	*birthday cake*
das Geburtstagsgeschenk	*birthday gift*

Ich habe ihm zum Geburtstag gratuliert.	*I wished him a happy birthday.*
Sie ist im Jahr 1988 geboren und lebt jetzt in Bonn.	*She was born in 1988 and now lives in Bonn.*

The verb **gebären** (*to bear*) is irregular and has the following third-person conjugation in the various tenses:

PRESENT	sie gebärt *or* gebiert
PAST	sie gebar
PRESENT PERFECT	sie hat geboren
FUTURE	sie wird gebären

Use **leben** to mean *to be alive* or *to live* in a general sense. Use **wohnen** to describe *where someone lives* or *where someone's home is.*

Lebt er noch?	*Is he still alive?*
Die alte Frau wohnt in Hamburg.	*The old woman lives in Hamburg.*
Wir wohnen seit Juni in Berlin.	*We've been living in Berlin since June.*

Tod

sterblich	*mortal*
sterben	*to die*
umkommen	*to die, get killed*
töten	*to kill*
umbringen	*to kill*
die Todesangst	*fear of death*
eines natürlichen Todes sterben	*to die a natural death*
die Todesanzeige	*death notice*
die Trauerfeier	*funeral*
die Beerdigung	*burial*
sich zu Tode schämen	*to be ashamed to death*

sich tödlich langweilen	*to be bored to death*
todmüde	*dead tired*
der Todfeind	*deadly enemy*
die Todesstrafe	*death penalty*

Und wenn sie nicht gestorben sind, dann leben sie noch heute.	*They lived happily ever after.*

Notice that both **sterben** and **umkommen** require **sein** as their auxiliary in the perfect tenses:

PRESENT	er stirbt	er kommt um
PAST	er starb	cr kam um
PRESENT PERFECT	er **ist** gestorben	er **ist** umgekommen
FUTURE	er wird sterben	er wird umkommen

In welchem Jahr?

When talking about the year in which someone was born or died, use the year alone or together with the prepositional phrase **im Jahr**. For example:

Sie ist 1975 geboren.	
Sie ist **im Jahr** 1975 geboren.	*She was born in 1975.*

Er ist 2001 gestorben.	
Er ist **im Jahr** 2001 gestorben.	*He died in 2001.*

With dates, use **am**. With months, use **im**.

Karl ist **am** vierten Oktober geboren.	*Karl was born on the fourth of October.*
Mein Onkel ist **im** Februar gestorben.	*My uncle died in February.*

However, if you are speaking about the birth of someone who is now dead, use **wurde** in place of the auxiliary **sein**. For example:

Mein Sohn **ist** im Mai geboren.	*My son was born in May.*
Beethoven **wurde** im Jahr 1770 geboren.	*Beethoven was born in 1770.*

ÜBUNG
7·3

Answer the following questions, based on your personal knowledge if possible. Sample answers are provided in the answer key.

1. In welchem Monat sind Sie geboren? _____

2. In welchem Jahr sind Sie geboren? _____

3. Was für Geburtstagsgeschenke hast du bekommen? _____

4. Was hat deine Mutter zum Geburtstag gebacken? _____

5. Wann ist sein Großvater gestorben? _____

6. Warum schämte sich der Junge zu Tode? _____

7. Wie ist die Frau umgekommen? _____

8. Wann war die Beerdigung des verstorbenen Kanzlers? _____

Rewrite each of the following sentences in the past, present perfect, and future tenses.

1. Wo feiern Sie Weihnachten?

   PAST _____

   PRESENT PERFECT _____

   FUTURE _____

2. Die Kinder tragen Kostüme.

   PAST _____

   PRESENT PERFECT _____

   FUTURE _____

3. Ich gratuliere ihr zum Geburtstag.

   PAST _____

   PRESENT PERFECT _____

   FUTURE _____

4. Heute schmücken sie den Weihnachtsbaum.

   PAST _____

   PRESENT PERFECT _____

   FUTURE _____

5. Zu Ostern bekommen sie Besuch.

   PAST _____

   PRESENT PERFECT _____

   FUTURE _____

6. Die Familie singt Weihnachtslieder.

   PAST _____

   PRESENT PERFECT _____

   FUTURE _____

7. Der Mann kommt um.

   PAST _____

   PRESENT PERFECT _____

   FUTURE _____

8. Der Dieb tötet ihn.

   PAST _____

   PRESENT PERFECT _____

   FUTURE _____

9. Er lebt sorgenfrei.

PAST _____

PRESENT PERFECT _____

FUTURE _____

10. Sie schämt sich zu Tode.

PAST _____

PRESENT PERFECT _____

FUTURE _____

ÜBUNG
7·5

Read each description of a holiday or event, and then fill in the blank with the name of the holiday, event, or other appropriate word.

1. Silvester, der 1. Januar _____

2. Er ist am 10. Mai geboren. _____

3. der 24. Dezember _____

4. der 3. Oktober _____

5. Geschenke für meine Mutter _____

6. die Trauerfeier, die Beerdigung _____

7. Der Osterhase bringt bunte Eier. _____

8. Kinder tragen im Oktober Kostüme. _____

9. Ein Mädchen feiert ihren Geburtstag. _____

10. eine südwestdeutsche Tradition _____

ÜBUNG
7·6

Circle the letter of the word or phrase that best completes each sentence.

1. An _____ haben wir Kostüme getragen.
   a. Weihnachten　　　b. Ostern　　　c. Reformationstag　　　d. Fasching

2. Meine Tante ist _____ 1970 geboren.
   a. gelebt　　　b. wohnen　　　c. im Jahre　　　d. todmüde

3. Der Dieb _____ sich zu Tode.
   a. schämte　　　b. kam um　　　c. bringt um　　　d. bekommt

4. Meine Schwester ist heute Abend _____ gekleidet.
   a. festlich   b. tödlich   c. gewohnt   d. gefeiert

5. Der alte Mann ist eines natürlichen _____ gestorben.
   a. Lebens   b. Todes   c. Beerdigung   d. Festtages

6. Am 6. Dezember brachte Nikolaus _____.
   a. Eier   b. Festansprache   c. Weihnachten   d. Geschenke

7. _____ Weihnachten!
   a. Feierlich   b. Fröhliche   c. Festlich   d. Kirchliche

8. Herzlichen _____ zum Geburtstag.
   a. Glückwunsch   b. Geburtstags-   c. Geburtstagstorte   d. Gesundheit
                              geschenke

9. Der Heiligabend ist am _____ Dezember.
   a. 6.   b. 24.   c. 25.   d. 26.

10. Meine Schwester ist _____ März geboren.
    a. im   b. am   c. zu   d. zum

11. Sein Freund ist bei einem Unglück _____.
    a. geboren   b. umgekommen   c. gewohnt   d. umgebracht

12. Alle Menschen sind _____.
    a. gefeiert   b. tödlich   c. gesetzlich   d. sterblich

13. Sie möchte ihnen zum _____ gratulieren.
    a. Trauerfeier   b. Geburt   c. Hochzeitstag   d. Halloween

14. Mein Neffe ist am _____ geboren.
    a. April   b. neunzehnten Juni   c. 2001   d. Jahre 2002

15. Der Tag der Deutschen Einheit ist ein _____ Festtag.
    a. Tradition   b. gesetzlicher   c. Neujahr   d. kirchlicher

Theater, music, radio, and television

Germany offers a great variety of entertainment. Germans go to the theater to see plays by many past and present German dramatists as well as works by international writers. Large cities have theaters that produce regular opera and ballet performances, as well as concert halls for the many fine German orchestras.

Das Theater

Let's look at some of the vocabulary necessary for talking about the theater:

die Bühne	*stage*
Gehen wir ins Theater!	*Let's go to the theater.*
das Schauspiel	*play*
das Theaterstück	*play*
das Drama	*drama*
die Komödie	*comedy*
die Oper	*opera*
das Ballett	*ballet*
der Schauspieler	*actor*
die Schauspielerin	*actress*
die Hauptrolle	*the main or starring role*
das Theaterabonnement	*season's ticket, subscription*
der Theaterbesucher	*theatergoer*
die Karte	*ticket*
die Eintrittskarte	*admission ticket*

Let's illustrate some of these words in sentences:

Wie oft gehen Sie ins Theater?	*How often do you go to the theater?*
Wir gehen jeden Freitag ins Theater.	*We go to the theater every Friday.*
Wir gehen selten in die Oper.	*We rarely go to the opera.*
Mein Freund geht manchmal ins Ballett.	*My friend sometimes goes to the ballet.*
Hat dir das Drama gefallen?	*Did you like the drama?*
Es hat mir sehr gut gefallen.	*I really liked it a lot.*
Diese Komödie hat uns nicht gefallen.	*We didn't like this comedy.*
Das Schauspiel gefiel ihm nicht.	*He didn't like the play.*
Ist die Kasse noch nicht offen?	*Isn't the box office open yet?*
Die Theaterbesucher nehmen ihre Plätze.	*The theatergoers take their seats.*
Der Vorhang geht hoch.	*The curtain goes up.*

Ein einziger Schauspieler steht auf der Bühne.	*A single actor is on the stage.*
Die Schauspielerin hat viel Applaus bekommen.	*The actress received a lot of applause.*
Das Publikum war begeistert.	*The audience was enthralled.*
Alle klatschen Beifall.	*Everyone applauds.*

ÜBUNG

8·1

Answer the following questions, based on your own experience if possible. Sample answers are provided in the answer key.

1. Gehst du oft ins Theater? _____

2. Was für Theaterstücke hast du gern? _____

3. Welches Schauspiel hat dir gefallen? _____

4. Hast du die Oper oder das Ballett lieber? _____

5. Welche Oper ist deine Lieblingsoper? _____

6. Was tut das Publikum am Ende des Theaterstücks? _____

7. Wer hat viel Applaus bekommen? _____

8. Wann ist die Kasse offen? _____

9. Habt ihr gute Plätze gehabt? _____

10. Wo sind die Eintrittskarten? _____

Das Konzert

Other important words are needed when discussing a musical performance:

der Konzertsaal	*concert hall*
der Konzertmeister, die Konzertmeisterin	*orchestra leader*
der Dirigent, die Dirigentin	*conductor*
der Sänger, die Sängerin	*singer*
der Bariton	*baritone*
der Bass	*bass*
das Orchester	*orchestra*
die Kapelle	*band*
der Chor	*chorus, choir*

Welches Instrument spielt Ihr Sohn?	*What instrument does your son play?*
Mein Sohn spielt ...	*My son plays . . .*
... eine Trommel.	*. . . a drum.*
... den Flügel.	*. . . the grand piano.*
... das Klavier.	*. . . the piano.*
... die Flöte.	*. . . the flute.*
... die Geige.	*. . . the violin.*
... die Klarinette.	*. . . the clarinet.*
... die Posaune.	*. . . the trombone.*

Let's illustrate some of these words in sentences:

Sollen wir ins Konzert gehen?	*Should we go to a concert?*
Ja, gerne. Was wird gespielt?	*Yes, gladly. What's playing?*
Eine Sinfonie von Mozart.	*A Mozart symphony.*
Das Orchester wird eine Ouvertüre spielen.	*The orchestra will play an overture.*
Die Kapelle wird Jazz spielen.	*The band will play jazz.*
Spielen Sie ein Instrument?	*Do you play an instrument?*
Als Kind spielte ich Ziehharmonika.	*I played the accordion as a child.*
Meine Tochter will Geige spielen.	*My daughter wants to play the violin.*
Herr Weber ist Musikant und spielt Flöte.	*Mr. Weber is a musician and plays the flute.*
In der Oper wurde „Tristan und Isolde" aufgeführt.	Tristan and Isolde *was performed in the opera.*
Die Sopranistin hat eine schöne Stimme.	*The soprano has a beautiful voice.*
Die Musik ist sehr traurig.	*The music is very sad.*
Die Marschmusik klingt lustig.	*The marching music sounds happy.*
Die Posaunen sind zu laut.	*The trombones are too loud.*

ÜBUNG
8·2

Answer the following questions, based on your own experience if possible. Sample answers are provided in the answer key.

1. Wie oft geht ihr ins Konzert? _____

2. Was für Musik habt ihr gern? _____

3. Wer steht auf der Bühne? _____

4. Wer hat eine gute Stimme? _____

5. Wer hat diese Sinfonie komponiert? _____

6. Welche Musik ist zu laut? _____

7. Welche Ouvertüre spielt das Orchester? _____

8. Welches Instrument hat Bach gespielt? _____

9. Was passiert, wenn der Dirigent erscheint? _____

10. Welches Instrument ist am größten? _____

Das Kino

Germany has a long tradition of moviemaking, starting with silent movies (**Stummfilme**) and continuing through the era of talking pictures (**Tonfilme**). Movies are, of course, shown in movie theaters, but the German names for these theaters vary:

das Lichtspielhaus
das Lichtspieltheater
das Filmtheater
der Filmpalast
das Kino

The word **der Film** in general means *photographic film*. But it also can be used to mean a *movie*. And if you're *in the movies*, you say:

Er ist seit Juli beim Film.	*He has been in the movies since July.*

Just as English doesn't use the word *nickelodeon* to describe a movie theater anymore (except to be clever or sound old-fashioned), German prefers to use the word **das Kino** (*cinema* or *film* as a medium) when talking about movie theaters. And that word, like the word **der Film**, can attach to numerous other words to form new vocabulary:

der Kinobesucher, die Kinobesucherin	*moviegoer*
der Kinogänger, die Kinogängerin	*moviegoer*
die Kinokarte	*ticket to the movies*
die Kinokasse	*movie box office*
die Kinoreklame	*on-screen advertising*
das Kinoprogramm	*film program, movie guide*
die Kinovorstellung	*(showing of a) movie*
die Filmvorstellung	*(showing of a) movie*
die Filmrolle	*part or role in a movie*
der Filmschauspieler	*movie actor*
die Filmschauspielerin	*movie actress*
der Filmstar	*movie star*
der Filmheld	*movie hero*
die Filmheldin	*movie heroine*
der Filmprojektor	*movie projector*
die Filmspule	*reel*
der Filmvorführer, die Filmvorführerin	*projectionist*
die Filmkunst	*art of cinema*
die Filmleinwand	*movie screen*
die Filmzensur	*film censorship*

Let's illustrate some of these words in sentences:

Gehen wir heute Abend ins Kino!	*Let's go to the show this evening!*
Was läuft heute im Kino?	*What's playing at the movies today?*
Heute läuft im Kino ein englischer Film.	*An English movie is playing today at the theater.*
Morgen läuft ein Dokumentarfilm.	*A documentary is playing tomorrow.*
Morgen läuft ein neuer Spielfilm.	*A new feature film is playing tomorrow.*
Ist dein Bruder noch beim Film?	*Is your brother still in the movies?*
Ja, er ist Regisseur.	*Yes, he's a director.*
Was für Filme siehst du gerne an?	*What kind of movies do you like to see?*
Ich sehe mir gerne Wildwestfilme an.	*I like to see cowboy movies.*
Hast du schon den alten Film „M" angesehen?	*Have you seen the old movie M?*
Das Kinoprogramm war sehr schlecht.	*The movie offerings were very bad.*
Mein Lieblingsfilmschauspieler war Heinz Rühmann.	*My favorite actor was Heinz Rühmann.*
Ihr Lieblingsfilmstar ist Brad Pitt.	*Her favorite actor is Brad Pitt.*
Wann beginnt die nächste Vorstellung?	*When does the next show begin?*
Der Film wird um 20 Uhr aus sein.	*The movie will be over at 8 P.M.*
Im Park wird ein Film gedreht.	*A movie is being shot in the park.*

The word *director* can be translated by two different German words:

der Dirigent	*music director, conductor*
der Regisseur	*film director*

Two words are used to mean *to see* or *to watch* a movie: **ansehen** and **anschauen**:

	ansehen	anschauen
PRESENT	sieht an	schaut an
PAST	sah an	schaute an
PRESENT PERFECT	hat angesehen	hat angeschaut
FUTURE	wird ansehen	wird anschauen

ÜBUNG
8·3

Answer the following questions, based on your own experience if possible. Sample answers are provided in the answer key.

1. Kannst du morgen ins Kino gehen? _____

2. Ist die Filmzensur in Deutschland streng? _____

3. Wer interessiert sich für die Filmkunst? _____

4. Was läuft im Kino? _____

5. Um wie viel Uhr ist die nächste Vorstellung? _____

6. Wie alt ist dieser Filmstar? _____

7. Was ist Ihr Lieblingsfilm? _____

8. Wie ist das neue Kinoprogramm? _____

9. Was für Filme sehen Sie sich gerne an? _____

10. Womit fängt die Vorstellung an? _____

Das Radio und das Fernsehen

Radio and television have become as much entertainment vehicles as they have been communication vehicles. These two forms of electronics are widespread in the German-speaking world and can be found in homes, cars, schools, restaurants, bars, and stores. They are even used in auditoriums or stadiums as part of events or presentations.

The word **das Radio** is used to mean a *radio set*, and the same meaning is derived when certain suffixes are attached:

der Radioapparat	*radio set*
das Radiogerät	*radio set*

Let's look at some useful phrases dealing with **das Radio**:

der Radiosender	*radio station*
im Radio	*on the radio*
Ich höre jeden Morgen Radio.	*I listen to the radio every morning.*

Another word for *radio* is **der Rundfunk**, which usually functions like **das Radio**:

das Rundfunkgerät	radio set
der Rundfunkempfänger	radio receiver
der Rundfunksender	radio station
die Rundfunksendung	radio program
die Rundfunkübertragung	radio broadcast
der Rundfunksprecher, die Rundfunksprecherin	radio announcer
das Rundfunkprogramm	radio program guide

Here are a few sentences that illustrate the use of **der Rundfunk**:

Was hören Sie gern im Rundfunk?	*What do you like listening to on the radio?*
Ich höre gern klassische Musik.	*I like listening to classical music.*
Mein Vater hört gern Sportübertragungen.	*My father likes listening to sports broadcasts.*
Was wird heute Abend übertragen?	*What will be broadcast tonight?*
Heute Abend wird ein Fußballspiel übertragen.	*A soccer game will be broadcast tonight.*
Bitte stelle das Radio ein bisschen lauter ein!	*Please turn the sound up a little on the radio.*
Sie sind auf Sendung.	*They're on the air.*
Um wie viel Uhr werden die Nachrichten gesendet?	*What time is the news on?*

The verb **fernsehen** has the separable prefix **fern-** and means *to watch television*. The principal parts of this verb in the third-person singular are as follows:

PRESENT	er sieht fern	*he watches television*
PAST	er sah fern	*he watched television*
PRESENT PERFECT	er hat ferngesehen	*he has watched television*
FUTURE	er wird fernsehen	*he will watch television*

The noun **der Fernseher** can mean the *television set* or the *television viewer*. But **der Fernsehapparat** and **das Fernsehgerät** mean only *television set*.

The form **Fernseh-** is used as a prefix for a variety of words dealing with television:

der Fernsehansager, die Fernsehansagerin	*television announcer*
die Fernsehaufzeichnung	*television recording*
der Fernsehempfang	*television reception*
die Fernsehkamera	*television camera*
der Fernsehkanal	*television channel*
das Fernsehprogramm	*television viewing guide*
der Fernsehsatellit	*television satellite*
der Fernsehschirm	*television screen*
die Fernsehsendung	*television program*
der Fernsehspot	*television commercial*
das Fernsehstudio	*television studio*
der Fernsehturm	*television tower*
die Fernsehübertragung	*television broadcast*

The words in the preceding list can be used without **Fernseh-** when it is understood that they refer to television. Instead of **die Fernsehsendung**, for example, you can say **die Sendung**.

Today, it is quite fashionable to use **TV** occasionally as a substitute for **das Fernsehen**:

der TV-Sender	*TV station*
das TV-Programm	*TV programming schedule*
neues aus TV	*the latest on TV*
die TV-Info	*TV information*
die TV-Tipps	*TV tips*

Let's look at a few phrases and sentences that illustrate the use of words related to **das Fernsehen**:

Seid ihr jetzt verkabelt?	*Do you have cable TV now?*
Ich sehe lieber Fernsehprogramme über die Politik.	*I prefer watching TV shows about politics.*
Die Olympischen Spiele wurden direkt aus Kanada übertragen.	*The Olympic Games were broadcast directly from Canada.*
Warum sitzt du den ganzen Tag vor dem Bildschirm?	*Why do you sit in front of the TV all day long?*
Was wird morgen im Fernsehen übertragen?	*What's going to be broadcast on TV tomorrow?*
Was kommt morgen im Fernsehen?	*What's on TV tomorrow?*

When watching television, it is convenient to have **die Fernbedienung** (*the remote control*) handy.

The verb **hören** means *to hear*:

Hörst du die Kinder singen?	*Do you hear the children singing?*
Ich habe nichts gehört.	*I didn't hear anything.*

But the same verb means *to listen to* when the object of the verb is **Radio** or something broadcast on the radio:

Wir hören jeden Abend Radio.	*We listen to the radio every evening.*
Die Jungen hörten Musik.	*The boys were listening to music.*

Notice that the definite article (***das* Radio**, ***die* Musik**) is not required with this kind of meaning. However, when *listen to* has a person as its object, the verb **zuhören** is required and the object is in the dative case:

Ich habe dem Professor zugehört.	*I listened to the professor.*
Die Kinder hörten ihr zu.	*The children listened to her.*

ÜBUNG
8·4

Answer the following questions, based on your own experience if possible. Sample answers are provided in the answer key.

1. Was hören Sie gern im Radio? _____

2. Haben Sie ein neues Radiogerät gekauft? _____

3. Um wie viel Uhr beginnt die Kindersendung? _____

4. Wie oft sieht Ihre Familie fern? _____

5. Wie viel Fernsehkanäle haben Sie? _____

6. Haben Sie eine Fernsehantenne? _____

7. Was wird heute Abend übertragen? _____

Place an X in the blanks that identify where you are most likely to encounter the items listed on the left: **ins Theater**, **ins Kino**, **ins Konzert**, **im Rundfunk**, *or* **im Fernsehen**.

	Theater	Kino	Konzert	Rundfunk	Fernsehen
1. Stück	_____	_____	_____	_____	_____
2. Spielfilm	_____	_____	_____	_____	_____
3. Chor	_____	_____	_____	_____	_____
4. Sinfonie	_____	_____	_____	_____	_____
5. Komödie	_____	_____	_____	_____	_____
6. Nachrichten	_____	_____	_____	_____	_____
7. Sportsendung	_____	_____	_____	_____	_____
8. Oper	_____	_____	_____	_____	_____
9. Dirigent	_____	_____	_____	_____	_____
10. Ballett	_____	_____	_____	_____	_____
11. Filmleinwand	_____	_____	_____	_____	_____
12. Bühne	_____	_____	_____	_____	_____
13. Flügel	_____	_____	_____	_____	_____

Rewrite each of the following sentences in the other three tenses.

1. ansehen

   PRESENT   <u>Er sieht oft fern.</u>

   PAST   _____

   PRESENT PERFECT   _____

   FUTURE   _____

2. zuhören

   PRESENT   _____

   PAST   _____

   PRESENT PERFECT   _____

   FUTURE   <u>Wir werden dem Lehrer zuhören.</u>

3. übertragen

PRESENT _____

PAST <u>Ein Konzert wurde übertragen.</u>

PRESENT PERFECT _____

FUTURE _____

4. stehen

PRESENT _____

PAST _____

PRESENT PERFECT <u>Der Chor hat auf der Bühne gestanden.</u>

FUTURE _____

5. schauen

PRESENT <u>Ich schaue mir gerne Spielfilme an.</u>

PAST _____

PRESENT PERFECT _____

FUTURE _____

ÜBUNG
8·7

Fill in each blank with an appropriate word.

1. Er sieht sich _____ Wildwestfilme an.

2. Meine Eltern gingen jeden Freitag _____ Theater.

3. Im Ballett hat Angelika Keller die _____ getanzt.

4. Die Tänzer sitzen auf der _____ und warten.

5. Im Kino _____ ein neuer Dokumentarfilm.

6. Wann beginnt die nächste _____?

7. Der _____ des Orchesters war Fritz Reiner.

8. Ruhe bitte! Wir sind auf _____.

9. Das Spiel wird direkt aus den USA _____.

10. Um 20 Uhr werden die _____ gesendet.

11. Die Kindersendung _____ um 17 Uhr.

12. Der _____ hat eine sehr gute Stimme.

13. Die Mädchen sitzen auf dem Boden und _____ Musik.

14. Meine Schwestern sehen jeden Abend _____.

15. Mein Mann sitzt das ganze Wochenende vor dem _____.

Circle the letter of the word or phrase that best completes each sentence.

1. Seine _____ ist Mozarts „die Zauberflöte."
   a. Lieblingskonzert   b. Lieblingsoper   c. Lieblingsfilmstar   d. Lieblingsfilm

2. Ihre _____ fangen erst um 5 Uhr an.
   a. Übertragungen   b. Ballett   c. Ouvertüre   d. Posaunen

3. Das _____ heißt „Nathan der Weise" von Lessing.
   a. Schauspiel   b. Sendung   c. Sender   d. Theaterabonnement

4. Ich habe die _____ verloren!
   a. Kinos   b. Komödie   c. Eintrittskarten   d. Drama

5. Die junge Sopranistin hat eine sehr schöne _____.
   a. Bariton   b. Stück   c. Kasse   d. Stimme

6. Was für ein _____ spielt Ihre Tochter?
   a. Geige   b. Instrument   c. Posaunen   d. Sport

7. Hier wird ein neuer _____ gebaut.
   a. Fernsehturm   b. Theaterstück   c. Radiogerät   d. Fernsehansager

8. Wir sind schon seit drei Wochen _____.
   a. gehört   b. zugehört   c. gesendet   d. verkabelt

9. Die letzte _____ beginnt in zehn Minuten.
   a. Konzert   b. Vorstellung   c. Ballett   d. Radiosender

10. Der _____ hat zu laut gesungen.
    a. Chor   b. Sopranistin   c. Kapelle   d. Kinoreklame

11. Dieses _____ ist sehr ausführlich.
    a. Fernsehapparat   b. Fernsehansagerin   c. Radioprogramm   d. Radiosender

12. Wir hören gern Rockmusik im _____.
    a. Komödie   b. Filmkunst   c. Flöte   d. Radio

13. Wir haben gute Plätze, weil wir ein _____ haben.
    a. Abonnement   b. Karte   c. Geige   d. Fernsehkanal

14. Was wurde gestern Abend _____?
    a. übertragen   b. zugehört   c. anschauen   d. interessiert

15. Meine Tante geht jede Woche _____ Ballett.
    a. vor   b. zu   c. ins   d. von

Transportation

People get around by various modes of transportation. But no matter how complicated or technical transportation may become, it all began with people getting around on their own two feet. Today, we call them *pedestrians*.

der Fußgänger, die Fußgängerin	*pedestrian*

Sie gehen zu Fuß nach Hause.	*They go home on foot.*
Gehst du immer zu Fuß?	*Do you always go on foot?*

Der Transport

Transportation moves not only people but also goods of every description. In the modern world, transportation involves many different vehicles, which fall into the following categories:

der Straßentransport	*ground (road) transportation*
der Bahntransport	*rail transportation*
der Seetransport	*sea transportation*
der Lufttransport	*air transportation*

Ground transportation takes place on a country's roads and highways. In German, the words for the types of roads are as varied as in English. For example:

der Pfad	*path*
der Weg	*path, way*
der Radweg	*bicycle path*
die Allee	*avenue, lane*
die Straße	*street*
die Einbahnstraße	*one-way street*
die Landstraße	*rural road*
die öffentliche Straße	*public road*
der Verkehrsweg	*main route*
die Autobahn	*highway, expressway*
die Ausfahrt	*exit ramp*
die Einfahrt	*entrance ramp*

English commonly uses the verb *to go* in general terms and does not specify whether a person is on foot or in some kind of vehicle. German, however, is specific and uses the verbs **gehen**, **fahren**, and **fliegen** precisely. Consider the following sentences:

Ich gehe ins Theater.	*I'm going to the theater. (on foot)*
Ich fahre nach Berlin.	*I'm going to Berlin. (by ground transportation)*
Ich fliege in die Schweiz.	*I'm going to Switzerland. (by plane)*

Der Straßentransport

Let's look at some of the vehicles that travel on roads:

das Fahrrad, das Rad	*bicycle*
das Motorrad	*motorcycle*
das Moped	*moped*
der Lastwagen	*truck*
der Wagen	*car*
das Auto	*automobile*
der Kombi	*stationwagon*
der Sportwagen	*sports car*
der Rennwagen	*racing car*
der Bus	*bus*
das Taxi, die Taxe	*taxi*

The noun **das Fahrrad** also has a verb form: **Rad fahren**. Here are sentences using the principal parts of this verb:

PRESENT	Er fährt Rad.	*He rides a bike.*
PAST	Er fuhr Rad.	*He rode a bike.*
PRESENT PERFECT	Er ist Rad gefahren.	*He has ridden a bike.*
FUTURE	Er wird Rad fahren.	*He will ride a bike.*

This same verb can be used as a noun, just as other German infinitives: **das Radfahren**. Let's look at how these words are used:

Martin hat sich ein neues Fahrrad gekauft.	*Martin bought himself a new bike.*
Wir sind zwei Stunden lang Rad gefahren.	*We were cycling for two hours.*
Radfahren macht Spaß.	*Cycling is fun.*

The following sentences illustrate how the words for various vehicles on the street can be used:

Sie fährt mit dem Motorrad in die Stadt.	*She goes to the city by motorcycle.*
Dieser Lastwagen ist zu schwer, um auf dieser Straße zu fahren.	*This truck is too heavy to travel on this street.*
Wer hat den großen Wagen gelenkt?	*Who drove (steered) the big car?*
Ich muß mein Auto reparieren lassen.	*I have to have my car repaired.*
Ein Moped darf nicht auf dem Radweg fahren.	*A moped isn't allowed on the bicycle path.*
Der Student nimmt den Bus, um an die Uni zu kommen.	*The student takes the bus to get to the university.*
Das Taxi wurde von der Polizei gestoppt.	*The taxi was stopped by the police.*

If you don't have your own vehicle, you can sometimes travel to a destination by *hitchhiking*. The German phrase is **per Anhalter fahren**:

Mein Bruder ist per Anhalter nach Köln gefahren.	*My brother hitchhiked to Cologne.*

If you go by car, you need to know what to do with your car when you arrive at your destination. The following words are useful for this situation:

parken	to park
die Parkuhr	parking meter
der Parkplatz	parking place
das Parkhaus	parking garage

Die Parkplätze sind alle belegt.	The parking places are all taken.
Bitte parken Sie im Parkhaus!	Please park in the parking garage.

9·1

Answer the following questions, based on your personal knowledge if possible. Sample answers are provided in the answer key.

1. Wohin gehen Sie oft zu Fuß? _____

2. Wo soll ein Fußgänger nicht spazieren gehen? _____

3. Wo kann man nur in eine Richtung fahren? _____

4. Was für ein Wagen ist schneller als ein Kombi? _____

5. Wer fährt oft per Anhalter? _____

6. Von wem wurde der Taxifahrer gestoppt? _____

7. Was willst du reparieren lassen? _____

8. Womit fahrt ihr in die Stadt? _____

9. Worauf wartest du? _____

10. Warum hat der Mann das Motorrad verkauft? _____

Der Bahntransport

Rail transportation includes more than just railroad trains; it includes any vehicle that rides on rails.

die Straßenbahn	streetcar
die Eisenbahn	railroad
die S-Bahn	city or local railway
die U-Bahn	subway
die Einschienenbahn	monorail
der Zug	train
der D-Zug	through train
der Eilzug	express train
der InterCity (or IC)	InterCity Express
der Güterzug	freight train

When traveling, you need some specific vocabulary to get on and off a mode of transport and to find the services you need:

die Station	a subway or local railway station
der Bahnhof	railway station

der Hauptbahnhof	*main railway station*
die Haltestelle	*stop*
die Bushaltestelle	*bus stop*
die Straßenbahnhaltestelle	*streetcar stop*
der Bahnsteig	*platform*
der Fahrschein	*ticket (bus, streetcar)*
die Fahrkarte	*ticket (train)*

The verb **steigen** combines with three prefixes to form important words relating to transportation:

einsteigen	*to get on board*
umsteigen	*to transfer*
aussteigen	*to get off*

In sentences, these verbs are used like this:

Wir können in der Nähe des Museums in die S-Bahn einsteigen.	*We can get on the S-Bahn near the museum.*
Ich muss in der nächsten Station umsteigen.	*I have to transfer at the next station.*
Steigen wir am Marktplatz aus!	*Let's get off on the market square.*

When you buy a ticket, you need to use the verb **lösen**:

Wo kann man einen Fahrschein lösen?	*Where can you buy a ticket?*

Here are a few more useful sentences that relate to public transportation:

Ich habe den letzten Bus verpasst.	*I missed the last bus.*
Die Straßenbahn hielt vor dem Hotel.	*The streetcar stopped in front of the hotel.*
Der IC nach Berlin fährt um 10 Uhr ab.	*The InterCity train to Berlin departs at 10 o'clock.*
Wann kommt der Güterzug an?	*When does the freight train arrive?*
Der Eilzug nach Hamburg hatte 40 Minuten Verspätung.	*The express to Hamburg is delayed by 40 minutes.*
Einen Fahrschein nach Bremen. Hin und zurück.	*A ticket to Bremen. Round-trip.*
Ich habe eine Rückfahrkarte nach München.	*I have a round-trip ticket to Munich.*

When traveling by train, you need a few more helpful words and phrases:

erste Klasse	*first class*
das Abteil	*compartment*
der Liegewagen	*couchette car*
der Nichtraucher	*nonsmoking car or compartment*
der Schlafwagen	*sleeper car*
die Gepäckaufbewahrung	*baggage check*

Ich möchte zweiter Klasse reisen.	*I want to travel second class.*
Der IC fährt auf Gleis 2 ab.	*The InterCity train departs from Track 2.*
Ich brauche einen Fahrplan.	*I need a schedule.*
Es ist verboten schwarzzufahren.	*Traveling without a ticket is not permitted.*

Der Seetransport

Before the great steamers were born, sailors used the wind to power them across the sea. Sailing was as much a dangerous adventure as it was a means of transportation. Of course, not everyone sailed across the ocean. Other bodies of water were also used for transportation.

der Ozean	*ocean*
die See	*sea*
das Meer	*sea*
der See	*lake*
der Teich	*pond*
der Fluss	*river*
der Bach	*stream*

The following are well-known bodies of water:

der Atlantische Ozean	*Atlantic Ocean*
der Pazifische Ozean	*Pacific Ocean*
das Mittelmeer	*Mediterranean Sea*
der Golf von Mexiko	*Gulf of Mexico*
der Persische Golf	*Persian Gulf*
die Nordsee	*North Sea*
die Ostsee	*Baltic Sea*
der Amazonas	*Amazon River*
der Nil	*Nile River*
der Rhein	*Rhine River*
die Elbe	*Elbe River*
die Wolga	*Volga River*

The verb *to sail* is **segeln**:

Auf diesem See wird oft gesegelt.	*People often sail on this lake.*
Kannst du segeln?	*Can you sail?*

Notice how **segeln** combines with other words to form new words:

das Segel	*sail*
segeln	*to sail*
das Boot	*boat*
das Segelboot	*sailboat*
das Schiff	*ship*
das Segelschiff	*sailing ship*
die Jacht	*yacht*
die Segeljacht	*sailing yacht*
die Segelfahrt	*voyage on a sailing vessel*
die Segelregatta	*sailing regatta*

There are more than just sailing vessels on the waterways of the world. Some are small pleasure boats; others are enormous freighters and liners:

das Paddelboot	*rowboat*
das Motorboot	*motorboat*
das Kajütboot	*cabin cruiser*
der Dampfer	*steamer*
der Frachter	*freighter*
der Öltanker	*oil tanker*
der Schaufelraddampfer	*paddle wheeler*
der Überseedampfer	*ocean liner*

Also, the navy has specialized military ships:

die Marine	*fleet, navy*
die Kriegsmarine	*navy (military)*

der Flugzeugträger	aircraft carrier
der Kreuzer	cruiser
das U-Boot (Unterseeboot)	submarine
der Zerstörer	destroyer

Now let's look at some sentences that illustrate the use of these words:

Mein Vater will ein Motorboot mieten.	My father wants to rent a motorboat.
Zwei Dampfer sind bei Flut ausgelaufen.	Two steamers sailed with the tide.
Alle Matrosen sind an Bord des Flugzeugträgers.	All the sailors are on board the aircraft carrier.
Der Kapitän war Offizier bei der Kriegsmarine.	The captain was an officer in the navy.
Der Schaufelraddampfer wird im Hafen anlegen.	The paddle wheeler will put into harbor.
Das alte Schiff hat kein Rettungsboot.	The old ship doesn't have a lifeboat.

Der Lufttransport

Air travel today is as common as rail travel was for previous generations. The variety of aircraft is great. Let's look at some of the most common forms:

das Flugzeug	airplane
der Doppeldecker	biplane
das Düsenflugzeug	jet plane
der Jumbojet	jumbo jet
das Segelflugzeug	glider
der Hubschrauber	helicopter
das Luftschiff	dirigible

The military has its own varieties of aircraft:

der Düsenjäger	jet fighter
der Bomber	bomber
der Truppentransporter	troop carrier
die Rakete	rocket
das Raumfahrzeug	spacecraft

Here are sentences that illustrate the use of words dealing with air travel:

Die Touristen fliegen um 11 Uhr ab.	The tourists leave at 11 o'clock.
Auf diesem Flughafen startet ein Flugzeug alle drei Minuten.	A plane takes off from this airport every three minutes.
Bald landen wir.	We'll land soon.
Jeder Fluggast muss ein Flugticket haben.	Each passenger must have a ticket.
Die Pilotin ist sehr erfahren.	The pilot (female) is very experienced.
Mit welcher Fluggesellschaft wollen Sie fliegen?	What airline do you want to fly on?
Bitte schnallen Sie sich an!	Please fasten your seat belt.
Der neue Hubschrauber fliegt ziemlich schnell.	The new helicopter flies rather fast.
Dieser Düsenjäger fliegt am schnellsten.	This fighter flies the fastest.

Answer the following questions, based on your personal knowledge if possible. Sample answers are provided in the answer key.

1. Wo soll man auf die Straßenbahn warten? _____

2. Welcher Zug kommt am schnellsten nach Freiburg? _____

3. Welcher Klasse reisen Sie lieber? _____

4. Was soll man vor der Fahrt lösen? _____

5. Was für ein Boot ist größer als ein Paddelboot? _____

6. Was trägt ein Flugzeugträger? _____

7. Wer ist noch nicht an Bord des Schiffes? _____

8. Was wird im Hafen anlegen? _____

9. Hast du je einen Doppeldecker gesehen? _____

10. Was startet alle fünf Minuten? _____

Rewrite each of the following sentences in the other three tenses.

1. gehen

   PRESENT   Er geht oft zu Fuß.

   PAST   _____

   PRESENT PERFECT   _____

   FUTURE   _____

2. machen

   PRESENT   _____

   PAST   Radfahren machte Spaß.

   PRESENT PERFECT   _____

   FUTURE   _____

3. fahren wollen

   PRESENT   _____

   PAST   _____

   PRESENT PERFECT   Er hat nicht per Anhalter fahren wollen.

   FUTURE   _____

4. verpassen

PRESENT _____

PAST _____

PRESENT PERFECT _____

FUTURE <u>Wird er den Bus verpassen?</u>

5. fliegen

PRESENT <u>Der Hubschrauber fliegt über der Stadt.</u>

PAST _____

PRESENT PERFECT _____

FUTURE _____

ÜBUNG

9·4

Fill in each blank with an appropriate word.

1. Sie ist zu Fuß zum Stadtpark _____.

2. Die Parkplätze waren alle _____.

3. Ein Rennwagen ist _____ als ein Moped.

4. Wir warten an der Haltestelle auf eine _____.

5. Auf der _____ kann man am schnellsten fahren.

6. Wir müssen am Marktplatz _____.

7. Schnell! Steige in die _____ ein!

8. Italien und Spanien liegen am _____.

9. Vor der Abfahrt musst du einen Fahrschein _____.

10. Du hast keine Fahrkarte. Wirst du _____?

11. Ich muss ein Hotel finden. Ich habe den letzten Zug _____.

12. Ein _____ hat zwei Flügel und sieht sehr altmodisch aus.

13. Der Dampfer ist bei _____ ausgelaufen.

14. Die Passagiere sind schon an _____ des Schiffes.

15. Sie sind lange geflogen, aber bald _____ sie.

Circle the letter of the word or phrase that best completes each sentence.

1. Es sind heute viele _____ im Stadtpark.
   a. Fahrgast   b. Fußgänger   c. Paddelboot   d. Teich

2. Der große _____ ist sehr schwer.
   a. Lastwagen   b. Motorboot   c. Segelschiff   d. Straßenbahn

3. Frau Keller wird ihr Moped _____.
   a. verkauft   b. abfahren   c. geflogen sein   d. reparieren lassen

4. Ein Sportwagen darf nicht _____ fahren.
   a. auf dem Radweg   b. auf die Autobahn   c. in der Eisenbahn   d. im Hauptbahnhof

5. Haben Sie _____ nach Bern?
   a. eine Rückfahrkarte b. ein Schlafwagen   c. den D-Zug   d. die U-Bahn

6. Wirst du in der Nähe des Rathauses _____?
   a. aussteigen   b. lösen   c. verpassen   d. starten

7. Die Wolga ist ein _____ in Russland.
   a. Teich   b. Mittelmeer   c. Fluss   d. Düsenjäger

8. Herr Schneider war Offizier bei _____.
   a. der Kriegsmarine b. einem U-Boot   c. dem Kapitän   d. einem Matrosen

9. Auf _____ sieht man oft Segelboote.
   a. diesen Fluss   b. diesem See   c. der Persische Golf d. Rhein

10. Der _____ ist das größte Schiff.
    a. Motorboot   b. Hubschrauber   c. Flut   d. Öltanker

11. _____ fliegt schneller als ein Doppeldecker.
    a. Eine Jacht   b. Ein   c. Ein Flugzeugträger d. Ein Hafen
                            Düsenflugzeug

12. Hier startet _____ alle sechs Minuten.
    a. die Marine   b. mit dem Luftschiff c. ein Flugzeug   d. das Flugticket

13. Es ist wichtig ein _____ zu haben.
    a. Fluggast   b. Rettungsboot   c. Bahnhof   d. Ausfahrt

14. Es ist zu teuer _____ zu reisen.
    a. auf dem Flughafen b. vor dem neuen   c. erster Klasse   d. die Nordsee
                            Hotel

15. Ich fahre nicht gern _____.
    a. per Anhalter   b. eine Haltestelle   c. das Paddelboot   d. im Abteil

Travel, vacation, and nationality

Like so many other Europeans, Germans love to travel. They enjoy hiking through forests and in the mountains, sunbathing on the island of Capri, or taking a three-week tour around the United States and Canada. In short, Germans have the "travel bug" and use their long vacation time from work (from three to six weeks!) to journey as far as their budget will allow.

Ferien und Reisen

The plural noun **die Ferien** is the *vacation time* a person has from school or work. But the singular noun **der Urlaub** can also be translated as *vacation*. Let's look at some phrases that illustrate how those two words are used:

in die Ferien fahren	*to go on a vacation*
in den großen Ferien	*during summer vacation*
das Ferienheim	*vacation home*
das Ferienlager	*vacation camp*
der Urlauber, die Urlauberin	*vacationer*
Urlaub haben	*have military leave, be on vacation*
Urlaub machen	*be on vacation*
das Urlaubsgeld	*money saved for vacation*
der Urlaubsschein	*pass for military leave*

The following sentences show how these words can be used:

Wann beginnen die Schulferien?	*When does (school) vacation begin?*
In den großen Ferien fahren wir jedes Jahr in die Alpen.	*During every summer vacation we go to the Alps.*
Er hat acht Urlaubstage.	*He has eight vacation days.*
Sie machen eine Urlaubsreise ans Meer.	*They're on a vacation trip to the sea.*
Herr Weber ist noch nicht aus dem Urlaub zurück.	*Mr. Weber isn't back from vacation yet.*
Wir haben jetzt genug Urlaubsgeld, um nach Italien zu reisen.	*We now have enough vacation money to go to Italy.*
Der junge Soldat ist auf Urlaub in Berlin.	*The young soldier is on leave in Berlin.*

Most vacations include a trip to a new place. In German, the noun **die Reise** (*trip, journey*) and the verb **reisen** (*to travel*) are used to describe the many aspects of travel. Let's look at some examples along with other vocabulary that deals with vacation plans:

das Reisebüro	travel agency
der Reisepass, der Pass	passport
das Visum	visa
das Reiseandenken	souvenir
der Reisebegleiter, die Reisebegleiterin	traveling companion, chaperone
die Spanienreise	trip to Spain
die Busreise	trip by bus
der Reiseführer	guidebook
der Reiseführer, die Reiseführerin	tour guide
der Reiseleiter, die Reiseleiterin	tour guide
die Reisekrankheit	travel sickness
die Reisegruppe	group of tourists
die Reisepläne	travel plans
die Reiseroute	itinerary
der/die Reisende	traveler
Besichtigungen machen	to go sightseeing
der Ausflug	excursion
der Besuch eines Museums	visit to a museum
der Besucher, die Besucherin	visitor
der Deutschlandbesuch	visit to Germany
der Tourist, die Touristin	tourist
die Hafenrundfahrt	a trip around the harbor
die Kreuzfahrt	cruise
die letzte Reise antreten	to meet one's Maker
die Sehenswürdigkeiten	sights (seen while sightseeing)
die Sightseeingtour	sightseeing tour
die Tour	tour

Now let's look at some sentences that illustrate the use of this vocabulary as well as some important new words:

Frau Berger ist viel gereist.	Mrs. Berger is a seasoned traveler.
Ich bin für einige Tage nach Luxemburg verreist.	I went to Luxemburg for a few days.
Meine Eltern sind verreist.	My parents are away on a trip.
Sie machen eine Reise um die Welt.	They're taking a trip around the world.
Habt ihr eine Rundreise durch die Stadt gemacht?	Did you take a tour around the city?
Ich fahre dieses Jahr zu einem Kurort in Dänemark.	This year I'm going to a resort in Denmark.
Brauchen Sie eine Landkarte?	Do you need a map?
Brauchst du einen Stadtplan?	Do you need a map of the city?
An der Grenze werden wir kontrolliert werden.	We'll be checked at the border.
Er musste Zoll bezahlen.	He had to pay duty.
In der Nähe der Autobahn gibt es eine Raststätte.	There's a rest stop in the vicinity of the highway.
Ich suche eine billige Pension.	I'm looking for a cheap guest house.
Wir können in einem Hotel übernachten.	We can stay overnight in a hotel.
Die Jugendherberge ist sehr weit von hier.	The youth hostel is very far from here.
Er hat ein neues Zelt und will jedes Wochenende zelten.	He has a new tent and wants to go camping (tenting) every weekend.

Ich mache nur im Sommer Camping.	*I only go camping in the summer.*
Mein Onkel hat eine Ferienwohnung am Bodensee.	*My uncle has a vacation place on Lake Constance.*
Ich habe an meine Schwester eine Ansichtskarte geschickt.	*I sent my sister a picture postcard.*

Die Sehenswürdigkeiten

When traveling in Germany, you can take in many different kinds of sights:

die Kunsthalle	*art museum*
das Gemälde	*painting*
die Statue	*statue*
das Denkmal	*monument*
die Burg	*castle*
das Schloss	*palace*
der Palast	*palace*
die Festung	*fortress*
die Stadtmauer	*city wall*
das Rathaus	*city hall*
die Kirche	*church*
der Dom	*cathedral*
die Brücke	*bridge*
das Stadion	*stadium*
der Bundestag	*federal parliament*
der Fernsehturm	*television tower*
der Irrgarten	*maze*
der zoologische Garten, der Zoo	*zoo*
das Harzgebirge, der Harz	*Hartz Mountains*
die Lüneburger Heide	*the Lueneburg Heath*
der Schwarzwald	*Black Forest* (mountain range)
die Seilbahn	*cable car*

Dieses Denkmal ist dem ersten Kanzler zu Ehren errichtet worden.	*This monument was put up in honor of the first chancellor.*
Freiburg liegt im Schwarzwald.	*Freiburg is located in the Black Forest.*
Der Bundestag ist in der Hauptstadt.	*The federal parliament is in the capital.*
Dieser Fernsehturm ist der Höchste in Europa.	*This television tower is the highest in Europe.*
Werden Sie das Olympische Stadion besuchen?	*Will you visit the Olympic Stadium?*
Die Touristen besichtigen eine mittelalterliche Burg.	*The tourists visit a castle from the Middle Ages.*

Answer the following questions, based on your personal knowledge if possible. Sample answers are provided in the answer key.

1. Wohin reisen Sie gern? _____

2. Wie viele Ferientage haben Sie jedes Jahr? _____

3. Waren Sie einmal in einem Ferienlager? _____

4. Wann macht Ihre Familie Urlaub? _____

5. Wer ist noch nicht aus dem Urlaub zurück? _____

6. Was macht Ihr Freund mit seinem Urlaubsgeld? _____

7. Wo kann man die Karten für eine Stadtrundfahrt kaufen? _____

_____

8. Wer begleitet die Schülergruppe im Museum? _____

9. Was wird an der Grenze passieren? _____

10. Was für ein Hotel suchen Sie? _____

Die Nationalität

When traveling, you will occasionally be asked for your travel documents, particularly at certain border crossings. Depending upon your nationality, you will have to provide an identification card, a passport, a visa, or a birth certificate.

Besides having a passport for international travel, Germans have their national identity card—**der Personalausweis**. Other forms of identification for travel include the following:

der Pass	*passport*
das Passbild	*passport photo*
das Visum	*visa*
der Führerschein	*driver's license*
die Geburtsurkunde	*birth certificate*

At a border crossing you will probably be confronted with certain general phrases:

Haben Sie Ihre Papiere bei sich?	*Do you have your papers on you?*
Meine Papiere sind in meinem Koffer.	*My papers are in my suitcase.*
Ihren Pass, bitte!	*Your passport, please.*
Ist Ihr Visum noch gültig?	*Is your visa still valid?*
Mein Visum ist gültig, und ich habe schon meine Aufenthaltserlaubnis bekommen.	*My visa is valid, and I have already received my residence permit.*
Wo ist Ihr Geburtsort?	*Where is your place of birth?*
Ich bin in den USA geboren.	*I was born in the USA.*
Ich bin Amerikaner (Amerikanerin).	*I'm an American.*

Depending upon whether you are in your own country or in a foreign land, you can be either a native of the country or a foreigner. Consider these words and phrases that deal with nationality:

die Staatsangehörigkeit	*nationality*
ein gebürtiger Amerikaner	*a native-born American (male)*
eine gebürtige Deutsche	*a native-born German (female)*
eine eingebürgerte Amerikanerin	*a naturalized American (female)*
ein eingebürgerter Deutscher	*a naturalized German (male)*
der Ausländer, die Ausländerin	*foreigner*
Ich bin amerikanischer Staatsbürger.	*I'm an American citizen.*
Meine Familie stammt aus Bayern.	*My family comes from Bavaria.*
Ich bin deutscher Abstammung.	*I'm of German descent.*
Meine Frau ist von Geburt Polin.	*My wife is Polish by birth.*
Mein Sohn ist im Ausland geboren.	*My son was born abroad.*
Wir fahren selten ins Ausland.	*We seldom travel abroad.*

When someone's nationality is German, the adjective **deutsch** is used as a noun but requires the appropriate adjective endings in each of the four cases:

	GERMAN (MALE)	GERMAN (FEMALE)	GERMANS (PLURAL)
NOMINATIVE	der Deutsche	die Deutsche	die Deutschen
ACCUSATIVE	den Deutschen	die Deutsche	die Deutschen
DATIVE	dem Deutschen	der Deutschen	den Deutschen
GENITIVE	des Deutschen	der Deutschen	der Deutschen

Other nationalities that end in **-er** are masculine and decline like nouns. The feminine form of the nationality ends in **-in**. Other masculine nouns of nationality end in **-e**, and their feminine forms end in **-in**. A brief list of masculine forms of nationality and their respective country names and adjective forms follows:

Nationalität	Land	Adjektiv
der Australier	Australien (*Australia*)	australisch
der Belgier	Belgien (*Belgium*)	belgisch
der Brasilianer	Brasilien (*Brazil*)	brasilianisch
der Chinese	China (*China*)	chinesisch
der Engländer	England (*England*)	englisch
der Franzose	Frankreich (*France*)	französisch
der Grieche	Griechenland (*Greece*)	griechisch
der Holländer	Holland (*Holland*)	holländisch
der Italiener	Italien (*Italy*)	italienisch
der Japaner	Japan (*Japan*)	japanisch
der Kanadier	Kanada (*Canada*)	kanadisch
der Mexikaner	Mexiko (*Mexico*)	mexikanisch
der Norweger	Norwegen (*Norway*)	norwegisch
der Österreicher	Österreich (*Austria*)	österreichisch
der Pole	Polen (*Poland*)	polnisch
der Russe	Russland (*Russia*)	russisch
der Schwede	Schweden (*Sweden*)	schwedisch
der Spanier	Spanien (*Spain*)	spanisch
der Tscheche	Tschechien (*Czech Republic*)	tschechisch
der Türke	die Türkei (*Turkey*)	türkisch
der Ukrainer	Ukraine (*Ukraine*)	ukrainisch

English can use a noun form or an adjective form to give a person's nationality. German uses a noun form without a definite article:

Ich bin Deutscher.	*I'm a German. I'm German.*
Sie ist Spanierin.	*She's a Spaniard. She's Spanish.*
Sind Sie Schwede?	*Are you a Swede? Are you Swedish?*

In English, names of countries, the names of their citizens, and the adjectives that describe their citizens are considered proper and thus are capitalized:

the United States of America
an American
the American flag

But in German, only the nouns are capitalized. Except in very special circumstances, the adjectives derived from country names are not capitalized:

Deutschland	*Germany*
ein junger Deutscher	*a young German*
die Deutsche Demokratische Republik	*the German Democratic Republic*
eine **deutsche** Zeitung	*a German newspaper*
Ägypten	*Egypt*
eine nette Ägypterin	*a nice Egyptian woman*
eine **ägyptische** Pyramide	*an Egyptian pyramid*

ÜBUNG
10·2

Put an X in the blanks that identify the country in which each place listed on the left is found.

	Deutschland	Russland	Polen	Österreich	Norwegen	Schweiz
1. Moskau	_____	_____	_____	_____	_____	_____
2. die Alpen	_____	_____	_____	_____	_____	_____
3. die Elbe	_____	_____	_____	_____	_____	_____
4. Warschau	_____	_____	_____	_____	_____	_____
5. Bremen	_____	_____	_____	_____	_____	_____
6. Wien	_____	_____	_____	_____	_____	_____
7. Bern	_____	_____	_____	_____	_____	_____
8. Fjord	_____	_____	_____	_____	_____	_____
9. Wolga	_____	_____	_____	_____	_____	_____
10. Salzburg	_____	_____	_____	_____	_____	_____
11. Harzgebirge	_____	_____	_____	_____	_____	_____

ÜBUNG
10·3

Answer the following questions, based on your personal knowledge if possible. Sample answers are provided in the answer key.

1. Wo bist du geboren? _____

2. Hast du die Geburtsurkunde für deine Tochter bekommen? _____

   _____

3. Warum braucht man einen Führerschein? _____

4. Hast du einen Freund, der im Ausland geboren ist? _____

   _____

5. Was für Papiere braucht man, um ins Ausland zu fahren? _____

   _____

6. Was ist deine Staatsangehörigkeit? _____

7. Welcher amerikanische Politiker ist von Geburt Österreicher? _____

   _____

8. Woher stammt deine Familie? _____

9. Welche Sprache spricht man in Belgien? _____

10. Was ist die Hauptstadt Norwegens? _____

ÜBUNG
10·4

Rewrite each of the following sentences in the other three tenses.

1. reisen

   PRESENT   Wir reisen nach Griechenland.

   PAST   _____

   PRESENT PERFECT _____

   FUTURE   _____

2. kontrollieren

   PRESENT   _____

   PAST   Hier wurden unsere Pässe kontrolliert.

   PRESENT PERFECT _____

   FUTURE   _____

3. suchen

   PRESENT   _____

   PAST   _____

PRESENT PERFECT	Er hat ein gutes Hotel gesucht.
FUTURE	_____

4. sein

PRESENT	_____
PAST	_____
PRESENT PERFECT	_____
FUTURE	Wird der Matrose auf Urlaub sein?

5. bekommen

PRESENT	Sie bekommt ihre Geburtsurkunde.
PAST	_____
PRESENT PERFECT	_____
FUTURE	_____

ÜBUNG
10·5

Fill in each blank with an appropriate word.

1. Du brauchst einen _____, um Auto fahren zu dürfen.

2. In den großen _____ fahren wir ins Ausland.

3. Wir machen im Herbst _____.

4. Ich habe die Fahrkarten im _____ gekauft.

5. Wir sind an der _____ kontrolliert worden.

6. Der _____ ist nicht so groß wie die Alpen.

7. Von wem hast du die schöne _____ bekommen?

8. Los Angeles in Kalifornien ist mein _____.

9. Sie brauchen nicht nur einen Pass, sondern auch ein _____.

10. Ich bin _____ Staatsbürger.

11. In Österreich spricht man _____.

12. Kairo ist die _____ Ägyptens.

13. Meine Verwandten stammen _____ Frankreich.

14. Amsterdam ist eine _____ Stadt.

15. Viele Kanadier sprechen Englisch und _____.

Circle the letter of the word or phrase that best completes each sentence.

1. Ich habe dir ein _____ in Mexiko gekauft.
   a. Visum   b. Andenken   c. Führerschein   d. Hauptstadt

2. Der Offizier ist auf _____ in Paris gewesen.
   a. Urlaub   b. der Grenze   c. ein Zelt   d. verreist

3. Wir haben eine _____ auf der Elbe gemacht.
   a. Sehenswürdigkeiten b. Reisebegleiterin c. Ausflug   d. Hafenrundfahrt

4. Wir sollen in einer Pension _____.
   a. verkaufen   b. verpassen   c. übernachten   d. zelten

5. Das _____ befindet sich am Marktplatz.
   a. Camping   b. deutscher   c. Schülergruppe   d. Rathaus
                           Abstammung

6. Die alte _____ ist vor 600 Jahren zerstört worden.
   a. Staatsangehörigkeit b. Burg   c. Urlaubsschein   d. Reiseroute

7. Ich kann keine _____ machen. Ich werde seekrank.
   a. Kreuzfahrt   b. Stadtrundfahrt   c. Besichtigung   d. Personalausweis
                                                der Kirche

8. Mein Großvater ist _____ Amerikaner.
   a. ins Ausland   b. an der Grenze   c. mittelalterlicher d. eingebürgerter

9. Hast du das große _____ in Wien besichtigt?
   a. Schloss   b. Brücke   c. Urlaubsgeld   d. Geburtsurkunde

10. Warum fährst du nach Moskau? Kannst du _____?
    a. reisen   b. russisch   c. kanadisch   d. zerstören

11. Mein Nachbar will ohne einen _____ fahren.
    a. Fahrrad   b. Tschechin   c. Führerschein   d. Fernsehturm

12. Eine _____ kann man in der Nähe von Kairo besichtigen.
    a. Palast   b. Schwarzwald   c. Hauptstadt   d. Pyramide

13. War Marlene Dietrich _____ oder Belgierin?
    a. Franzose   b. Deutsche   c. amerikanisch   d. englisch

14. Habt ihr eure _____ bei euch?
    a. Papiere   b. Ferientage   c. Abstammung   d. Geburtsort

15. Meine Tante ist _____ Mexikanerin.
    a. amerikanischer   b. von Geburt   c. stammen   d. im Ausland
       Abstammung

•11• Geography and history

There are many words that describe the many aspects of geography and history. Such words are important not only to enrich one's vocabulary but also to help in understanding Germany and the world.

Die Erdkunde

Just like English, German has more than one word to describe the universe:

der Kosmos	*cosmos*
das Universum	*universe*
das Weltall	*universe*

In that great expanse of space exist numerous astronomical bodies, including the planet upon which human beings live:

die Erde	*Earth*
der Asteroid	*asteroid*
der Komet	*comet*
der Meteor	*meteor*
der Mond	*moon*
der Planet	*planet*
der Stern	*star*
die Milchstraße	*the Milky Way*
die Sonne	*sun*
das Sonnensystem	*solar system*

The major land masses and continents (**der Kontinent**) of the earth are as follows:

Asien	*Asia*
Afrika	*Africa*
Australien	*Australia*
Europa	*Europe*
Mittelamerika	*Central America*
Nordamerika	*North America*
Südamerika	*South America*
der Nahe Osten	*Middle East*
die Antarktis	*Antarctica*

The word **das Land** means both *land* and *country*. Its plural form is **die Länder**. The following list names some well-known places and countries found on the major land masses:

Thailand und die Philippinen sind in Asien.	Thailand and the Philippines are in Asia.
Simbabwe und Südafrika sind afrikanische Länder.	Zimbabwe and South Africa are African countries.
Tasmanien ist eine Insel und ist ein Teil Australiens.	Tasmania is an island and is part of Australia.
Irland ist die „Grüne Insel" Europas.	Ireland is the Emerald Isle of Europe.
Portugal liegt an der Westküste Europas.	Portugal is on the west coast of Europe.
Helgoland ist eine deutsche Insel in der Nordsee.	Helgoland is a German island in the North Sea.
Costa Rica ist ein mittelamerikanisches Land.	Costa Rica is a Central American country.
Der Panamakanal verbindet das Karibische Meer (die Karibik) mit dem Pazifischen Ozean.	The Panama Canal connects the Caribbean Sea with the Pacific Ocean.
Kanada, die USA und Mexiko liegen in Nordamerika.*	Canada, the U.S.A., and Mexico are located in North America.
Argentinien und Kolumbien sind südamerikanische Länder.	Argentina and Colombia are South American countries.
In der Antarktis gibt es mehrere wissenschaftliche Siedlungen.	In Antarctica there are several scientific settlements.

ÜBUNG 11·1

Place an X in the blanks that identify the continents on which the countries and cities listed on the left are located.

	Afrika	Asien	Europa	Nordamerika	Südamerika
1. Ägypten	_____	_____	_____	_____	_____
2. Brasilien	_____	_____	_____	_____	_____
3. Großbritannien	_____	_____	_____	_____	_____
4. Indien	_____	_____	_____	_____	_____
5. Kalkutta	_____	_____	_____	_____	_____
6. Leipzig	_____	_____	_____	_____	_____
7. Manila	_____	_____	_____	_____	_____
8. Mexiko	_____	_____	_____	_____	_____
9. Minsk	_____	_____	_____	_____	_____
10. Mongolien	_____	_____	_____	_____	_____
11. Peru	_____	_____	_____	_____	_____
12. Polen	_____	_____	_____	_____	_____
13. Thailand	_____	_____	_____	_____	_____
14. Toronto	_____	_____	_____	_____	_____

*Für Deutsche ist Mexiko in Mittelamerika. (Germans consider Mexico to be in Central America.)

Answer the following questions, based on your personal knowledge if possible. Sample answers are provided in the answer key.

1. Welche Staatsangehörigkeit haben Sie? _____

2. Welcher Kontinent ist der Größte? _____

3. Welcher Kontinent ist der Kleinste? _____

4. Welches Land feirert am 3. Oktober die politische Einheit? _____

   _____

5. Wie viele Planeten gibt es im Sonnensystem? _____

6. Auf welchem Kontinent liegt Morokko? _____

7. Was verbindet das Karibische Meer mit dem Pazifischen Ozean? _____

   _____

8. Welches Land liegt an der Westküste Europas? _____

9. Welches europäische Land ist eine Insel? _____

10. Zu welchem Land gehört Tasmanien? _____

Geographische Merkmale

The land features of the earth are varied and occur in different combinations from continent to continent. Some of these features—both man-made and natural—are as follows:

die Ebene	*plain*
die Prärie	*prairie*
das Tal	*valley*
die Wüste	*desert*
die Oase	*oasis*
der Hügel	*hill*
der Berg	*mountain*
das Gebirge	*mountain range*
der Wald	*woods, forest*
der Regenwald	*rain forest*
die Felswand	*cliff*
das Kliff	*cliff (seaside)*
der Bach	*stream*
der Fluss	*river*
der Wasserfall	*waterfall*
der Gletscher	*glacier*
der Eriekanal	*Erie Canal*
der Sueskanal	*Suez Canal*

Within the great land masses are smaller regional and political communities. Let's look at some useful vocabulary that describes these places:

das Gebiet	*region*
die Region	*region*
der Staat	*state*
das Bundesland	*federal state*
der Kanton	*canton (of Switzerland)*
die Provinz	*province*
der Bezirk	*district*
die Stadt	*city, town*
das Dorf	*village*

The word **das Klima** means *climate*. Like the natural features of the earth, climate comes in various forms. The following words can be used to describe climate:

das Wetter	*weather*
tropisch	*tropical*
trocken	*dry*
die Temperatur	*temperature*
5 Grad Wärme	*5 degrees above 0*
5 Grad Kälte	*5 degrees below 0*
kalt	*cold*
kühl	*cool*
warm	*warm*
heiß	*hot*
sonnig	*sunny*
feucht	*humid, damp*
die Wolke	*cloud*
bewölkt	*cloudy*
der Regen	*rain*
regnerisch	*rainy*
das Gewitter	*storm*
der Wind	*wind*
windig	*windy*
der Schnee	*snow*
der Schneesturm	*blizzard*

The following sentences describe the weather:

Heute steigen die Temperaturen.	*The temperature is rising today.*
Es ist 18 Grad Celsius.	*It's 18 degrees centigrade.*
Es ist 70 Grad Fahrenheit.	*It's 70 degrees Fahrenheit.*
Es regnet.	*It's raining.*
Es nieselt.	*It's drizzling.*
Es fängt an zu hageln.	*It's starting to hail.*
Es ist neblig geworden.	*It's gotten foggy.*
Es blitzt und donnert.	*There's lightning and thunder.*
Es schneit.	*It's snowing.*

Die Himmelsrichtungen

Directions and points on a compass are formed differently in English and German. German directions, such as **der Norden** (*north*), are always masculine. But when they are used as points on a compass, they do not show their gender. In addition, the directions can be used as prefixes to form new German words where in English the directions are shown as adjectives. But German also has adjectival forms of the directions. Let's look at these forms:

DIRECTION	COMPASS POINT	ADJECTIVE	
Norden	Nord	nördlich	*north*
Süden	Süd	südlich	*south*
Osten	Ost	östlich	*east*
Westen	West	westlich	*west*
Nordosten	Nordost	nordöstlich	*northeast*
Nordwesten	Nordwest	nordwestlich	*northwest*
Südosten	Südost	südöstlich	*southeast*
Südwesten	Südwest	südwestlich	*southwest*

The forms shown for the points on a compass can be used as prefixes:

der Nordwind	*the north wind*
Südamerika	*South America*
Osteuropa	*Eastern Europe*
Westdeutschland	*West Germany*

When the adjectival forms of the directions are used, they decline as normal adjectives.

Winde aus nördlichen Richtungen	*winds from a northerly direction*
ein südliches Klima	*a southern climate*
ein östliches Gebirge	*an eastern mountain range*
westliche Winde	*westerly winds*

The following sentences illustrate vocabulary related to directions:

Ein kalter Wind kommt von Norden.	*A cold wind is coming from the north.*
Morgen reisen sie nach Norden.	*Tomorrow they're traveling north.*
Baumwolle wächst im tiefen Süden.	*Cotton grows in the Deep South.*
Wir fahren jetzt in Richtung Süden.	*We're traveling south now.*
Sie hat ein Haus im Osten Italiens.	*She has a house in eastern Italy.*
Er wohnt 20 Kilometer östlich von Hamburg.	*He lives 20 kilometers east of Hamburg.*
Das Dorf liegt etwas westlich von Köln.	*The village is a little west of Cologne.*
Mein Schlafzimmer geht nach Westen.	*My bedroom faces west.*
Die Düsenjäger fliegen nach Nordosten.	*The fighter planes are flying northeast.*
Das Schiff fährt nach Südwesten.	*The ship is heading southwest.*

ÜBUNG
11·3

Answer the following questions, based on your personal knowledge if possible. Sample answers are provided in the answer key.

1. Wie viel Grad sind es? _____

2. Liegt Hamburg in Nord- oder Süddeutschland? _____

3. Welche Großstadt liegt im Westen der USA? _____

4. Ist Bremerhaven an der Küste oder in der Wüste? _____

5. Wo befindet sich ein großer Regenwald? _____

6. Was für Wetter haben wir heute? _____

7. Was für ein Wind kommt von Süden? _____

8. Wo kann man Gletscher finden? _____

9. Ist Mongolien ein westliches oder ein östliches Land? _____

10. In welche Richtung fährt der Zug? _____

Die Geschichte

Germany has enjoyed a long history. The region's earliest beginnings were described by the Roman historian Tacitus in his essay on the Germanic people called *Germania*. In general, the history of Germany can be divided into three eras:

Alte Geschichte	*ancient history*
Mittlere Geschichte	*medieval history*
Neue Geschichte	*modern history*

As the German nation evolved, it became part of a great empire in the year A.D. 800. This empire was ruled by **Karl der Große** (*Charlemagne*). In the nineteenth century a second empire was formed by the strength and determination of Otto von Bismarck. This second empire collapsed with the end of World War I. Then in 1933 Adolf Hitler began the third empire—his so-called Thousand-Year Empire. Let's look at the vocabulary that deals with these three empires:

das Reich	*empire*
das Heilige Römische Reich Deutscher Nation	*the Holy Roman Empire of the German Nation*
das Mittelalter	*Middle Ages*
das Königtum	*kingdom*
der König	*king*
die Königin	*queen*
der Prinz	*prince*
die Prinzessin	*princess*
das zwanzigste Jahrhundert	*the twentieth century*
die Weimarer Republik	*the Weimar Republic*
das Dritte Reich	*the Third Reich*
das Tausendjährige Reich	*the Thousand-Year Empire*
der Erste Weltkrieg	*First World War*
der Zweite Weltkrieg	*Second World War*
der Kalte Krieg	*Cold War*
der eiserne Vorhang	*the Iron Curtain*
die Bundesrepublik Deutschland	*the German Federal Republic*
die Deutsche Demokratische Republik	*the German Democratic Republic*
der Kanzler	*chancellor*
das Wirtschaftswunder	*the economic miracle*
die Wiedervereinigung	*reunification*
das einundzwanzigste Jahrhundert	*the twenty-first century*
die Europäische Union (EU)	*the European Union*

Karl der Große wurde zum Kaiser gekrönt.	*Charlemagne was crowned emperor.*
Kolumbus hat 1492 Amerika entdeckt.	*Columbus discovered America in 1492.*
Gutenberg hat die Druckerpresse erfunden.	*Gutenberg invented the printing press.*
Das Zweite Deutsche Reich wurde 1871 gegründet.	*The Second German Empire was founded in 1871.*

Wilhelm II. war der letzte deutsche Kaiser.	*Wilhelm II was the last German emperor.*
Adolf Hitler war Führer des Dritten Reiches.	*Adolf Hitler was the leader of the Third Reich.*
Deutschland wurde 1945 in vier Zonen geteilt.	*Germany was divided into four zones in 1945.*
Im Jahr 1961 wurde in Berlin die Mauer gebaut.	*The Wall was built in Berlin in 1961.*

ÜBUNG 11·4

Answer the following questions, based on your personal knowledge if possible. Sample answers are provided in the answer key.

1. Wer hat „Germania" geschrieben? _____

2. Wer wurde im Jahr 800 zum Kaiser gekrönt? _____

3. Was hat Gutenberg erfunden? _____

4. In welchem Jahr wurde das Zweite Deutsche Reich gegründet? _____

5. Welcher Krieg endete 1918? _____

6. Welche Republik wurde in der russischen Zone gegründet? _____

7. Was wurde 1961 in Berlin gebaut? _____

8. Wann feiert Deutschland den Tag der Deutschen Einheit? _____

9. Zu welcher politischen Union gehört jetzt Deutschland? _____

ÜBUNG 11·5

In each blank provided, write the historical era in which the event occurred: **Alte Geschichte, Mittlere Geschichte,** *or* **Neue Geschichte.**

1. _____ Kolumbus entdeckte Amerika.

2. _____ Tacitus beschrieb das germanische Volk.

3. _____ Die Mauer wurde in Berlin gebaut.

4. _____ Das Zweite Deutsche Reich wurde gegründet.

5. _____ Das Dritte Reich wurde gegründet.

6. _____ Die Druckerpresse wurde erfunden.

7. _____ Karl der Große wurde zum Kaiser gekrönt.

8. _____ Deutsche feiern den Tag der Deutschen Einheit.

9. _____ Wilhelm II. war Kaiser des Deutschen Reiches.

10. _____ Der Zweite Weltkrieg endete.

Rewrite the following sentences in the past, present perfect, and future tenses.

1. Der Kanal verbindet zwei Seen.

   PAST _____

   PRESENT PERFECT _____

   FUTURE _____

2. Die Temperaturen steigen.

   PAST _____

   PRESENT PERFECT _____

   FUTURE _____

3. Die Hauptstadt liegt im Osten.

   PAST _____

   PRESENT PERFECT _____

   FUTURE _____

4. Er erfindet eine neue Maschine.

   PAST _____

   PRESENT PERFECT _____

   FUTURE _____

5. Hier wird eine Mauer gebaut.

   PAST _____

   PRESENT PERFECT _____

   FUTURE _____

Circle the letter of the word or phrase that best completes each sentence.

1. Die Erde ist einer der neun _____.
   a. Weltall   b. Planeten   c. Kontinente   d. Teile

2. _____ ist der kleinste Kontinent.
   a. Europa   b. Die Antarktis   c. Nordamerika   d. Asien

3. _____ verbindet das Karibische Meer mit dem Pazifischen Ozean.
   a. Der Panamakanal   b. Die Nordsee   c. Die Ostsee   d. Der Sueskanal

4. Helgoland ist _____.
   a. nördlich von   b. westlich von   c. die Hauptstadt   d. eine Insel
       Norwegen   Amerika

5. Wo gibt es mehrere _____ Siedlungen?
   a. wissenschaftliche   b. Universum   c. geographisch   d. südöstliche

6. In Nordafrika gibt es eine große _____.
   a. See   b. Wüste   c. Mittelalter   d. Königtum

7. Es ist schon _____ Celsius.
   a. 20 Grad   b. die grüne Insel   c. die Mittlere Geschichte   d. regnerisch

8. Julius Caesar war _____.
   a. die Neue   b. feucht   c. in der   d. Römer
       Geschichte   Europäischen
                                         Union

9. Karl der Große war Kaiser _____.
   a. des Dritten   b. der Weimarer   c. des Heiligen   d. des
       Reiches   Republik   Römischen Reiches   Tausendjährigen
                                           Deutscher Nation   Reiches

10. Es blitzt und _____.
    a. Schnee   b. hageln   c. donnert   d. bewölkt

11. Das Zweite Deutsche Reich wurde _____ gegründet.
    a. die Mittlere   b. 1871   c. die Neue   d. 1918
        Geschichte   Geschichte

12. Wer hat _____ erfunden?
    a. Amerika   b. die Druckerpresse   c. die Bundesrepublik   d. Kolumbus

13. Wilhelm II. war der _____.
    a. letzte deutsche   b. Otto von   c. Zweite Deutsche   d. Kanzler
        Kaiser   Bismarck   Reich

14. Im Jahr 1961 wurde _____.
    a. entdeckt   b. die Druckerpresse   c. die Mauer gebaut   d. gegründet
                             erfinden

15. _____ wird im Oktober gefeiert.
    a. Der Tag der   b. Das Wirtschafts-   c. Der Kalte Krieg   d. Das
        Deutschen Einheit   wunder   einundzwanzigste
                                                            Jahrhundert

Farms and gardens

A wide variety of plants and crops are grown on small private farms or enormous corporate plantations. These crops are used by the individual farmer or are prepared for distribution across an entire region or country.

Der Bauernhof

The farm has been central to German life for centuries. But in the twenty-first century, agricultural production has become an industry, and most Germans now live in towns and cities. **Das Bauerndorf**, *the farming village*, still exists, but its place in farming is no longer as prominent as it once was. Let's look at some vocabulary that describes agriculture in general:

landwirtschaftlich	*agricultural*
die Landwirtschaft	*agriculture*
das Landwirtschaftsministerium	*the ministry of agriculture*
die Landwirtschaftsschule	*college of agriculture*
der Landarbeiter	*agricultural worker*
die Agrarindustrie	*agricultural business*
der Landwirt	*farmer*
die Landwirtin	*farmer's wife*

Several verbs describe agricultural activities:

anbauen	*to grow, cultivate*
bebauen	*to cultivate (land)*
düngen	*to fertilize*
ernten	*to harvest*
jäten	*to weed*
kultivieren	*to cultivate (crops)*
mähen	*to mow*
pflanzen	*to plant*
säen	*to sow*
schneiden	*to cut, prune*
umpflanzen	*to transplant*
wachsen	*to grow*

Notice how these verbs are used in sentences:

Auf diesem Bauernhof wird Roggen angebaut.	*Rye is grown on this farm.*
Dieses Feld muss bebaut werden.	*This field has to be cultivated.*

Wir haben den Boden gedüngt.	We fertilized the soil.
Kartoffeln werden im Herbst geerntet.	Potatoes are harvested in the fall.
Welche Feldfrucht wird hier kultiviert?	What crops are cultivated here?
Die Wiesen müssen gemäht werden.	The meadows have to be mown.
Man pflanzt Mais im Frühling.	You plant corn in the spring.
Getreide wird auch im Frühling gesät.	Grain is also sown in the spring.
Diese Pflanzen sollen umgepflanzt werden.	These plants should be transplanted.
Auf unserem Bauernhof wachsen Rüben und Möhren.	Beets and carrots grow on our farm.

Whether a farm is large or small, you can find numerous kinds of crops grown there:

das Gemüse	vegetables
das Getreide	grain, cereal
das Heu	hay
das Korn	grain
das Stroh	straw
der Hafer	oats
der Weizen	wheat
die Gerste	barley
die Luzerne, die Alfalfa	alfalfa

A vegetable farm can also have many varieties:

der Blumenkohl	cauliflower
der Kohl	cabbage
der Lauch	leek
der Rosenkohl	brussels sprouts
der Salat (Kopfsalat)	lettuce
der Spinat	spinach
die Bohne	bean
die Erbse	pea
die Gurke	cucumber (pickle)
die Karotte (Möhre)	carrot
die Rübe	beet
die Tomate	tomato
die Zwiebel	onion

All crops require care. They are fed, watered, and protected from disease and insects. A list of vocabulary that describes these functions follows:

die Fruchtfolge	crop rotation
die Düngung mit Chemikalien	using chemical fertilizers
die Pflanznahrung	plant food
die Pflanzen wässern	to water plants
das Land bewässern	to irrigate the land
das Pestizid	pesticide
die Schädlingsbekämpfung aus der Luft	crop dusting
die Schädlingsbekämpfung	crop spraying

Answer the following questions, based on your personal knowledge if possible. Sample answers are provided in the answer key.

1. Was wird auf diesem Bauernhof angebaut? _____

2. Womit kann man den Boden düngen? _____

3. Was für Gemüse wächst in Ihrem Garten? _____

4. Wann soll Mais gesät werden? _____

5. Welche Feldfrucht wird auf diesem Bauernhof kultiviert? _____

_____

Die Plantage

Certain crops are usually grown on large farms or plantations. Some of these include the following:

das Zuckerrohr	*sugarcane*
der Bambus	*bamboo*
der Kaffee	*coffee*
der Reis	*rice*
der Tee	*tea*
die Baumwolle	*cotton*
die Zuckerrübe	*sugar beet*

To cultivate the land, it must first be plowed. Let's look at some words that deal with *plowing*:

der Pflug	*plow*
pflügen	*to plow*
umpflügen	*to plow up (crops in the soil)*
Furchen pflügen	*to plow furrows*
unterpflügen	*to plow in*
zerpflügen	*to plow up (the soil)*

Die Bäume und Sträucher

It is impossible to list all the kinds of trees and shrubs that exist in the world. But certain varieties are known universally and should be part of one's active German vocabulary:

der Baum	*tree*
der Busch	*bush*
der Strauch	*bush, shrub*
die Birke	*birch*
die Eiche	*oak*
die Esche	*ash*
die Kastanie	*chestnut*
die Kiefer	*pine*
die Palme	*palm*
die Tanne	*fir*
die Ulme	*elm*

| die Weide | willow |
| die Zeder | cedar |

When these names of trees are used as prefixes for other words, the letter **-n** is often added to the name of the tree. The result is words such as these:

das Eschenholz	ash wood
der Eichenwald	oak woods
der Tannenbaum	fir tree
die Birkenrinde	birch bark
kastanienbraun	chestnut brown (adjective)

Let's look at how some of these words can be used in sentences:

Der Indianer baute ein Kanu aus Birkenrinde.	The Indian made a canoe out of birch bark.
Die alten Kiefern sind gefällt worden.	The old pines have been cut down.
Dieser Schrank ist aus Eichenholz.	This cabinet is made of oak.
Kiefernholz ist ziemlich weich.	Pine is rather soft.
Man kann Palmen auf einer tropischen Insel finden.	You can find palms on a tropical island.
Tannen sind das ganze Jahr über grün.	Firs are green all year long.
Tannenbäume werden als Weihnachtsbäume verkauft.	Fir trees are sold as Christmas trees.
Überall liegen Kiefernzapfen.	There are pinecones everywhere.
Weiden wachsen oft am Rand eines Flusses.	Willows often grow at the edge of a river.

Many trees are fruit-bearing. They are called **Obstbäume**. Consider these examples and how the name of the tree differs from the name of the fruit:

Der Kirschbaum trägt Kirschen.	The cherry tree bears cherries.
Der Apfelbaum trägt Äpfel.	The apple tree bears apples.
Der Birnbaum trägt Birnen.	The pear tree bears pears.
Der Pflaumenbaum trägt Pflaumen.	The plum tree bears plums.
Der Pfirsichbaum trägt Pfirsiche.	The peach tree bears peaches.
Die Aprikose trägt Aprikosen.	The apricot tree bears apricots.
Die Apfelsine trägt Apfelsinen.	The orange tree bears oranges.

The singular nouns for the names of the fruits are **die Kirsche**, **der Apfel**, **die Birne**, **die Pflaume**, **der Pfirsich**, **die Aprikose**, and **die Apfelsine**. The following words describe certain bushes and shrubs:

der Flieder	lilac
der Fliederstrauch	lilac bush
die Forsythie	forsythia
die Rose	rose
der Rosenstrauch	rosebush
der Liguster	privet
die Hecke	hedge

The parts of a tree or shrub are as follows:

das Blatt	leaf
der Ast	branch
der Samen	seed
der Stachel	thorn
der Stamm	trunk
der Stengel	stalk

der Zweig	*twig*
die Astgabel	*fork (of a tree)*
die Blüte	*blossom*
die Knospe	*bud*
die Rinde	*bark*
die Wurzel	*root*

Der Garten

A private garden is usually much smaller than the crop fields of a farm or plantation. Let's look at the vocabulary that can be developed from the word **Garten**:

der Garten	*garden*
die Gartenanlage	*garden layout*
der Gärtner, die Gärtnerin	*gardener*
die Gartenarbeit	*gardening*
der Gartenarchitekt, die Gartenarchitektin	*landscape architect*
der Gartenbau	*horticulture*
das Gartengerät	*gardening tool*
der Gartenschlauch	*garden hose*
der Gartenzaun	*garden fence*
der Gartenzwerg	*garden gnome*

Many gardens contain edible plants such as herbs, vegetables, fruits, and berries. Some of these include the following:

der Thymian	*thyme*
das Basilikum	*basil*
die Petersilie	*parsley*
der Sellerie	*celery*
der Kürbis	*gourd, pumpkin*
das Obst	*fruit*
die Banane	*banana*
die Brombeere	*blackberry*
die Erdbeere	*strawberry*
die Heidelbeere	*blueberry*
die Himbeere	*raspberry*
die Johannisbeere	*currant*
die Melone	*melon*
die Weintraube	*grape*

Grapes are cultivated in vineyards, and much of the crop is made into wine. A small vineyard is **der Weingarten**. A large-scale vineyard is called **das Weingut**.

Depending upon where a person lives, certain unwanted plants can encroach upon a garden:

das Unkraut	*weed*
der Kaktus	*cactus*
der Löwenzahn	*dandelion*
die Distel	*thistle*

Die Blumen

Perhaps the most attractive part of a garden is the flower beds. The climate in which someone lives determines the kinds of flowers that can be grown. Here are just some of the most commonly cultivated flowers:

die Blume	*flower*
die Gardenienblüte	*gardenia*
die Gladiole	*gladiola*
die Jonquille	*jonquil*
die Lilie	*lily*
das Maiglöckchen	*lily of the valley*
die Nelke	*carnation*
die Petunie	*petunia*
die Schwertlilie	*iris*
die Sonnenblume	*sunflower*
die Tulpe	*tulip*
das Veilchen	*violet*

Let's look at some sentences that illustrate some of these new words:

Mein Nachbar hat mir einen Rosenstrauß gegeben.	*My neighbor gave me a bouquet of roses.*
In unserem Garten wachsen nur Tulpen und Nelken.	*Only tulips and carnations grow in our garden.*
Ich muss das Blumenbeet besser pflegen.	*I have to take better care of the flower bed.*
Die Schwertlilie blüht am Ende des Monats Mai.	*The iris blooms at the end of May.*
Man soll die Petunien nicht pflücken.	*You shouldn't pick the petunias.*
In seinem Garten hat er nur Gewürzkraut.	*He only has herbs in his garden.*
Ich möchte die Maiglöckchen dorthin umpflanzen.	*I want to transplant the lilies of the valley there.*
Das Veilchen wächst in einem Topf.	*The violet is growing in a pot.*
Die Gardenienblüte riecht sehr schön.	*The gardenia smells very nice.*
Die Sonnenblumen sind sehr groß geworden.	*The sunflowers have gotten very big.*
Sie pflückte Erdbeeren in einen Korb.	*She picked strawberries and put them in a basket.*
Die Himbeeren schmecken sehr süß.	*The raspberries taste very sweet.*
Die Kinder haben viele Pfirsiche gepflückt.	*The children picked a lot of peaches.*
Ich habe Kirschen am liebsten.	*I like cherries the best.*

Some flowers and plants are grown for commercial purposes in large nurseries. The German word for this kind of nursery is **die Gärtnerei**. However, a nursery for trees is **die Baumschule**.

If plants and flowers are exceptionally delicate and have to be grown in a climate of extreme temperatures, they can be safely cultivated in **das Treibhaus** (*hothouse*):

der Efeu	*ivy*
der Farn	*fern*
die Orchidee	*orchid*

Well-manicured gardens are often surrounded by lawns of verdant grass. Consider these vocabulary words that deal with the *lawn*:

das Gras	*grass*
der Grashalm	*blade of grass*
der Rasen	*lawn*
die Rasenfläche	*patch of grass*
die Rasenschere	*grass clippers*
der Rasenmäher	*lawn mower*
der Rasensprenger	*lawn sprinkler*

Answer the following questions, based on your personal knowledge if possible. Sample answers are provided in the answer key.

1. Was für Blumen wachsen in deinem Blumengarten? _____

2. Was ist dein Vater von Beruf? _____

3. Was gibst du deiner Freundin? _____

4. Wann blühen die Rosen? _____

5. Was tun die Kinder? _____

6. Was wächst in einem Topf? _____

7. Was riecht so schön? _____

8. Was machst du heute im Garten? _____

9. Was schmeckt süß? _____

10. Was für Obst hast du am liebsten? _____

Place an X in the blanks that identify where you would find the items listed on the left.

	Bauernhof	Plantage	Gemüsegarten	Blumengarten
1. Rosenstrauch	_____	_____	_____	_____
2. Veilchen	_____	_____	_____	_____
3. Getreide	_____	_____	_____	_____
4. Kaffee	_____	_____	_____	_____
5. Blumenkohl	_____	_____	_____	_____
6. Kartoffeln	_____	_____	_____	_____
7. Schwertlilien	_____	_____	_____	_____
8. Fruchtfolge	_____	_____	_____	_____
9. Hafer	_____	_____	_____	_____
10. Tee	_____	_____	_____	_____
11. Obstbaum	_____	_____	_____	_____
12. Nelken	_____	_____	_____	_____

Rewrite each of the following sentences in the past, present perfect, and future tenses.

1. Was wird hier angebaut?

    PAST _____

    PRESENT PERFECT _____

    FUTURE _____

2. Die Bauern säen Weizen.

    PAST _____

    PRESENT PERFECT _____

    FUTURE _____

3. Der Mann fällt die alte Ulme.

    PAST _____

    PRESENT PERFECT _____

    FUTURE _____

4. Hier wächst Gewürzkraut.

    PAST _____

    PRESENT PERFECT _____

    FUTURE _____

5. Diese Blumen blühen nur im Sommer.

    PAST _____

    PRESENT PERFECT _____

    FUTURE _____

Complete each sentence with an appropriate word.

1. Auf dieser _____ wird Reis kultiviert.

2. _____ haben weiches Holz.

3. Der Rosenstrauch blüht im _____.

4. Er hat ein Kanu aus _____ gebaut.

5. Das Gras sieht trocken aus. Wo ist der _____?

6. Die Gardenienblüten _____ wunderbar.

7. Der Apfelbaum _____ Äpfel.

8. Meine Tochter hat viele Himbeeren _____.

9. Martin hat seiner Mutter einen _____ gegeben.

10. Erbsen und Bohnen wachsen im _____.

Circle the letter of the word or phrase that best completes each sentence.

1. Auf dieser Plantage wird _____ geerntet.
   a. der Eichenwald   b. Baumwolle   c. eine Weide   d. Tannenbäume

2. Auf unserem Bauernhof wuchsen _____.
   a. eine Kiefer   b. Rüben und Mais   c. das Eschenholz   d. ein Fliederstrauch

3. Morgen müssen wir Unkraut _____.
   a. bebauen   b. Furchen pflügen   c. tragen   d. jäten

4. Mais wird im April _____.
   a. erfunden   b. fällen   c. pflegen müssen   d. gesät

5. Das alte Bett ist aus _____.
   a. Eichenholz   b. einem   c. dem Korb   d. Kirschen
                          Gemüsegarten

6. Die Kinder haben da _____ gepflanzt.
   a. Sonnenblumen   b. ein Gartengerät   c. einen Rasenmäher   d. Veilchen im Topf

7. Die _____ dieses Baumes sehen sehr trocken aus.
   a. Birkenrinde   b. Blätter   c. Sträucher   d. Gemüse

8. _____ sind kleine, weiße Blumen.
   a. Aprikosen   b. Zeder   c. Maiglöckchen   d. Blumenkohl

9. Auf dem _____ sitzt ein kleiner Vogel.
   a. Gartenzaun   b. Blumengarten   c. Weintraube   d. Rasenschere

10. Diese Banane _____ nicht gut.
    a. schmeckt   b. wird angebaut   c. plückte   d. blühen

11. Die Blumen in dieser Vase _____ sehr schön.
    a. bebauten   b. riechen   c. düngen   d. tragen

12. Die _____ ist in vielen Ländern eine Industrie.
    a. Gartenarchitektin   b. Erbsen   c. Bauerndörfer   d. Landwirtschaft

13. Weizen wird im Herbst _____.
    a. geerntet   b. kultivieren   c. schneiden   d. gewachsen

14. Kannst du mir _____ pflücken helfen?
    a. Pflaumen   b. eine Weide   c. die Gartenanlage   d. Hecke

15. Im _____ wachsen exotische Orchideen.
    a. Gärtnerei   b. Bauernhof   c. Pfirsichbaum   d. Treibhaus

The human body

Vocabulary dealing with the body and its functions is essential when discussing health, exercise, or medicine.

Der Körper

Der menschliche Körper is *the human body*. The body is not just a bunch of body parts linked together but rather a system of organs, limbs, tissues, and functions working in concert to perform the many acts that we call *life*.

Let's look at some basic words that deal with the word **der Körper**:

der (die) Körperbehinderte	*the physically handicapped*
der (die) Körperbeschädigte	*the disabled*
der Körperbau	*physique*
der Körpergeruch	*body odor*
der Körperteil	*body part*
die Körperbehaarung	*body hair*
die Körperfülle	*corpulence*
die Körperflüssigkeit	*bodily fluid*
die Körperfunktion	*bodily function*
die Körperhaltung	*posture*
die Körperöffnung	*orifice*
die Körperverletzung	*bodily harm*
körperlich	*physical*

These words describe the parts of the body, organs, and tissues:

der Kopf	*head*
das Gesicht	*face*
die Stirn	*forehead*
das Kinn	*chin*
die Backe	*cheek (of the face or buttocks)*
die Wange	*cheek (of the face)*
die Lippe	*lip*
die Zunge	*tongue*
das Handgelenk	*wrist*
der Arm	*arm*
der Ellenbogen	*elbow*
die Schulter	*shoulder*
der Busen	*chest, bosom*
der Bauch	*belly*
der Magen	*stomach*

der Hintern	*backside, butt*
das Knie	*knee*
das Bein	*leg*
das Fußgelenk	*ankle*
die Zehe	*toe*
das Herz	*heart*
die Leber	*liver*
die Haut	*skin*
der Knochen	*bone*
der Schädel	*skull*
das Blut	*blood*
der Muskel	*muscle*
der Nerv	*nerve*

The noun **der Nagel** (*nail*) can refer to *fingernail* or *toenail*: **der Fingernagel** or **der Fußnagel**:

Ich schneide mir die Fingernägel.	*I cut my fingernails.*
Meine Mutter lackiert sich die Fußnägel.	*My mother polishes her toenails.*

Let's look at other sentences that discuss the parts of the body:

Karl hat sich einen Knochen gebrochen.	*Karl broke a bone.*
Ihm tut der Magen weh.	*His stomach hurts.*
Ihre Haut ist weich.	*Her skin is soft.*
Das Baby will nicht auf dem Rücken schlafen.	*The baby doesn't want to sleep on its back.*
Ihr Blutdruck ist normal.	*Your blood pressure is normal.*
Der Sportler trainiert seine Bauchmuskeln.	*The athlete is working on his abdominals.*
Der alte Mann ist nervenkrank.	*The old man has a nervous disorder.*
Mein Vater hat ein Problem mit der Leber gehabt.	*My father had a liver problem.*
Er hat den Dieb in die Knie gezwungen.	*He forced the thief to his knees.*
Mir ist das Blut in die Wangen gestiegen.	*The blood rose to my cheeks.*
Die Frau brachte es nicht über die Lippen.	*The woman couldn't bring herself to say that.*
Du bist mir auf die Zehen getreten!	*You stepped on my toes.*

The following sentences illustrate the functions of certain body parts and organs:

Man sieht mit den Augen.	*You see with your eyes.*
Man riecht mit der Nase.	*You smell with your nose.*
Man hört mit den Ohren.	*You hear with your ears.*
Man denkt mit dem Gehirn.	*You think with your brain.*
Man hält etwas mit den Händen.	*You hold something with your hands.*
Man spricht mit dem Mund.	*You speak with your mouth.*
Man kaut mit den Zähnen.	*You chew with your teeth.*
Man schluckt mit dem Hals.	*You swallow with your throat.*
Man berührt etwas mit den Fingern.	*You touch something with your fingers.*
Man steht auf den Beinen.	*You stand on your legs.*
Man atmet mit den Lungen.	*You breath with your lungs.*

Answer the following questions, based on your personal experience if possible. Sample answers are provided in the answer key.

1. Wer hat einen guten Körperbau? _____

2. Was tut die Krankenschwester? _____

3. Was ist passiert? _____

4. Warum kann das Kind nicht durch die Nase atmen? _____

_____

5. Warum hinkst du so? _____

6. Warum geht deine Frau zum Zahnarzt? _____

7. Warum kratzt sich Erik den Kopf? _____

8. Womit sieht man? _____

Der Kopf

Let's look at some words that describe the parts of the head:

das Haar	*hair*
der Bart	*beard*
der Backenbart	*sideburns*
der Schnurrbart	*moustache*
der Augapfel	*eyeball*
die Augenfarbe	*eye color*
die Augenbraue	*eyebrow*
die Augenwimper	*eyelash*
aus den Augenwinkeln	*out of the corner of one's eyes*
die Falte	*wrinkle*
das Muttermal	*mole*
das Genick	*nape of the neck*
das Nasenloch	*nostril*
das Zahnfleisch	*gum*
die Mandeln	*tonsils*
flüstern	*to whisper*
lachen	*to laugh*
lächeln	*to smile*

Here are some sentences referring to parts of the head:

Er kämmt sich die Haare.	*He combs his hair.*
Sie hat wellige Haare.	*She has wavy hair.*
Er zieht die Stirn in Falten.	*He knits his brow.*
Er wäscht sich das Gesicht.	*He washes his face.*
Sie putzt sich die Zähne.	*She brushes her teeth.*
Halt den Mund!	*Shut up!*

Der Rumpf

The *torso* is the trunk of the body from which the limbs extend and where important organs are located. The following list of words and phrases relate to **der Rumpf**:

das Glied	*limb*
der Brustkorb	*rib cage*
die Rippe	*rib*
die Brustwarze	*nipple*
der Nabel	*navel*
der Rücken	*back*
die Hüfte	*hip*
der Blinddarm	*appendix*
der Dickdarm	*large intestine*
der Dünndarm	*small intestine*
die Niere	*kidney*

Der Läufer hat eine breite Brust.	*The runner has a broad chest.*
Der Kranke konnte kein Glied rühren.	*The patient couldn't move a muscle.*

Different parts of the body function in different ways. Here are just a few examples of those functions:

schwitzen	*to sweat*
spucken	*to spit*
speicheln	*to salivate*
verdauen	*to digest*
niesen	*to sneeze*
schnarchen	*to snore*
erbrechen	*to vomit*
urinieren	*to urinate*
defäkieren	*to defecate*
Kot ausscheiden	*to defecate*

The following words and phrases have a more limited use but are helpful in describing the body:

das Grübchen	*dimple*
der Pickel	*pimple*
der Wundschorf	*scab*
die Hautfarbe	*skin color*
die Pigmentierung	*pigmentation*
die Sommersprosse	*freckle*
die Krähenfüße	*crow's-feet*

Er hat sehr behaarte Beine.	*He has very hairy legs.*
Das ist eine alte Narbe.	*That's an old scar.*
Ich habe eine Gänsehaut.	*I've got goose bumps.*
Ihre Körperhaltung ist sehr schlecht.	*Her posture is very bad.*
Sie hatte eine Mandelentzündung.	*She had tonsilitis.*
Er hatte eine Blinddarmentzündung.	*He had appendicitis.*

Answer the following questions, based on your personal experience if possible. Sample answers are provided in the answer key.

1. Was tut der Junge vor dem Spiegel? _____

2. Wer trägt einen Bart? _____

3. Welche Augenfarbe hast du? _____

4. Wer hat Krähenfüße? _____

5. Was für einen Körperbau hat der Sportler? _____

6. Warum hinkt der Mann? _____

7. Was tun die Kinder jeden Morgen? _____

8. Warum hat sie sich erbrochen? _____

Let's look at a variety of adjectives that help describe the body:

dunkelbraun gebrannt	deeply tanned
groß	big, tall
klein	small, short
dick	fat
dünn	thin
muskulös	muscular
hager	scrawny
schön	pretty
hübsch	beautiful, handsome
attraktiv	attractive
hässlich	ugly
graziös	graceful
schwerfällig	clumsy
kahl	bald

Place an X in the blanks matching the adjectives listed on the left with the appropriate body parts and persons.

	Bein	Blutdruck	Fuß	Haut	Knochen	Sportler
1. behaart	_____	_____	_____	_____	_____	_____
2. dünn	_____	_____	_____	_____	_____	_____
3. gebrochen	_____	_____	_____	_____	_____	_____
4. muskulös	_____	_____	_____	_____	_____	_____
5. normal	_____	_____	_____	_____	_____	_____
6. verrenkt	_____	_____	_____	_____	_____	_____
7. weich	_____	_____	_____	_____	_____	_____

Rewrite each of the following sentences in the past, present perfect, and future tenses.

1. Sie bricht sich das Bein.

   PAST _____

   PRESENT PERFECT _____

   FUTURE _____

2. Mein Onkel trägt einen Schnurrbart.

   PAST _____

   PRESENT PERFECT _____

   FUTURE _____

3. Die Kinder kämmen sich die Haare.

   PAST _____

   PRESENT PERFECT _____

   FUTURE _____

4. Sie atmet durch die Nase.

   PAST _____

   PRESENT PERFECT _____

   FUTURE _____

5. Es tut ihm weh.

   PAST _____

   PRESENT PERFECT _____

   FUTURE _____

Fill in each blank with an appropriate word.

1. Was ist los? Hast du dir den Fuß _____?

2. Meine Tochter hat große blaue _____.

3. Ihr _____ schlägt jetzt normal.

4. Der alte Herr hat Probleme mit der _____.

5. Ich muss dem Kind die _____ schneiden.

6. Du bist mir wieder auf die _____ getreten!

7. Man _____ mit den Lungen.

8. Die Jungen haben sich die _____ gewaschen.

9. Der junge Sportler hat eine breite _____.

10. Die alte Dame hat keine _____.

11. Sie hat sich das Bein gebrochen und _____.

12. Der Läufer hat sehr _____ Beine.

13. Mein Bruder _____ wenn er schläft.

14. Dieser ältere Mann hat immer einen _____ getragen.

15. Die Lehrerin hat die Stirn in _____ gezogen.

ÜBUNG 13·6

Circle the letter of the word or phrase that best completes each sentence.

1. Man hört mit den _____.
   a. Haut   b. Ohren   c. Rücken   d. Körperfülle

2. Man kann wirklich nichts gegen _____ tun.
   a. Falten   b. das Knie   c. den Ellenbogen   d. die Augenbrauen

3. Vorsicht! Sonst _____ du dir wieder den Fuß.
   a. erbrachst   b. ziehst   c. tust   d. verrenkst

4. Deine Haare sind sehr _____ und wellig.
   a. weich   b. muskulös   c. gelächelt   d. kämmt

5. Es ist kalt. Ich habe eine _____.
   a. Schuppen   b. Gänsehaut   c. Körperteile   d. Augenfarbe

6. Die Sportlerin ist graziös und _____.
   a. Krähenfüße gehabt   b. über die Lippen   c. kahl   d. hübsch

7. Mir tut _____ weh.
   a. der Schnurrbart   b. der Magen   c. das Problem   d. die Augenwimper

8. Er hat keine _____ und kann nicht sprechen.
   a. Nasenloch   b. Haut   c. Hals   d. Zunge

9. Warum ist deine _____ so schlecht?
   a. Körperhaltung b. Blinddarm   c. Krähenfüße   d. Körperbau

10. Die jungen Männer haben sehr breite _____.
    a. Schultern   b. Handgelenk   c. Knie   d. Zehen

11. Die kranke Frau kann kein _____ rühren.
    a. Stirn   b. Glied   c. Niere   d. Brustkorb

12. Der Junge ist faul und sehr _____ geworden.
    a. normal   b. gewaschen   c. dick   d. kahl

13. Von dieser Verletzung sind _____ zurückgeblieben.
    a. Hautfarbe   b. Narben   c. Rippen   d. Wangen

14. Sprich lauter! Warum _____ du?
    a. kautest   b. trägst   c. lachtest   d. flüsterst

15. Erik hat sich noch nicht _____ geputzt.
    a. das Zahnfleisch   b. das Gehirn   c. den Körperbau   d. die Zähne

Dining, foods, and beverages

When dining out, people might go to an elegant establishment for a fine meal or to the corner café for less-expensive fare. Here is a list of places to buy a meal:

das Café	*café*
das Esslokal	*restaurant*
das Restaurant	*restaurant*
die Gaststätte	*small restaurant*
das Imbisslokal	*snack bar*
der Imbissraum	*lunch room*
die Imbissbude	*hot dog stand*
das Lokal	*tavern, pub*
das Gasthaus	*inn*
der Gasthof	*inn*
der Speisesaal	*dining room (of a hotel), dining hall*
der Ratskeller	*restaurant (in the city hall basement)*
die Kantine	*cafeteria (at work)*
die Mensa	*student cafeteria (at a college)*
der Speisewagen	*dining car (of a train)*

The three mealtimes are called:

das Frühstück	*breakfast*
das Mittagessen	*lunch, dinner*
das Abendessen (Abendbrot)	*supper, dinner*

But when you *have* or *eat* these meals, verbs are formed from the previous nouns:

frühstücken	*to have or eat breakfast*
zu Mittag essen	*to have or eat lunch*
zu Abend essen	*to have or eat supper*

Here are some example sentences:

Ich frühstücke um 8 Uhr.	*I have breakfast at 8 o'clock.*
Ich esse um 12 Uhr zu Mittag.	*I eat lunch at 12 o'clock.*
Ich esse um 18 Uhr zu Abend.	*I have supper at 6 P.M.*
Mittags essen wir meist im Imbisslokal.	*For lunch we usually eat at a snack bar.*
Abends gehen wir oft ins Restaurant.	*We often go to a restaurant in the evening.*
Ich gehe lieber in eine Gaststätte.	*I prefer going to a small restaurant.*

114

Können Sie mir sagen, wo der Speisewagen ist?	*Can you tell me where the dining car is?*
Was gibt's heute in der Mensa?	*What's there to eat in the cafeteria today?*
Mein Bruder ist Kellner in einem Café.	*My brother is a waiter in a cafe.*
Sie gehen nie in dieses Gasthaus.	*They never go to this inn.*

The following phrases help illustrate the kinds of vocabulary needed when speaking about a restaurant or dining out.

Gehen wir heute abend essen!	*Let's go out to eat this evening.*
Essen Sie nie chinesisch?	*Don't you ever eat Chinese food?*
Essen wir heute italienisch!	*Let's have Italian food today.*
Heute Abend essen wir mexikanisch.	*This evening we're having Mexican food.*
Dieses Restaurant hat eine gute Küche.	*This restaurant has good food.*
Haben Sie eine Reservierung?	*Do you have a reservation?*
Wir haben einen Tisch auf den Namen Keller reserviert.	*We reserved a table in the name of Keller.*
Die Tische sind mit weißen Tischtüchern gedeckt.	*The tables are covered with white tablecloths.*
Könnten Sie mir bitte die Weinkarte bringen?	*Could you bring me the wine list, please?*
Könnten Sie mir bitte die Speisekarte bringen?	*Could you bring me the menu, please?*
Könnten Sie mir bitte eine Serviette bringen?	*Could you bring me a napkin, please?*
Die Kellnerin kann etwas Gutes empfehlen.	*The waitress can recommend something good.*
Er ist der Koch.	*He's the chef (cook).*
Sie ist die Köchin.	*She's the chef (cook).*
Guten Appetit!	*Have a good meal. Enjoy your food.*
Zahlen, bitte!	*Check, please.*
Ich gebe nicht mehr als zehn Prozent Trinkgeld.	*I don't give more than a 10 percent tip.*
Die Bedienung war ausgezeichnet.	*The service was excellent.*

The following words will also come in handy:

der Appetit	*appetite*
das Essen	*food*
die Speise	*dish, food*
die Beilage	*side dish*
die Spezialität	*specialty*
die Kneipe	*bar, tavern*
der Wirt, die Wirtin	*proprietor, innkeeper*
der Schankkellner, die Schankkellnerin	*bartender*
die Theke	*bar, counter*
die Selbstbedienung	*self-service*
die Rechnung	*bill*
servieren	*serve*
probieren	*try, have a taste*

On the table in a German restaurant, you will most likely find the following items:

die Tischdecke	*tablecloth*
das Menü	*menu*
die Flasche Mineralwasser	*bottle of mineral water*
das Glas	*glass*
das Weinglas	*wine glass*
das Geschirr	*dishes*
der Teller	*plate*
die Tasse	*cup*

die Untertasse	saucer
das Besteck	utensils
das Messer	knife
die Gabel	fork
der Löffel	spoon
der Esslöffel	soup spoon, tablespoon
der Teelöffel	teaspoon
der Pfefferstreuer	pepper shaker
der Salzstreuer	salt shaker
das Salzfässchen	salt cellar

ÜBUNG
14·1

Answer the following questions, based on your personal experience if possible. Sample answers are provided in the answer key.

1. Wo gibt es ein gutes Restaurant in der Nähe? _____

2. Wie ist die Küche in diesem Gasthof? _____

3. Wo ist der Speisewagen? _____

4. Um wie viel Uhr frühstücken die Kinder? _____

5. Essen Sie gern italienisch? _____

6. Wer hat Ihnen die Weinkarte gebracht? _____

7. Was hat der Kellner empfohlen? _____

8. Wie viel Trinkgeld haben Sie gegeben? _____

9. Brauchen Sie einen anderen Löffel? _____

10. Was trinken Sie gern? _____

Das Essen

The Germans have two ways to express that you are *hungry*: **Ich habe Hunger** or **Ich bin hungrig**. More than one verb means *to eat*, but not all of them can be used in the same way:

essen	to eat
speisen	to eat, dine (formal speech)
dinieren	to dine (formal speech)
fressen	to eat, feed (of animals)

Ich habe einen Bärenhunger!	I could eat a horse!
Ich bin satt.	I had enough to eat. (I'm full.)
Er hat uns arm gegessen.	He ate us out of house and home.

The verb **essen** also combines with **vegetarisch** as follows:

| Meine Freundin isst nur vegetarisch. | My girlfriend is a vegetarian. (My girlfriend eats only a vegetarian diet.) |

The same word combines with other vocabulary to form a variety of useful phrases:

essen gehen	*to go out for a meal*
kalt essen	*to have a cold meal*
von etwas essen	*to have a bite of something*
warm essen	*to have a hot meal*
Was gibt es zu essen?	*What's there to eat?*
Ich mache dir etwas zu essen.	*I'll make you something to eat.*

These phrases are formed with the noun **das Essen** or its prefix form **Ess-**:

beim Essen sein	*to be at dinner (breakfast, lunch)*
beim Essen stören	*to disturb someone's meal*
zum Essen einladen	*to invite someone to dinner*
das Essen warm stellen	*to keep the food hot*
das Essgeschirr	*pots and pans*
das Essstäbchen	*chopstick*
die Esskultur	*gastronomy*
Essen auf Rädern	*Meals on Wheels*
Essen fassen!	*Come and get it! Chow time!*

Of course, all kinds of dishes can be prepared at home or ordered in a restaurant. Let's look at some of the most common ones as well as other vocabulary that relates to them:

die Lebensmittel	*groceries*
das Lebensmittelgeschäft	*grocery store*
der Supermarkt	*supermarket*
einkaufen gehen	*to go shopping*
das Brot	*bread*
das Roggenbrot	*rye bread*
das Vollkornbrot	*whole grain bread*
das Weißbrot	*white bread*
das Weizenbrot	*wheat bread*
die Orangenmarmelade	*orange marmalade*
die Butter	*butter*
der Käse	*cheese*
das Ei (die Eier)	*egg (eggs)*
das Hähnchen	*chicken*
das Kalbfleisch	*veal*
das Rindfleisch	*beef*
das Schweinefleisch	*pork*
das Steak	*steak*
das Wiener Schnitzel	*Viennese-style cutlet*
die Wurst	*sausage*
der Aufschnitt	*sliced cold cuts*
der Knödel	*dumpling*
der Pilz	*mushroom*
die Nudel	*noodle*
die Suppe	*soup*
backen	*bake*
braten	*roast*
kochen	*cook, boil*
Ich esse gern ein Omelett.	*I like eating an omelet.*
Martin isst lieber Spiegeleier.	*Martin prefers to eat fried eggs.*
Sonja isst am liebsten Rühreier.	*Sonja's favorite is scrambled eggs.*

When you purchase foods at a store, they usually come in some kind of container:

das Fass	*keg, barrel*
der Korb	*basket*
der Sack	*bag, sack*
die Tüte	*bag*
die Büchse	*can*
die Konserve	*canned goods*
die Flasche	*bottle*
die Kiste	*box, case*
die Schachtel	*box*
die Tafel (Seife, Schokolade)	*bar (of soap, chocolate)*

Here are a few more useful sentences that relate to foods:

Du musst den Kohl in Wasser kochen.	*You have to boil the cabbage in water.*
Er hat die Zwiebeln braun gebraten.	*He browned the onions.*
Mein Onkel hat eine Pfirsichtorte gebacken.	*My uncle baked a peach tort.*
Hast du das Mittagessen schon vorbereitet?	*Did you already make lunch?*
Ich werde den Gulasch würzen.	*I'll season the goulash.*
Sie hat die Kartoffeln noch nicht geschält.	*She still hasn't peeled the potatoes.*
Er rührt seinen Kaffee.	*He's stirring his coffee.*
Wer hat die Pommes frites bestellt?	*Who ordered the French fries?*

There are many foods to order off a restaurant menu:

Ich möchte ... bestellen.	*I'd like to order the . . .*
... das Fondue ...	*. . . fondue.*
... das Butterbrot ...	*. . . sandwich.*
... den Eintopf ...	*. . . stew.*
... den Rehbraten ...	*. . . venison.*
... die Forelle ...	*. . . trout.*
... den Salat ...	*. . . salad.*
... Kartoffelsalat ...	*. . . potato salad.*
... Pfannkuchen ...	*. . . pancakes.*
... Rotkohl ...	*. . . red cabbage.*
... das Sauerkraut ...	*. . . sauerkraut.*
... Würstchen ...	*. . . sausages.*

Dessert is **der Nachtisch**.

Haben Sie ...	*Do you have . . .*
... Kompott?	*. . . stewed fruit?*
... Apfelmus?	*. . . applesauce?*
... Apfelstrudel?	*. . . apple strudel?*
... eine Schokoladetorte?	*. . . chocolate cake?*
... Pudding?	*. . . pudding?*
... Kekse?	*. . . cookies?*
... Kuchen?	*. . . cake?*
... Eis?	*. . . ice cream?*

Answer the following questions, based on your personal experience if possible. Sample answers are provided in the answer key.

1. Was haben Sie im Supermarkt gekauft? _____

2. Was essen Sie gern zum Frühstück? _____

3. Wer kocht für Ihre Familie? _____

4. Was bestellen Sie, wenn Sie im Restaurant essen? _____

5. Was essen sie gern zum Nachtisch? _____

Let's look at a list of a few other foods that can be found in either a restaurant or a grocery store:

das Öl	oil
das Schmalz	lard
der Honig	honey
der Joghurt	yogurt
der Quark	curd cheese
der Schinken	ham
der Senf	mustard
der Speck	bacon
die Brezel	pretzel
die Margarine	margarine
die Soße	gravy, sauce
die Spätzle	spaetzle (southern German pasta)
die Nuss	nut

Das Getränk

You can order beverages from the **Getränkkarte** (*beverage menu*) in a restaurant or from a beverage stand.

die Getränkebude	beverage stand
der Getränkestand	beverage stand
der Getränkeautomat	beverage vending machine (pop/soda machine)

Let's look at some words and sentences that deal with beverages:

der Orangensaft	orange juice
der Apfelwein	cider
das Bier	beer
das Pils	pilsner beer
der Wein	wine
das Sprudelwasser	sparkling mineral water
die Brause	carbonated drink
der Kognak	cognac
der Portwein	port
der Likör	liqueur
der Rum	rum

der Schnaps	schnapps
der Sekt	champagne (sparkling wine)
der Weinbrand	brandy
der Weißwein	white wine
der Wodka	vodka

Was trinken Sie gern?	*What do you like to drink?*
Ich trinke gern kalte Milch.	*I like to drink cold milk.*
Erik trinkt lieber schwarzen Kaffee.	*Erik prefers to drink black coffee.*
Ist der Kaffee koffeinfrei?	*Is the coffee decaffeinated?*
Tanja trinkt am liebsten Tee mit Zucker.	*Tanja's favorite drink is tea with sugar.*
Geben Sie mir bitte eine Flasche Saft!	*Give me a bottle of juice, please.*
Mein Sohn trinkt Kakao.	*My son is drinking cocoa.*
Was für Limonade trinkt sie?	*What kind of soft drink is she drinking?*
Sie trinkt Fanta.	*She's drinking Fanta (orange soda).*
Ist dieses Bier alkoholfrei?	*Is this beer alcohol-free?*
Ich habe einen guten Rotwein bestellt.	*I ordered a good red wine.*

ÜBUNG
14·3

Answer the following questions, based on your personal experience if possible. Sample answers are provided in the answer key.

1. Wo kann man ein Glas Wein bestellen? _____

2. Trinken Sie lieber Kaffee oder Tee? _____

3. Was gibt es in der Flasche? _____

4. Trinken Sie alkoholfreies Bier? _____

5. Was trinken die Gäste auf einer Party? _____

ÜBUNG
14·4

Place an X in the blanks that identify the meals when the foods and drinks listed on the left are eaten or drunk.

	Frühstück	Mittagessen	Abendessen
1. Milch	_____	_____	_____
2. Spargel	_____	_____	_____
3. Blumenkohl	_____	_____	_____
4. Wiener Schnitzel	_____	_____	_____
5. Kompott	_____	_____	_____
6. Sekt	_____	_____	_____
7. Pils	_____	_____	_____

8. Tee   _____   _____   _____

9. Brot mit Butter   _____   _____   _____

10. Apfelstrudel   _____   _____   _____

11. Limonade   _____   _____   _____

12. Orangensaft   _____   _____   _____

13. Schweinefleisch   _____   _____   _____

14. Suppe   _____   _____   _____

15. Schokoladetorte   _____   _____   _____

ÜBUNG 14·5

Rewrite each of the following sentences in the past, present perfect, and future tenses.

1. Sie frühstücken um halb 8.

   PAST   _____

   PRESENT PERFECT   _____

   FUTURE   _____

2. Er isst keine Butter.

   PAST   _____

   PRESENT PERFECT   _____

   FUTURE   _____

3. Ich trinke gern Limonade.

   PAST   _____

   PRESENT PERFECT   _____

   FUTURE   _____

4. Mein Vater bestellt das Sauerkraut.

   PAST   _____

   PRESENT PERFECT   _____

   FUTURE   _____

5. Sie kocht den Kohl 20 Minuten.

   PAST   _____

   PRESENT PERFECT   _____

   FUTURE   _____

Fill in each blank with an appropriate word.

1. Heute Abend essen wir _____.

2. Ich habe ein Messer und einen Löffel, aber keine _____.

3. Ich gebe immer 15 Prozent _____.

4. Mittags esse ich meist im _____.

5. Der Student fragt, wo die _____ ist.

6. Mein Vater hilft meiner Mutter das _____ vorbereiten.

7. Die Kinder essen oft Brot mit _____.

8. Der kleine Junge trinkt gern _____.

9. Ich habe einen Tisch auf den Namen Schmidt _____.

10. Onkel Peter hat ein Fass _____ gekauft.

11. Trinken Sie lieber Rotwein oder _____?

12. Frau Kamps hat uns zum Essen _____.

13. Ich will keine _____. Ich habe Eier nicht gern.

14. Ist der _____ koffeinfrei?

15. Der Mann ist betrunken. Er hat zu viel _____ getrunken.

Circle the letter of the word or phrase that best completes each sentence.

1. Der _____ hat eine sehr gute Küche.
   a. Lokal   b. Apfelwein   c. Ratskeller   d. Theke

2. Wir _____ selten im Esszimmer.
   a. frühstücken   b. bestellen   c. am liebsten   d. rühren

3. Guten _____!
   a. Appetit   b. Essen   c. fassen   d. dinieren

4. Die Kellnerin hat _____ verdient.
   a. das Mittagessen   b. ein gutes   c. diese Mensa   d. ein
                           Trinkgeld   Lebensmittelgeschäft

5. Tante Gerda hat eine Kirschtorte _____.
   a. reserviert   b. essen gegangen   c. zahlen   d. gebacken

6. Ich habe keinen Hunger. _____.
   a. Ich gehe ins   b. Ich bin satt   c. Ich werde fünf   d. Ich habe keinen Tee
      Restaurant   Würstchen bestellen   getrunken

7. Möchten Sie ein Glas _____?
   a. Soße   b. Milch   c. Flasche   d. Zucker

8. Unser Nachbar hat uns wieder _____ gestört.
   a. ins Lokal   b. vom Cafe   c. beim Essen   d. in der Tasse

9. Ist _____ gesunder als Weißbrot?
   a. Sekt   b. Margarine   c. der Gasthof   d. Vollkornbrot

10. Er hat Schweinefleisch mit _____ bestellt.
    a. Knödeln   b. ein Teller   c. dieser Theke   d. der Schankkellner

11. Zum Frühstück isst er gern _____
    a. Hähnchen   b. Rühreier   c. eine Untertasse   d. die Schachtel

12. Ich trinke lieber _____ Bier.
    a. neu   b. ausgezeichnet   c. Sprudelwasser   d. alkoholfreies

13. Ich habe nur drei _____ gekauft.
    a. Weingläser   b. Weinkarte   c. Speisewagen   d. Speisekarte

14. Sie hat Apfelstrudel _____ gebacken.
    a. mit Zwiebeln   b. zum Nachtisch   c. Orangensaft   d. und Servietten

15. Diese _____ ist schmutzig.
    a. Pilz   b. Suppe   c. Tasse   d. Eis

 # Days, months, and years

People watch the passage of time with great interest. They record events that have taken place and assign them dates in the calendar to analyze and compare them to present events or even to predict future events. For millennia, the words that describe days, months, and years have been among the tools for the recording of time.

The word **der Tag** (*day*) is the basis for vocabulary and phrases relating to *days*:

täglich	*daily*

Es wird Tag.	*It's getting light.*
Ein neuer Tag bricht an.	*A new day is breaking.*
Der Tag graut.	*The day is dawning (breaking).*
Im Frühling werden die Tage länger.	*In spring the days get longer.*
Im Herbst werden die Tage kürzer.	*In fall the days get shorter.*

The Germans have a little expression that uses the word **der Tag** and is quite similar to the English expression:

Die Brüder sind wie Tag und Nacht.	*The brothers are like day and night.*

Of course, this same noun is used as a greeting:

Guten Tag!	*Hello! Good day!*

The noun **der Morgen** means *morning*, but written as **morgen** it means *tomorrow*. This noun is used to generate new words and phrases:

am frühen Morgen	*early in the morning*
am folgenden Morgen	*the following morning*
bis in den frühen Morgen	*until the early hours of the morning*
das Morgenland	*East, Orient*
morgenländisch	*Eastern, Oriental*

Use this noun as a greeting:

Guten Morgen!	*Good morning.*

Der Nachmittag means *afternoon* and can be used in forming new vocabulary or phrases that relate to *afternoon*:

nachmittäglich	*afternoon* (adjective)
ein Nachmittagsspaziergang	*an afternoon stroll*

am frühen Nachmittag	*in the early afternoon*
am späten Nachmittag	*in the late afternoon*

The noun **der Abend** means *evening* and can be used to form new vocabulary or phrases:

gegen Abend	*toward evening*
am nächsten Abend	*the following evening*
während des Abends	*during the evening*
das Abendland	*West, Occident*
abendländisch	*Western, occidental*

You can greet someone with this noun:

Guten Abend!	*Good evening.*

The word **die Nacht** means *night* and is the basis for some new vocabulary that relates to *nighttime*:

nächtlich	*nightly, every night*
in der Nacht, bei Nacht	*at night*
bis spät in der Nacht	*until late in the night*
Die Nacht ist hereingebrochen.	*Night has fallen.*

You can say *good night* by using the noun **die Nacht**. This expression is usually said to someone who is going to bed:

Gute Nacht! Schlaf gut!	*Good night. Sleep well.*

The nouns **der Morgen**, **der Abend**, and **die Nacht** are used in three special expressions that describe which morning, evening, or night is being talked about: yesterday's, today's, or tomorrow's:

gestern Morgen	*yesterday morning*
heute Morgen	*this morning*
morgen früh (*not* Morgen)	*tomorrow morning*
gestern Abend	*yesterday evening, last night*
heute Abend	*this evening*
morgen Abend	*tomorrow evening*
gestern Nacht	*last night*
heute Nacht	*tonight*
morgen Nacht	*tomorrow night*

Die Wochentage

The German days of the week are all masculine (**der**) because the word *day* is masculine: **der Tag**.

Sonntag	*Sunday*
Montag	*Monday*
Dienstag	*Tuesday*
Mittwoch	*Wednesday*
Donnerstag	*Thursday*
Freitag	*Friday*
Samstag, Sonnabend	*Saturday*

With a few exceptions, the German days of the week are used much in the same way as the English days of the week. Let's look at some example phrases:

sonntags (*adverb*)	*Sundays, every Sunday*
am Montag	*on Monday*
ein schwarzer Freitag	*a black Friday*
ab kommenden Montag	*from next Monday*

Er kommt am Dienstag.	*He's coming on Tuesday.*
Er kommt Mittwoch.	*He's coming on Wednesday.*
Er kommt nächsten Donnerstag.	*He's coming next Thursday.*
Es ist an einem Sonnabend geschehen.	*It happened on a Saturday.*

In colloquial language, you will hear *on [a day]* said without the preposition **an: Er kommt Mittwoch.**

Use these expressions to describe the time of day:

Sonntagmorgen	*Sunday morning*
Montagmittag	*Monday noon*
Dienstagnachmittag	*Tuesday afternoon*
Mittwochabend	*Wednesday evening*
Donnerstagnacht	*Thursday night*

If you tell *at* what time of day something occurs, use **an: am Freitagmorgen, am Samstagabend,** and so on. Each of these expressions has an adverbial form that ends in **-s:**

montagmittags	*on Mondays at noon*
mittwochabends	*on Wednesday evenings*

Expressions of time that are not the subject of the sentence or do not follow a preposition most often appear in the accusative case:

Er kommt nächsten Freitag.	*He is coming next Friday.*

Words derived from the noun **die Woche** refer to *week*:

wöchentlich	*weekly, every week*
heute in einer Woche	*a week from today*
heute vor einer Woche	*a week ago today*
dreimal die Woche	*three times a week*
das Wochenende	*weekend*

The last noun can be used in an expression:

Schönes Wochenende!	*Have a nice weekend!*

ÜBUNG

15·1

Answer the following questions, based on your personal experience if possible. Sample answers are provided in the answer key.

1. In welcher Jahreszeit werden die Tage länger? _____

2. Ist Japan im Morgenland oder im Abendland? _____

3. Wie lange arbeitet dein Vater im Büro? _____

4. Welchen Tag haben wir heute? _____

5. Wann ist dein Geburtstag? _____

Der Monat

The twelve months of the year are all masculine (**der**):

Januar	*January*
Februar	*February*
März	*March*
April	*April*
Mai	*May*
Juni	*June*
Juli	*July*
August	*August*
September	*September*
Oktober	*October*
November	*November*
Dezember	*December*

Let's look at some vocabulary that deals with the word **der Monat**:

monatlich	*monthly, every month*
monatweise	*by the month*
monatelang	*for months*
das Monatseinkommen	*monthly income*
das Monatsende	*end of the month*
im Monat Mai	*in the month of May*
Frau Benz ist im sechsten Monat.	*Mrs. Benz is in her sixth month (of pregnancy).*

When you say that something occurs *in* a particular month, use the preposition **in**: **im Oktober** (*in October*). But when **das Datum** (*the date*) is included, there are a few variations. When you ask for the date, it is expressed in the nominative case. Notice that there are two ways of asking for the date:

Welches Datum haben wir heute?	*What is today's date?*
Heute ist der erste Januar.	*Today is the first of January.*
Der Wievielte ist heute?	*What is today's date?*
Heute ist der elfte Juni.	*Today is the eleventh of June.*

When you ask *when* something is taking place, use the preposition **an** and the dative case. Notice again that there are two ways of asking this:

Wann ist das Examen?	*When is the exam?*
Das Examen ist am vierten April.	*The exam is on the fourth of April.*
Am Wievielten ist die Party?	*On what date is the party?*
Die Party ist am zwanzigsten März.	*The party is on the twentieth of March.*

Let's look at some phrases that illustrate the use of dates with the months:

ab dem zwölften August	*from August twelfth*
vom zweiten Februar an	*from February second (and on)*
vom sechsten bis zum elften Mai	*from the sixth to the eleventh of May*
am Dienstag, dem fünften April	*on Tuesday, the fifth of April*
Er ist am achten Juli geboren.	*He was born on July eighth.*
Sie ist am siebten September gestorben.	*She died on September seventh.*

Das Jahr

Several interesting words and phrases are derived from the word **das Jahr** (*year*):

jährlich	*yearly, annually, every year*
ein halbes Jahr	*half a year, six months*
jedes Jahr	*every year*
alle vier Jahre	*every four years*
von Jahr zu Jahr	*from year to year*
im Alter von vierzig Jahren	*at the age of forty*
Jahraus, Jahrein	*year in, year out*
das Jahrzehnt	*decade*
das Jahresabonnement	*annual subscription*
das Jahreseinkommen	*annual income*
die mittlere Jahrestemperatur	*the mean temperature of a year*

Er ist achtzehn Jahre alt.	*He's eighteen years old.*
Er ist schon jahrelang krank.	*He has been ill for many years.*
Sie feierten den Jahresbeginn.	*They celebrated the New Year.*
Mein Vater ist Jahrgang 1955.	*My father was born in 1955.*
Die vier Jahreszeiten sind der Sommer, der Herbst, der Winter und der Frühling (das Frühjahr).	*The four seasons are summer, fall, winter, and spring.*
Es wird Frühling.	*Spring is coming.*
Anfang Sommer war es dieses Jahr sehr heiß.	*The beginning of summer was very hot this year.*
Letzten Herbst machten wir eine Europareise.	*Last fall we took a trip around Europe.*
Im Winter gehe ich oft Ski laufen.	*I often go skiing in winter.*
Alle vier Jahre gibt es ein Schaltjahr.	*Leap year comes every four years.*

Years are rarely written out as words. For example, 1999 would be one long word if written out: **neunzehnhundertneunundneunzig**. The numerical form is preferred. Use the preposition **in** to express *in* what year something occurs:

im zweiten Jahr	*in the second year*
Er wurde im Jahr 1850 geboren.	*He was born in 1850.*

But be aware that the expression **im Jahr** can be omitted from sentences that tell in what year something occurs. Only the year itself is stated. Compare the following two examples:

Sie besuchte uns im Jahr 2002.	*She visited us in 2002.*
Sie besuchte uns 2002.	*She visited us in 2002.*

If you add the expression B.C. or A.D. to a year, it will appear like this:

im Jahr 65 v. Chr. (vor Christi)	*in 65 B.C.*
im Jahr 1890 n. Chr. (nach Christi)	*in A.D. 1890*

Answer the following questions, based on your own experience if possible. Sample answers are provided in the answer key.

1. In welchem Monat ist deine Tochter geboren? _____

2. Am Wievielten ist der alte Herr gestorben? _____

3. Wie lange blieb Onkel Thomas zu Besuch? _____

4. Welcher Jahrgang ist deine Frau? _____

5. Was feiern Amerikaner am vierten Juli? _____

6. Am Wievielten beginnt der neue Film? _____

7. Wie lange spielt der Film? _____

8. Wie bezahlst du deine Miete? _____

9. Wann kam Erik aus Irak zurück? _____

10. Wann bist du geboren? _____

Das Jahrhundert

Vocabulary that deals with *centuries* occurs primarily in a few forms: one with prepositions and others in a genitive-case construction. Look at these examples:

das 21. (einundzwanzigste) Jahrhundert	*the twenty-first century*
das 11. (elfte) Jahrhundert	*the eleventh century*
Es gab viele Kriege im 20. Jahrhundert.	*There were a lot of wars in the twentieth century.*
Sie lebte im 15. Jahrhundert.	*She lived in the fifteenth century.*
Das ist ein Denkmal aus dem 14. Jahrhundert.	*That's a monument from the fourteenth century.*
Die Krise dauerte bis zum 17. Jahrhundert.	*The crisis lasted until the seventeeth century.*
Er war Schriftsteller des 19. Jahrhunderts.	*He was a nineteenth-century writer.*
Das ist eine Sinfonie des 18. Jahrhunderts.	*That's an eighteenth-century symphony.*

Notice that English can use a century in a modifying position. German, however, puts the century in the genitive case:

ein Dichter des 20. Jahrhunderts	*a twentieth-century poet*
ein Roman des 19. Jahrhunderts	*a nineteenth-century novel*

ÜBUNG
15·3

Answer the following questions, based on your personal experience if possible. Sample answers are provided in the answer key.

1. In welchem Jahrhundert betrat der erste Mensch den Mond? _____

2. In welchem Jahrhundert wurde George Washington geboren? _____

3. Wie viele Jahre hat ein Jahrhundert? _____

ÜBUNG
15·4

Rewrite each of the following sentences in the past, present perfect, and future tenses.

1. Die Tage werden länger.

   PAST _____

   PRESENT PERFECT _____

   FUTURE _____

2. Sie kommt am Freitag.

   PAST _____

   PRESENT PERFECT _____

   FUTURE _____

3. Es geschieht im Winter.

   PAST _____

   PRESENT PERFECT _____

   FUTURE _____

4. Wir feiern den Jahresbeginn.

   PAST _____

   PRESENT PERFECT _____

   FUTURE _____

5. Sie bleibt den ganzen Winter zu Besuch.

   PAST _____

   PRESENT PERFECT _____

   FUTURE _____

Fill in each blank with an appropriate word.

1. Tokio ist eine Stadt im _____.

2. Ich arbeitete bis in den frühen _____.

3. Morgen _____ gehen wir ins Kino.

4. Der Unfall ist an einem _____ geschehen.

5. Karl ist noch nicht da. Er kommt _____ Montag.

6. Die Jungen trainieren viermal die _____.

7. Ich habe im Oktober _____.

8. Welches _____ haben wir heute?

9. Seine Party ist _____ achten März.

10. Ihre ältere Schwester ist _____ 1979.

11. Alle vier Jahre gibt es ein _____.

12. Mozart wurde im _____ 1756 geboren.

13. Ein _____ hat hundert Jahre.

14. Der Film läuft vom vierten bis zum neunten _____.

15. In welchem _____ ist der Schriftsteller gestorben?

Circle the letter of the word or phrase that best completes each sentence.

1. Während _____ liege ich auf meinem Bett und lese.
   a. die Nacht   b. ein Wochenende   c. des Abends   d. der Jahre

2. Ich versuche _____ zu trainieren.
   a. täglich   b. monatweise   c. in diesem Jahrzehnt d. der Morgen

3. Er ist endlich am späten _____ nach Hause gekommen.
   a. morgen   b. Frühling   c. Jahreszeit   d. Nachmittag

4. Unsere Gäste kommen nächsten _____.
   a. Jahr   b. wöchentlich   c. Jahrhundert   d. Dienstag

5. Im _____ werden die Tage kürzer.
   a. Wochenende   b. 20. Jahrhundert c. Herbst   d. Samstag

6. Der _____ ist heute?
   a. Wievielte   b. Nächste   c. Abendländische   d. Wochentag

7. Sie musste bis spät _____ arbeiten.
   a. in der Nacht   b. morgen   c. jährlich   d. vom zehnten Juni

8. Wann haben Sie _____?
   a. Geburtstag   b. geboren   c. Freitagmittag   d. früh

9. Das nächste Examen ist am einunddreißigsten _____.
   a. Februar   b. bis zum Sommer c. Oktober   d. Sonntag

10. Zum Anfang des_____ war es dieses Jahr sehr kalt.
    a. Mittwoch   b. Winters   c. Schaltjahr   d. Abends

11. Beethoven war ein Komponist des 19. _____.
    a. Jahres   b. Tages   c. Jahrhunderts   d. Schaltjahres

12. Thomas ist _____ Jahr 1990 geboren.
    a. von   b. vom   c. in   d. im

13. Er wollte _____ in der Hauptstadt bleiben.
    a. den ganzen Monat b. April und Juli c. der letzte Tag   d. morgenländisch

14. Ich bin _____ 1988.
    a. alt   b. Geburtstag   c. früh   d. Jahrgang

15. Das ist eine Burg aus dem 15. _____.
    a. Wochentag   b. Jahrhundert   c. Monat   d. Dezember

Health

Just like Americans, Germans are very health-conscious. The German language contains an enormous variety of words that deal with wellness and illness.

Bleib gesund!

Most English speakers have heard **Gesundheit!** said after someone sneezes. Note that the word means *health*, although in English we say *Bless you!* The word's adjectival form is **gesund**, and both words are the basis for some helpful vocabulary:

wieder gesund werden	*to get well again*
gesund und munter	*hale and hearty*
der Gesunde	*healthy person*
auf seine Gesundheit trinken	*to drink to his health*
ihr gesundheitlicher Zustand	*the state of her health*
das Gesundheitsamt	*health department*
die Gesundheitsgefährdung	*health risk*
die Gesundheitspflege	*health care*
das Gesundheitszeugnis	*health certificate*
Seine Frau hat ihn gesund gepflegt.	*His wife nursed him back to health.*
Meine Schwester ist von zarter Gesundheit.	*My sister has a delicate constitution.*
Er ist wieder bei bester Gesundheit.	*He's in the best of health again.*
Wie geht es dir gesundheitlich?	*How's your health been?*
Das kann Gesundheitsschäden bewirken.	*That can damage your health.*

Wie geht's is the common way of asking how someone is. The words **geht es** are frequently written as a contraction: **geht's**. And when a noun or pronoun is added to the phrase, the dative case is required.

Wie geht's?	*How are things?*
Wie geht es Ihnen?	*How are you?*
Es geht mir gut, danke.	*I'm fine, thanks.*
Wie geht's Ihrer Frau?	*How's your wife?*
Es geht so.	*Just so-so.*
Sie fühlt sich zur Zeit nicht wohl.	*She hasn't been feeling well lately.*
Nicht schlecht.	*Not bad.*
Ziemlich gut.	*Rather well.*
Sehr gut. Und Ihnen?	*Very well. And you?*

Mir geht es auch gut.   *I'm fine, too.*
Ich glaube, dass ich krank werde.   *I think I'm getting sick.*

Krankheiten

The following words and phrases apply to common illnesses and conditions:

das Fieber	*fever*
das Halsweh	*sore throat*
der Durchfall	*diarrhea*
der Stuhlgang	*bowel movement*
der Husten	*cough*
heiser	*hoarse*
schmerzhaft	*painful, achy*
die Erkältung	*cold*
die Grippe	*flu, influenza*
blind	*blind*
stumm	*mute*
taub	*deaf*

Sie hat sich wieder erkältet.	*She got another cold.*
Diese Krankheit ist nicht ansteckend.	*This disease is not contagious.*

Several words and phrases describe how someone feels when he or she is more seriously ill:

die häufigsten Krankheitsprobleme	*the most frequent health problems*
die Lungenentzündung	*pneumonia*
die Mandelentzündung	*tonsillitis*
die Gelenkentzündung	*arthritis*
der Heuschnupfen	*hay fever*
das Geschwür	*ulcer*
geschwollene Beine	*swollen legs*
der Bluthochdruck	*high blood pressure, hypertension*
der Herzanfall, Herzinfarkt	*heart attack*
der Herzschlag	*heart attack (fatal)*
der Schlaganfall	*stroke*
der Krebs	*cancer*
der Tumor	*tumor*
das Aids	*AIDS*

Sind Sie krank?	*Are you sick?*
Wie fühlst du dich?	*How do you feel?*
Ich fühle mich wieder sehr schwach.	*I feel very weak again.*
Ich bin immer müde.	*I'm always tired.*
Ich schwitze.	*I'm sweating.*
Sie fror an den Händen.	*Her hands were ice cold.*
Zwei Tage in der Wüste machten sie kaputt.	*Two days in the desert took its toll on them.*
Wo haben Sie Schmerzen?	*Where is the pain?*
Wo tut es dir weh?	*Where does it hurt?*
Ich habe mich am Arm verletzt.	*I hurt my arm.*
Er hat sich den Daumen verbrannt.	*He burned his thumb.*

Sie hat ...	*She has . . .*
... Kopfschmerzen.	*. . . a headache.*

... Magenschmerzen.	. . . *a stomachache.*
... Zahnschmerzen.	. . . *a toothache.*

Sie leidet an Sodbrennen.	*She suffers from heartburn.*
Immer mehr Kinder leiden an Allergien.	*More and more children have allergies.*
Das Hautkrebsrisiko bei jungen Erwachsenen wächst.	*The risk of skin cancer is increasing among young adults.*
Die Pollenflugsaison hat begonnen.	*Pollen allergy season has begun.*

If someone is ill or in the hospital, you can wish him or her a speedy recovery with this phrase:

Gute Besserung!	*Get well soon.*

ÜBUNG
16·1

Answer the following questions, based on your personal experience if possible. Sample answers are provided in the answer key.

1. Sind Ihre Kinder wieder gesund geworden? _____

2. Wer in Ihrer Familie ist von zarter Gesundheit? _____

3. Wie geht es Ihnen gesundheitlich? _____

4. Was kann Gesundheitsschäden bewirken? _____

5. Wer hat die Grippe gehabt? _____

6. Woran leidet Ihr Mann? _____

7. Warum waren Sie im Krankenhaus? _____

8. Was für ein Risiko wächst bei jüngeren Leuten? _____

9. Was für Schmerzen haben Sie? _____

10. Wo tut es Ihnen weh? _____

Das Heilmittel

The remedy for illness and disease is treatment. Let's look at some vocabulary that relates to **der Arzt**:

der Arzt, die Ärztin	*doctor, physician*
ärztlich	*medical*
auf ärztliche Verordnung	*on doctor's orders*
die (Arzt)praxis	*practice*
die Ärzteschaft	*medical profession*
die Arzneikunde	*pharmacology*
der Facharzt, die Fachärztin	*specialist*

There is more than one word for *medicine* and *drugs*. Take a close look at the differences illustrated in the following sentences and phrases:

aus dem medizinischen Bereich	*from the field of medicine*
medizinisch behandlungsbedürftig	*in need of medical treatment*
der Ozonalarm	*ozone alert*
die erste Hilfe	*first aid*
die Notfallmaßnahme	*emergency measure*

Der Kranke muss Medikamente nehmen.	*The patient has to be on drugs.*
Der Arzt hat ein starkes Medikament verschrieben.	*The doctor prescribed a strong medicine.*
Diese Drogen sind nur auf Rezept zu erhalten.	*These drugs can only be obtained with a prescription.*
Diese Medizin ist verschreibungspflichtig.	*This medicine requires a prescription.*
Es ist gefährlich Rauschgift zu nehmen.	*It's dangerous to take (illicit) drugs.*
Er steht unter Drogen.	*He's on (illicit) drugs.*
Die neue Medizin wirkt langsam.	*The new medicine works slowly.*

The following verbs can be used to describe what a doctor does:

untersuchen	*to examine*
diagnostizieren	*to diagnose*
behandeln	*to treat*
heilen	*to heal*
verbinden	*to dress with a bandage*
impfen	*to inoculate*
röntgen	*to x-ray*
operieren	*to operate*

Der Zahnarzt (*dentist*) has a few specialized functions, illustrated by the following words and phrases:

die Zahnprothese	*denture*
die Teilprothese	*partial denture*
die Zahnbrücke	*dental bridge*
das künstliche Gebiss	*false teeth*

Die Zahnärztin muss einen Zahn ziehen.	*The dentist has to pull a tooth.*
Kann er plombiert werden?	*Can it be filled?*

The payment for medical treatment usually comes from an insurance provider: **die Krankenkasse**. They provide you with health insurance: **die Krankenversicherung**. Let's look at some general treatments and options that relate to health:

die Klinik	*clinic*
die Sprechstunde	*office hours*
die Krankenschwester	*nurse*
der Krankenpfleger	*nurse (male)*
der Kinderarzt, die Kinderärztin	*pediatrician*
der Frauenarzt, die Frauenärztin	*gynecologist*
der Augenarzt, die Augenärztin	*ophthalmologist*
der Chirurg, die Chirurgin	*surgeon*
der Notarzt, die Notärztin	*emergency room doctor*
der Krankenwagen	*ambulance*
das Pflaster	*bandage*
die Salbe	*salve, ointment*
die Tropfen	*drops*

die Tablette	*pill, tablet*
das Zäpfchen	*suppository*
die Impfung	*vaccination*
die Spritze	*injection*
die Krone	*crown (for a tooth)*
die Brille	*eyeglasses*
das Hörgerät	*hearing aid*
die Akupunktur	*acupuncture*
die Heilpflanze	*medicinal plant, herb*
die Kur	*spa treatment*
jemanden auf Diät setzen	*to put someone on a diet*
kosmetische Chirurgie	*cosmetic surgery*
Mein Sohn ist fit.	*My son is in good shape.*
Eine frühzeitige Therapie verhindert ernste Folgen.	*Early therapy avoids serious consequences.*

The following sentences and phrases can be used for certain aspects of an illness or health problem:

Er hatte ...	*He had . . .*
... eine hartnäckige Halsinfektion.	*. . . a persistent throat infection.*
... eine schlimme Grippe.	*. . . a bad flu.*
... einen Asthmaanfall.	*. . . an asthma attack.*
... bohrende Schmerzen.	*. . . gnawing pains.*
Er ist ...	*He suffers from . . .*
... ein Krebskranker.	*. . . cancer (a cancer sufferer).*
... ein Aidskranker.	*. . . AIDS.*
... ein Allergiekranker.	*. . . allergies.*
... ein Asthmakranker.	*. . . asthma.*
... ein Diabetiker.	*. . . diabetes.*
... ein Emphysemkranker.	*. . . emphysema.*
... ein Epileptiker.	*. . . epilepsy.*
Sie wird wegen ... behandelt.	*She's being treated for . . .*
... eines Magengeschwürs ...	*. . . a stomach ulcer.*
... der Gallensteine ...	*. . . gallstones.*
... Lungenkrebs ...	*. . . lung cancer.*
... Rückenschmerzen ...	*. . . back pain.*
... Verstopfung ...	*. . . constipation.*
Das Kind ist auf dem Wege der Besserung.	*The child is on the way to getting better.*
Er wird sich vollständig erholen.	*He'll make a full recovery.*
Die alte Frau war unheilbar krank.	*The old woman was terminally ill.*
Sie ist dreimal operiert worden.	*She's been operated on three times.*
Sie war unter ...	*She was under . . .*
... Vollnarkose.	*. . . general anesthesia.*
... Lokalanästhesie.	*. . . local anesthesia.*

Answer the following questions, based on your personal experience if possible. Sample answers are provided in the answer key.

1. Wo hat Ihr Arzt seine Praxis? _____

2. Ist Dokor Meier Facharzt? _____

3. Wie oft müssen Sie das Medikament nehmen? _____

4. Warum sind diese Drogen nur auf Rezept zu erhalten? _____

_____

5. Was hat der Kinderarzt empfohlen? _____

6. Wirkt diese Medizin gut? _____

7. Woran leidet der arme Mann? _____

8. Was hat der Arzt gegen Ihr Übergewicht gemacht? _____

9. Sind Sie noch krank? _____

10. Warum hat der Chirurg den alten Mann nicht operiert? _____

_____

Der Tod

When health cannot be restored, when an operation fails, or when someone just gets too old, death occurs. To wish someone condolences upon the death of a loved one, use this phrase:

Herzliches Beileid! *My deepest sympathies.*

The following words and phrases describe what may just precede death and what follows:

sterben	*to die*
umkommen	*to die, get killed*
töten	*to kill*
Selbstmord begehen	*to commit suicide*
tot	*dead*
die Leiche	*body, corpse*
der Tote, die Tote	*deceased, dead person*
der Sarg	*coffin*
das Grab	*grave*
die Beerdigung	*burial, funeral*
beerdigen	*to bury*
in tiefer Trauer	*in deep mourning*
der Beerdigungsunternehmer	*funeral director*
der Leichenzug	*funeral procession*
die Totenwache	*wake*

Sie trauerten um den verstorbenen Mann. *They grieved for the deceased man.*

Rewrite each of the following sentences in the past, present perfect, and future tenses.

1. Es geht ihm viel besser.

   PAST _____

   PRESENT PERFECT _____

   FUTURE _____

2. Der Junge erkältet sich.

   PAST _____

   PRESENT PERFECT _____

   FUTURE _____

3. Tut es weh?

   PAST _____

   PRESENT PERFECT _____

   FUTURE _____

4. Der Krankenpfleger impft das Kind.

   PAST _____

   PRESENT PERFECT _____

   FUTURE _____

5. Sie leidet an Krebs.

   PAST _____

   PRESENT PERFECT _____

   FUTURE _____

Fill in each blank with an appropriate word.

1. Meine Mutter war von _____ Gesundheit.

2. Wie geht es Ihnen _____?

3. _____ geht es sehr gut.

4. Sie hat eine Mandelentzündung und muss _____ werden.

5. Mein Onkel _____ an Sodbrennen.

6. _____ kann Gesundheitsschäden bewirken.

7. Gute _____!

8. Es tut mir am rechten Arm _____.

9. Die Operation ist teuer, aber ich habe eine _____.

10. Der Arzt behandelt meine Magenschmerzen und will mich _____ lassen.

11. Kann der Zahn _____ werden?

12. Diese Medizin _____ viel schneller.

13. Der kranke Mann hatte eine _____.

14. Sie werden sich vollständig _____.

15. Mein Freund im Altersheim ist leider _____.

ÜBUNG

16·5

Circle the letter of the word or phrase that best completes each sentence.

1. Ich möchte auf Ihre _____ trinken.
   a. Lungenentzündung   b. Krankheit   c. Gesundheit   d. Erwachsenen

2. Ich fühle mich zur Zeit _____.
   a. nicht wohl   b. Schmerzen   c. weh   d. am Finger verletzt

3. Du _____, weil es sehr heiß ist.
   a. hustest   b. Fieber   c. frierst   d. schwitzt

4. Meine neue Patientin hat _____ Beine.
   a. geschwollene   b. tote   c. kaputte   d. geschrumpft

5. Eine frühzeitige Therapie wird ernste Folgen _____.
   a. wachsen   b. verbrennen   c. verbrannt   d. verhindern

6. Die Kinder haben _____ gehabt.
   a. erkältet   b. die Grippe   c. ansteckend   d. die Krankenkasse

7. Der Zahnarzt muss noch zwei Zähne _____.
   a. ziehen   b. schwitzen   c. fühlen   d. gepflegt werden

8. Der sterbende Mann muss sofort _____ werden.
   a. auf Diät gesetzt   b. impfen   c. operiert   d. plombiert

9. Sie brauchen keine _____.
   a. Halsweh   b. Gesundheitsamt   c. kosmetische Chirurgie   d. starkes Medikament

10. Ich soll wegen eines _____ behandelt werden.
    a. Magengeschwürs   b. Gesundheitszeugnis   c. Diabetikers   d. Altersheims

11. Die _____ wird morgen um 11 Uhr stattfinden.
    a. Salbe   b. Beerdigung   c. Übergewicht   d. Leiche

12. Der Zahnarzt hat eine _____ in der Hauptstadt.
    a. Zahnschmerzen   b. Erkältung   c. Leichenzug   d. Praxis

13. Diese Drogen sind nur _____ zu erhalten.
    a. an Heuschnupfen   b. auf Rezept   c. unter   d. mit einer
                                                     Lokalanästhesie   Gesundheitsgefährdung

14. Alle Schüler werden nächsten Dienstag _____.
    a. geimpft werden   b. langsam wirken   c. den Daumen   d. einen Asthmaanfall
                                                         verbrennen

15. Sein Sohn hat lange um ihn _____.
    a. leiden   b. erwachsen   c. getrauert   d. umgekommen

 # Numbers, measurements, and dimensions

Two German words translate into the English word *number*: **die Zahl** and **die Nummer**. Use **die Zahl** for any numeral, amount, or figure in general, such as in counting: **eins, zwei, drei, vier**, and so on. Use **die Nummer** to designate something by its assigned number: for example, **Zimmer Nummer sechs** (*room number six*). Let's look at other phrases and words that use these two nouns:

in die roten Zahlen kommen	*to get into the red*
aus den roten Zahlen kommen	*to get out of the red*
in den schwarzen Zahlen	*in the black*
in großer Zahl	*in large numbers*
das Zahlenschloss	*combination lock*
die Zahlenkombination	*combination for a lock*
die Zahlenfolge	*sequence of numbers*
zahlbar	*payable*
zahllos	*countless*
zahlreich	*numerous*
nummerieren	*to number*
das Nummernkonto	*numbered account*
das Nummernschild	*license plate*
die Nummernscheibe	*dial*

Er ist unter der Nummer 555-0043 zu erreichen.	*He can be reached at 555-0043.*
Ich bin bloß eine Nummer.	*I'm just a number.*
Peter ist eine Nummer für sich.	*Peter is quite a character.*

The verb **zählen** is derived from the noun **die Zahl** and is used like its English counterpart *to count*:

Der vierjährige Erik kann bis zwanzig zählen.	*Four-year-old Erik can count to twenty.*

Die Kardinalzahlen

Let's look at *cardinal numbers* and the spelling variations that occur as numbers are combined to form new numbers:

null	*0*
eins	*1*
zwei	*2*
drei	*3*
vier	*4*

fünf	*5*
sechs	*6*
sieben	*7*
acht	*8*
neun	*9*
zehn	*10*
elf	*11*
zwölf	*12*
dreizehn	*13*
vierzehn	*14*
fünfzehn	*15*
sechzehn	*16*
siebzehn	*17*
achtzehn	*18*
neunzehn	*19*
zwanzig	*20*
einundzwanzig	*21*
dreißig	*30*
zweiunddreißig	*32*
vierzig	*40*
dreiundvierzig	*43*
fünfzig	*50*
vierundfünfzig	*54*
sechzig	*60*
fünfundsechzig	*65*
siebzig	*70*
sechsundsiebzig	*76*
achtzig	*80*
siebenundachtzig	*87*
neunzig	*90*
achtundneunzig	*98*
hundert, einhundert	*100*
zweihundert(und)eins	*201*
fünfhundert(und)achtundvierzig	*548*
tausend (eintausend)	*1,000*
dreitausend(und)dreiundzwanzig	*3,023*
vierhunderttausend	*400,000*
eine Million	*1,000,000*
fünf Millionen	*5,000,000*
sechs Millionen dreihunderttausend	*6,300,000*
eine Milliarde	*1,000,000,000 (1 billion)*
sieben Milliarden	*7,000,000,000 (7 billion)*
eine Billion	*1,000,000,000,000 (1 trillion)*
acht Billionen	*8,000,000,000,000 (8 trillion)*

You'll notice that numbers are written as one word except after **Million**, **Milliarde**, and **Billion**, which are nouns and thus are capitalized. In certain cases the addition of the word **und** is optional: **zweihundert(und)eins**. Be sure not to confuse the English number *billion* with the German number **die Billion**, which means *trillion*.

Large numbers are rarely written as words. A space or a period rather than a comma is used to separate the thousands:

8 000 504	*8,000,504*
7.000	*7,000*

When stating a year, the word **hundert** cannot be removed from the number as it is in English:

neunzehnhundertachtzehn   *nineteen eighteen*

Die Brüche

Fractions are formed quite simply in German. Just add the suffix **-tel** to most numbers and **-stel** to numbers that end in **-t**, **-d**, or **-g**:

ein fünftel	*fifth*
ein zehntel	*tenth*
ein hundertstel	*hundredth*
ein tausendstel	*thousandth*
ein dreißigstel	*thirtieth*

There are a few specialized fractions to consider separately:

ein halb (*adjective*)	*half*
die Hälfte (*noun*)	*a half*
das Drittel	*a third*
das Viertel	*a fourth*
das Dreiviertel	*three-fourths*
dreiviertel (*adjective*)	*three-quarter*
eineinhalb	*one and a half*
anderthalb	*one and a half*

If the fraction is part of a calculation or with a unit of measure, write the fraction with a lowercase letter or write the fraction and noun as one word and capitalized. Write fractions with a capital letter when combined with another noun in the genitive case.

ein fünftel Meter, ein Fünftelmeter	*a fifth of a meter*
zwei Drittel der Autobahn	*two-thirds of the highway*
ein Zehntel des Betrages	*a tenth of the amount*

You need certain arithmetic expressions to use numbers in calculations:

rechnen	*to calculate*
plus	*plus*
gibt, macht	*is, makes, equals*
minus	*minus*
mal	*times*
(geteilt) durch	*divided by*

The following sentences illustrate how the previous vocabulary can be used:

Hast du in der Schule Rechnen gelernt?	*Did you learn to do math in school?*
Vier und vier sind acht.	*Four and four is eight.*
Zwei plus drei sind fünf.	*Two plus three is five.*
Eins und drei macht vier.	*One and three equals four.*
Sieben plus eins gibt acht.	*Seven plus one is eight.*
Zehn minus sechs sind vier.	*Ten minus six is four.*
Sieben mal zwei sind vierzehn.	*Seven times two is fourteen.*
Zwölf (geteilt) durch vier sind drei.	*Twelve divided by four is three.*

Die Dezimalzahlen

Decimals are formed with a comma and not a period. Use the word **Komma** when saying the numbers.

0,2 (null Komma zwei)	*0.2*
2,58 (zwei Komma fünf acht)	*2.58*
10,40 (zehn Komma vier null)	*10.40*

Die Potenzen

Powers are primarily expressed by the word **hoch**:

fünf hoch zwei, fünf im Quadrat	*five squared*
acht hoch drei	*eight cubed*
elf hoch fünf	*eleven to the power of five*
sechs hoch zehn	*six to the power of ten*

The square root is expressed by the term **die Quadratwurzel**:

die Quadratwurzel aus neun	*the square root of nine*
die Quadratwurzel aus fünfzehn	*the square root of fifteen*

Note that the word **Quadrat** can be omitted from the expression:

die Wurzel aus fünfzehn	*the square root of fifteen*

Die Ordinalzahlen

Ordinal numbers are formed from numbers but are used and declined like adjectives. The numbers one through nineteen add the suffix **-t-** plus the appropriate adjective ending, and the numbers from twenty and higher add the suffix **-st-** plus the appropriate adjectival ending. The following ordinal numbers are shown with the adjectival **-e** ending:

CARDINAL	ORDINAL	
zwei	zweite	*second*
vier	vierte	*fourth*
fünf	fünfte	*fifth*
zehn	zehnte	*tenth*
neunzehn	neunzehnte	*nineteenth*
zwanzig	zwanzigste	*twentieth*
dreiundvierzig	dreiundvierzigste	*forty-third*
(ein)hundert	(ein)hundertste	*hundredth*
zweitausend	zweitausendste	*two-thousandth*
Million	millionste	*millionth*
Milliarde	milliardste	*billionth*
Billion	billionste	*trillionth*

A few ordinal numbers are formed irregularly:

eins	erste	*first*
drei	dritte	*third*
sieben	siebte	*seventh*

Answer the following questions. Sample answers are provided in the answer key.

1. Wie viel ist sieben mal drei? _____

2. Ist ein Viertel größer als ein Drittel? _____

3. Wer hat den ersten Preis gewonnen? _____

4. Wie viel Milch brauchst du? _____

5. Ist heute der erste Juli? _____

Der Meter

A meter is approximately 3 feet 3.4 inches long and is the starting point for measurements in the decimal system, which is used in many parts of the world, including Germany. Long-distance measurements use **der Kilometer** (0.62 of a mile). Shorter measurements use **der Zentimeter** (a tenth of a meter) and **der Millimeter** (a hundredth of a meter). The following words are useful when discussing these measurements:

die Breite	*width*
die Länge	*length*

Let's look at some phrases that illustrate the use of these words:

Von Hamburg nach Bremen sind es ungefähr 100 Kilometer.	*It's about 100 kilometers from Hamburg to Bremen.*
Hast du dieses Zimmer ausgemessen?	*Did you measure this room?*
Ja, es ist 4 Meter mal 5,25 Meter.	*Yes, it's 4 meters by 5.25 meters.*
Sein neues Haus hat mehr als 100 Quadratmeter.	*His new house has more than 100 square meters.*
Sie kann das Ziel aus einer Entfernung von 25 Metern treffen.	*She can hit the target from a distance of 25 meters.*
Das Brett ist 6 Zentimeter breit.	*The board is 6 centimeters wide.*
Die Nadel ist nur 30 Millimeter lang.	*The needle is only 30 millimeters long.*
Wie breit ist die Küche?	*How wide is the kitchen?*
Die Küche ist 3,5 Meter breit.	*The kitchen is 3.5 meters wide.*
Wie lang ist der Tisch?	*How long is the table?*
Der Tisch ist 75 Zentimeter lang.	*The table is 75 centimeters long.*
Wie weit ist Berlin entfernt?	*How far away is Berlin?*
Berlin ist 600 Kilometer entfernt.	*Berlin is 600 kilometers away.*

Das Gewicht

Weight in the metric system is measured in grams. But the measurement of weight involves a few other terms as well:

das Milligram	*milligram (0.000035 ounces)*
das Gramm	*gram (0.035 ounces)*
das Kilogramm, das Kilo	*kilogram (2.2 pounds)*

das Pfund	pound
ein halbes Pfund	half a pound
die Tonne	ton

The following sentences illustrate how weight is discussed and expressed:

Wie viel wiegst du?	How much do you weigh?
Ich wiege 80 Kilogramm.	I weigh 80 kilograms.
Hast du zugenommen?	Did you put on weight?
Hast du abgenommen?	Did you lose weight?
Die Zwillinge haben das gleiche Gewicht.	The twins are the same weight.
Wie viel wiegen diese Bücher?	How much do these books weigh?
Sie wiegen ungefähr 10 Kilo.	They weigh about 10 kilograms.
Geben Sie mir bitte 100 Gramm Käse!	Give me 100 grams of cheese, please.
Sie kaufte 10 Pfund Kartoffeln.	She bought 10 pounds of potatoes.
Dieses Paket ist ziemlich schwer.	This package is rather heavy.
Dieser Sack ist sehr leicht.	This bag is very light.
Mit mehr als 100 Kilo hat der Mann Übergewicht.	At over 100 kilograms, the man is overweight.

Die Höhe und die Tiefe

The height and depth of things are also measured in the metric system.

| die Höhe | height |
| die Tiefe | depth |

Here are some sentences discussing and expressing height and depth:

Wie hoch ist das Gebäude?	How tall is the building?
Es ist ungefähr 8 Meter hoch.	It's about 8 meters tall.
Die Garage ist niedriger.	The garage is lower.
Die Markise ist am niedrigsten.	The awning is the lowest.
Das Dach ist höher.	The roof is higher.
Der Turm ist am höchsten.	The tower is the tallest.
Dieses Flugzeug kann in einer Höhe von 3 000 Metern fliegen.	This airplane can fly at an altitude of 3,000 meters.
Dieser Berg ist mehr als 5.000 Meter hoch.	This mountain is over 5,000 meters tall.
Wie tief ist der Teich?	How deep is the pond?
Er ist nicht mehr als 1 Meter tief.	It's no more than 1 meter deep.
Welche Tiefe hat dieser See?	How deep is this lake?
Er hat eine Tiefe von 10 Metern.	It's 10 meters deep.
Hier ist der Rhein tiefer.	The Rhine is deeper here.
Dieser Kanal ist am tiefsten.	This canal is the deepest.

When speaking about the height of a human being, you cannot use a form of the word **hoch** (*high, tall*). Instead, use **groß**:

| Wie groß ist der Mann? | How tall is the man? |
| Er ist beinahe 2 Meter groß. | He's almost 2 meters tall. |

Answer the following questions, based on your personal experience if possible. Sample answers are provided in the answer key.

1. Wie breit ist dein Schlafzimmer? _____

2. Wie lang ist die Bank? _____

3. Wie viel Quadratmeter hat deine neue Wohnung? _____

   _____

4. Wie viel wiegt das Kind? _____

5. Wie groß ist dein Sohn? _____

6. Wie viel Zucker brauchst du? _____

7. Wie hoch ist die Markise? _____

8. Wie tief ist der See? _____

9. Wie weit ist München entfernt? _____

10. Wie viel wiegt dieser Wagen? _____

Rewrite each of the following sentences in the past, present perfect, and future tenses.

1. Er zählt bis zehn.

   PAST _____

   PRESENT PERFECT _____

   FUTURE _____

2. Sie misst das Zimmer aus.

   PAST _____

   PRESENT PERFECT _____

   FUTURE _____

3. Der dicke Mann nimmt ab.

   PAST _____

   PRESENT PERFECT _____

   FUTURE _____

4. Sie wiegt mehr als 50 Kilo.

   PAST _____

   PRESENT PERFECT _____

   FUTURE _____

5. Der Junge kann gut rechnen.

   PAST _____

   PRESENT PERFECT _____

   FUTURE _____

ÜBUNG
17·4

Fill in each blank with an appropriate word.

1. Wir brauchen Geld. Wir müssen aus den roten _____ kommen.

2. Eine _____ ist eine größere Zahl als eine Milliarde.

3. Meine Mutter hat nur ein _____ Brot gekauft.

4. Die Kinder lernen _____ in der Schule.

5. Sechs _____ drei sind achtzehn.

6. Zwanzig geteilt _____ fünf sind vier.

7. Bis zum nächsten Dorf sind es noch eineinhalb _____.

8. Elf minus _____ sind vier.

9. Seine _____ Frau war Französin.

10. Ist heute der Fünfzehnte oder der _____?

11. Wie viel _____ dieses Paket?

12. Der kleine Tisch ist nur 60 _____ lang.

13. Ist der Bodensee _____ als die Donau?

14. Ich möchte 5 _____ Käse kaufen.

15. Das Museum ist ungefähr 10 _____ hoch.

Circle the letter of the word or phrase that best completes each sentence.

1. Ich habe die _____ vergessen.
   a. Milliarde   b. Zahlenkom-   c. fünfte Tag   d. Rechnen
                         bination

2. Hast du _____ verloren?
   a. Quadrat   b. das   c. das Übergewicht   d. Millimeter
                        Nummernschild

3. Wir brauchen zwei _____ fünf Pfund.
   a. ungefähr   b. Komma   c. breit   d. Länge

4. Achtzehn _____ zehn sind achtundzwanzig.
   a. mal   b. aus   c. durch   d. plus

5. Wie viel ist sechs _____ drei?
   a. anderthalb   b. tausend   c. hoch   d. tief

6. Ich möchte dieses große Zimmer _____.
   a. ausmessen   b. nummerieren   c. entfernt   d. treffen

7. Der kleine Teich ist nur 1,5 Meter _____.
   a. bloß   b. tief   c. höher   d. am niedrigsten

8. Wie viel _____ das Kind?
   a. zahlen   b. zählen   c. wiegt   d. gemessen

9. Die kleine Wohnung hat nicht mehr als 40 _____.
   a. Millimeter   b. Quadratmeter   c. Zentimeter   d. Milligramm

10. _____ hat dieser Fluss?
    a. Welche Tiefe   b. Keine Höhe   c. Wohin   d. Wie lange

11. Dreißig _____ durch zehn macht drei.
    a. mal   b. hoch   c. geteilt   d. gewogen

12. Der Basketballspieler ist mehr als 2 Meter _____.
    a. hoch   b. tief   c. Pfund   d. groß

13. Die dünne Frau soll ein bisschen _____.
    a. abgenommen   b. sehr leicht   c. zunehmen   d. ziemlich schwer

14. Der Hund _____ 9 Kilo.
    a. trifft   b. wiegt   c. zählt   d. braucht

15. Die Grenze ist 25 Kilometer von hier _____.
    a. breit   b. aus   c. geteilt   d. entfernt

Clothing and fashion

There are three important German verbs for putting on and taking off clothes. They all come from the same base verb: **ziehen** (**er zieht, er zog, er hat gezogen, er wird ziehen**). The prefixes modify the base verb:

anziehen	*to put on (clothes), to dress*
ausziehen	*to take off (clothes), to undress*
umziehen	*to change (clothes)*

Use these verbs to tell what clothing is being put on or taken off:

Ich ziehe eine warme Jacke an.	*I put on a warm jacket.*
Rolf zog sein Hemd aus.	*Rolf took off his shirt.*

You can omit the mention of a particular kind of clothing by using an accusative reflexive pronoun:

Ich werde mich anziehen.	*I'll get dressed.*
Hast du dich noch nicht ausgezogen?	*Haven't you undressed yet?*
Sie soll sich umziehen.	*She should change clothes.*

But when you use a dative reflexive pronoun, an article of clothing can be included again:

Ich ziehe mir eine Jacke an.	*I put on a jacket.*
Ziehst du dir das Hemd aus?	*Are you taking off your shirt?*

Use **tragen** to mean *wear*:

Der Mann trägt eine Brille.	*The man is wearing glasses.*

The verb **haben** also plays a role when you talk about what someone wears:

Er hat eine Mütze auf.	*He has a cap on (his head).*
Er hat ein Hemd an.	*He has a shirt on (his torso).*
Er hat einen Gürtel um.	*He has a belt on (around his waist).*

Now that you have the essential verbs for talking about clothing, let's look at some useful words of apparel for covering the head and shoulders:

die Kopfbedeckung	*headgear*
das Kopftuch	*head scarf*
der Hut	*hat*
die Mütze	*cap*
die Badekappe	*bathing cap*
die Schirmmütze	*cap with visor*

der Schal	scarf
das Halstuch	scarf, muffler
das Schultertuch	shawl

Die Kleidung

Before looking at other kinds of apparel, let's look at some important words that are derived from the verb **kleiden** (*to dress*):

das Kleid	dress
die Kleider	dresses, clothes
die Kleidung	clothing
das Kleidungsstück	article of clothing, garment
der Kleiderbügel	coat hanger
der Kleiderhaken	clothes hook
der Kleiderschrank	wardrobe, dresser
die Kleiderbürste	clothes brush
die Kleiderpuppe	tailor's dummy
die Kleiderstange	clothes rack
kleidsam	becoming (attractive)

ÜBUNG
18·1

Answer the following questions, based on your personal experience if possible. Sample answers are provided in the answer key.

1. Wer zieht die Kinder am Morgen an? _____

2. Was ziehen Sie an? _____

3. Was haben Sie auf? _____

4. Was trägt die alte Dame? _____

5. Welches Kleidungsstück ist sehr kleidsam? _____

6. Was tragen Sie, wenn der Tag sonnig ist? _____

There is a myriad of vocabulary for men's and women's garments. Let's look at some of the most commonly used words for such clothing:

die Unterwäsche (*or* Wäsche)	underwear
das Unterhemd	undershirt
die Unterhose	underpants
der Büstenhalter	brassiere
der Schlüpfer	panties
die Strumpfhose	panty hose
der Strumpf	stocking
die Socke	sock
das T-Shirt	T-shirt
das Sweatshirt	sweatshirt
die Bluse	blouse
der Pullover	sweater

die Hose	*pants, trousers*
die Jeans	*jeans*
der Rock	*skirt*
das Kleid	*dress*
der Sakko	*sports coat*
der Anzug	*suit*
das Kostüm	*formal suit*
das Jackett	*formal jacket*
der Smoking	*tuxedo*
die Fliege	*bow tie*
die Frackschleife	*bow tie (for formal wear)*
die Krawatte	*tie*
die Uniform	*uniform*
der Mantel	*coat*
der Regenmantel	*raincoat*
der Pelzmantel	*fur coat*
der Handschuh	*glove*
der Stiefel	*boot*
die Sandale	*sandal*
der Badeanzug	*swimsuit*
der Bikini	*bikini*
der Schlafanzug	*pajamas*
das Nachthemd	*nightgown*
der Bademantel	*bathrobe*

The following sentences illustrate how these words can be used in sentences:

Wo hast du die neue ... gekauft?	*Where did you buy the new . . .*
... Hose ...	*. . . pants?*
... Strumpfhose ...	*. . . panty hose?*
... Bluse ...	*. . . blouse?*
... Unterhose ...	*. . . underpants?*
... Krawatte ...	*. . . tie?*

... muss gewaschen werden.	*The . . . has to be washed.*
Der Rock ...	*. . . skirt . . .*
Der Bademantel ...	*. . . bathrobe . . .*
Der Pullover ...	*. . . sweater . . .*
Der Schlüpfer ...	*. . . panties . . .*
Der Regenmantel ...	*. . . raincoat . . .*

Warum tragen sie keine ...	*Why aren't they wearing any . . .*
... Socken?	*. . . socks?*
... Strümpfe?	*. . . stockings?*
... Sweatshirts?	*. . . sweatshirts?*
... Anzüge?	*. . . suits?*
... Unterhemden?	*. . . undershirts?*

Katrin hat ... an.	*Katrin has . . . on.*
... eine schöne Bluse ...	*. . . a pretty blouse . . .*
... einen neuen Bikini ...	*. . . a new bikini . . .*
... braune Handschuhe ...	*. . . brown gloves . . .*
... eine Lederjacke ...	*. . . a leather jacket . . .*
... ein rotes Abendkleid ...	*. . . a red evening dress . . .*

Er trägt ...	He's wearing . . .
... eine karierte Fliege.	. . . a checkered bow tie.
... eine alte Strickjacke.	. . . an old cardigan.
... einen gestreiften Mantel.	. . . a striped coat.
... weiße Turnschuhe.	. . . white sneakers.
... einen schwarzen Anorak.	. . . a black windbreaker.
... zerlumpte Jeans.	. . . tattered jeans.

Was für ein Muster hat ...	What pattern does . . . have?
... deine Jacke?	. . . your jacket . . .
... deine Bluse?	. . . your blouse . . .
... dein Hemd?	. . . your shirt . . .

ÜBUNG
18·2

Answer the following questions, based on your personal experience if possible. Sample answers are provided in the answer key.

1. Was tragen Sie heute? _____

2. Welche Farbe hat der neue Büstenhalter? _____

3. Schlafen Sie in einem Nachthemd? _____

4. Hat Ihre Mutter einen Bikini gekauft? _____

5. Was hat Ihr Freund an? _____

6. Tragen die Kinder Stiefel im Sommer? _____

7. Trägt Ihr Mann heute eine Krawatte? _____

8. Was für ein Hemd trägt Ihr Nachbar? _____

9. Was für ein Muster hat sein Pullover? _____

10. Was waschen Sie heute? _____

Die Mode

Some people don't just want to be dressed; they want to be dressed up in the latest fashion. Let's look at some words and phrases that relate to fashion:

nach der neuesten Mode	in the latest fashion
große Mode sein	to be all the rage
in Mode sein	to be in fashion
modebewusst	fashion conscious
modisch	fashionable
altmodisch	old-fashioned
die Sommermodelle	summer fashions
die Wintermodelle	winter fashions
die Herrenmodelle	men's fashions
das Modehaus	fashion boutique

der Modeartikel	fashion accessory
der Modeschöpfer	fashion designer
die Schickeria	the fashionable people, the in-crowd

Karin macht immer jede Mode mit.	Karin always follows every fashion.
Das ist aus der Mode gekommen.	That has come out of fashion.
Es ist nicht mehr modern.	It's not fashionable anymore.

Fashionable and ordinary clothing can be purchased at various stores:

das Geschäft	store
das Hutgeschäft	hat store
das Juweliergeschäft	jewelry shop
das Kaufhaus	department store
das Modegeschäft	fashion store
das Versandhaus	mail-order company
der Damenschneider, die Damenschneiderin	dressmaker
der Laden	shop
die Boutique	boutique

The following words and phrases are useful when shopping for and trying on new things:

der Schlussverkauf	sale
die Qualität	quality
die Sachen	things
der Schmuck	jewelry
die Ohrringe	earrings
die Halskette	necklace
das Armband	bracelet
der Ring	ring
die Hutnadel	hat pin
die Handtasche	handbag

Es passt mir nicht.	It doesn't fit me.
Die Bluse steht dir gut.	The blouse really suits you.
Sie können es gerne anprobieren.	You're welcome to try it on.
Die Auswahl ist groß.	They have a large selection.
Das ist zu teuer.	That's too expensive.
Haben Sie etwas Billigeres?	Do you have something cheaper?
Welche Größe brauchen Sie?	What size do you need?
Diese Bluse können Sie nicht umtauschen.	You can't exchange this blouse.
Die Schuhe sind nicht nach meinem Geschmack.	The shoes aren't to my taste.
Sie sehen sehr schick aus.	You look very smart (fashionable).
Haben Sie eine Umkleidekabine?	Do you have a changing room?

If you're shopping for baby items, you might want to purchase some of the following:

die Babykleidung	baby clothes
das Lätzchen	bib
die Babyschuhe	booties
die Windel	diaper
das Babypuder	baby powder
die Rassel	rattle
der Kinderwagen	buggy

Rewrite each of the following sentences in the past, present perfect, and future tenses.

1. Ich ziehe mir die Hose an.

   PAST _____

   PRESENT PERFECT _____

   FUTURE _____

2. Er trägt neue Turnschuhe.

   PAST _____

   PRESENT PERFECT _____

   FUTURE _____

3. Sie hat einen Pelzmantel an.

   PAST _____

   PRESENT PERFECT _____

   FUTURE _____

4. Der Schauspieler zieht sich um.

   PAST _____

   PRESENT PERFECT _____

   FUTURE _____

5. Diese Sachen müssen gewaschen werden.

   PAST _____

   PRESENT PERFECT _____

   FUTURE _____

Fill in each blank with an appropriate word.

1. Der schüchterne Junge will sich nicht _____.

2. Der Clown hat eine komische _____ auf.

3. Wie lange haben Sie eine Brille _____?

4. Du bist nackt! Zieh _____ an!

5. Dieses Kleidungsstück ist nicht _____.

6. Der Läufer _____ teure Turnschuhe.

7. Warum haben Sie keinen Gürtel _____?

8. Ich habe nur ein Unterhemd und zwei _____.

9. Mein Sohn schläft in einem _____.

10. Diese Blusen sind schon aus der _____ gekommen.

11. Sie lässt sich ein neues Kleid beim _____ machen.

12. Sie können es in der Umkleidekabine _____.

13. Die Fliege gefällt mir nicht. Ich kaufe lieber eine _____.

14. Halsketten kann man im _____ kaufen.

15. Wie _____ mir diese Ohrringe?

ÜBUNG
18·5

Circle the letter of the word or phrase that best completes each sentence.

1. Warum willst du dich wieder _____?
   a. tragen   b. anhaben   c. umziehen   d. anprobieren

2. Der alte Mann hat einen karierten _____ auf.
   a. Hut   b. Mantel   c. Regenmantel   d. Unterwäsche

3. Ich finde Ihren neuen Rock sehr _____.
   a. die Mode   b. kleidsam   c. angezogen   d. getragen

4. Sie ist zu alt _____ zu tragen.
   a. den Laden   b. keine Babyschuhe   c. altmodisch   d. einen Bikini

5. Jeder Soldat bekommt eine neue _____.
   a. Schal   b. Qualität   c. Schlussverkauf   d. Uniform

6. Sie können sich _____ umziehen.
   a. nach der   b. in der   c. etwas Billiges   d. mit einem Anorak
      neuesten Mode   Umkleidekabine

7. Tragt ihr lieber Schuhe oder _____?
   a. Stiefel   b. Handtaschen   c. Armband   d. die Sachen

8. T-Shirts sind _____ gewesen.
   a. eine Hutnadel   b. zerlumpt   c. im Juweliergeschäft   d. große Mode

9. Ich habe dem neuen Baby _____ gekauft.
   a. Ohrringe   b. ein Lätzchen   c. meinen Geschmack   d. dieses Abendkleid

10. Nach einer Dusche trage ich _____.
    a. den Schlussverkauf   b. die Auswahl   c. einen Bademantel   d. einen Stiefel

11. Katrin kennt die neuesten Trends. Sie ist sehr _____.
    a. altmodisch   b. modebewusst   c. gestreift   d. kariert

12. Die hübsche Dame sieht sehr _____ aus.
    a. zerlumpt   b. schick   c. altmodisch   d. billig

13. Es ist zu klein. Haben Sie es in einer anderen _____?
    a. Größe   b. Geschäft   c. Handschuh   d. Versandhaus

14. Ich möchte gerne diesen Anzug _____. Er ist zu groß.
    a. tragen   b. umtauschen   c. gewaschen werden   d. waschen

15. Im großen Kaufhaus kann man auch _____ kaufen.
    a. Boutique   b. das Hutgeschäft   c. Babykleidung   d. den Modenschöpfer

Colors and contrasts

·19·

You may believe that colors and qualities refer strictly to adjectives, for example: *a red dress, a strong man,* and so on. But adjectives often also have nominal forms or are combined with other words to form new nouns and even verbs.

Die Farbe

Let's look at how **die Farbe** (*colors*) are used in various forms. First, colors can be nouns, and the German colors are all neuter (**das**). Some of the basic colors follow:

das Blau	*blue*
das Braun	*brown*
das Gelb	*yellow*
das Grau	*gray*
das Grün	*green*
das Rot	*red*
das Schwarz	*black*
das Weiß	*white*

The following sentences illustrate how the noun forms can be used:

Zeigt die Ampel Grün oder Rot?	*Is the traffic light green or red?*
Er ist bei Gelb über die Ampel gefahren!	*He drove through the light on yellow!*
Sie will aus Schwarz Weiß machen.	*She's trying to argue that black is white.*
Das Braun steht dir nicht.	*Brown doesn't look good on you.*

When German colors begin with a lowercase letter, they are adjectives; they decline and must show gender, number, and case unless they are predicate adjectives. For example, a predicate adjective can stand at the end of a phrase:

Sein neuer Pullover ist rot.	*His new sweater is red.*

Compare the predicate adjective with the following declined adjectives:

	a red sweater	*the yellow blouse*
NOMINATIVE	ein roter Pullover	die gelbe Bluse
ACCUSATIVE	einen roten Pullover	die gelbe Bluse
DATIVE	einem roten Pullover	der gelben Bluse
GENITIVE	eines roten Pullovers	der gelben Bluse

But remember that adjectives can be used as nouns. When they are, they are still declined as adjectives, unlike the nominal form of the colors, which are declined as nouns. **Das Grün** means *green* and is a noun. **Das Grüne** means *the green one* (something that is neuter, such as **das Kleid**) and is an adjective used as a noun. Let's look at the use of a few more colors. Take special note of their English translations.

der blaue Hut, der Blaue	*the blue hat, the blue one*
die graue Katze, die Graue	*the gray cat, the gray one*
das weiße Haus, das Weiße	*the white house, the white one*
die braunen Bären, die Braunen	*the brown bears, the brown ones*
Hast du das weiße Hemd gekauft?	*Did you buy the white shirt?*
Nein, das Blaue.	*No, the blue one.*
Welchen Hut möchtest du?	*Which hat do you want?*
Ich möchte den Schwarzen.	*I'd like the black one.*

Colors can be modified by two important prefixes: **dunkel-** (*dark*) and **hell-** (*bright, light*):

dunkelblau	*dark blue*
dunkelbraun	*dark brown*
dunkelgrau	*dark gray*
dunkelrot	*dark red*
hellblau	*bright blue*
hellgelb	*bright yellow*
hellgrün	*bright green*
hellrot	*bright red*

The following adjectives are also helpful in describing colors:

bunt	*colorful*
farbig	*colorful*
einfarbig	*solid color*
vielfarbig	*multicolored*

And the following vocabulary is derived from the word **die Farbe** (*color*):

die Farbigkeit	*colorfulness*
das Farbnegativ	*color negative*
das Farbfoto	*colored photo*
der Farbstift	*colored pencil*
der Farbstoff	*pigment, dye*
der Farbton	*shade*
färben	*to dye*
farbenblind	*color-blind*
farblos	*colorless*

These following sentences illustrate how colors are used as verbs:

Sie errötet vor Scham.	*She blushed in shame.*
Kannst du diese alten Schuhe weißen?	*Can you whiten these old shoes?*
Er schwärzt ein paar Wörter.	*He blots out a couple of words.*
Die alten Dokumente sind vergilbt.	*The old documents have yellowed.*
Ihm graut es, wenn er nur daran denkt.	*He dreads the very thought of it.*
Die Sonne hat ihren Körper stark gebräunt.	*The sun gave her body a deep tan.*
Kannst du diesen Stoff bläuen?	*Can you dye this material blue?*

So far you've encountered the most common colors. But in today's world colors have shades and tones that require more specific names. Here are a few of these special colors:

beige	*beige*
burgunderrot	*burgundy*
gebrochen weiß	*off-white*
gelbbraun	*tan*
golden	*gold*
indigoblau	*indigo*
lila	*lilac, purple*
metallgrau	*gunmetal gray*
olivgrün	*olive green*
orange	*orange*
pinkfarben	*shocking pink*
purpurrot	*crimson*
rosa	*pink*
scharlachrot	*scarlet*
silbern	*silver*
stahlgrau	*steel gray*
türkisblau	*turquoise blue*
türkisfarben	*turquoise*
türkisgrün	*turquoise green*
violett	*violet (purple)*

In German, colors are used to form a variety of other words and are used in special ways in certain phrases. Let's look at some of the important ones:

gelbsüchtig	*jaundiced*
das Gelbfieber	*yellow fever*
das Gelbkreuz	*mustard gas*
ein Roter, eine Rote	*redhead*
lieber rot als tot	*better red than dead*
rotbäckig	*red-cheeked*
das Rotkäppchen	*Little Red Riding Hood*
der Grünschnabel	*young whippersnapper*
blau	*drunk, wasted* (slang)
blauäugig	*blue-eyed* (also, *naïve*)
braunäugig	*brown-eyed*
die Bräune	*suntan*
der Weißwandreifen	*whitewall tire*
schwarz wie Ebenholz	*black as pitch (black as ebony)*
graubärtig	*gray-bearded*

Das Papier ist grünstichig.	*The paper has a greenish cast.*
Er machte ihr blauen Dunst vor.	*He pulled the wool over her eyes.*
Der alte Mann ist weißhaarig.	*The old man has white hair.*
Er hat sich endlich weißgewaschen.	*He finally cleared his name.*
Der Kerl ist Schwarzfahrer.	*The guy is a fare dodger.*
Hör auf mit dieser ewigen Schwarzmalerei!	*Stop always looking at the dark side of things.*
Der Tag graut.	*Day is dawning.*

Place an X in the blanks under the words that make sense when used with the adjectives on the left.

	Großvater	Auto	Augen	Hemd	See	Himmel
1. blauäugig	_____	_____	_____	_____	_____	_____
2. burgunderrot	_____	_____	_____	_____	_____	_____
3. errötet	_____	_____	_____	_____	_____	_____
4. gelb	_____	_____	_____	_____	_____	_____
5. gelbsüchtig	_____	_____	_____	_____	_____	_____
6. grau	_____	_____	_____	_____	_____	_____
7. grün	_____	_____	_____	_____	_____	_____
8. rot	_____	_____	_____	_____	_____	_____
9. schwarz	_____	_____	_____	_____	_____	_____
10. türkisblau	_____	_____	_____	_____	_____	_____
11. weißhaarig	_____	_____	_____	_____	_____	_____

Die Gegensätze

Contrasts show an opposing relationship between two things. Sometimes these words are true antonyms, but often they are just two strongly opposing ideas. Obviously, the opposite of *white* is *black*. These two words are true antonyms. But *strange* and *ordinary* can contrast something even though they are not antonyms: for example, *a strange concept* and *an ordinary concept*. This section presents true antonyms and numerous other contrasting words. Let's look at some useful contrasting nouns and phrases:

der Mann, die Frau	*man, woman*
der Junge, das Mädchen	*boy, girl*
der Vater, die Mutter	*father, mother*
das Kind, der Erwachsene	*child, adult*
der Himmel, die Hölle	*heaven, hell*
das Gute, das Böse	*good, evil*
das kleinere Übel	*the lesser evil*
die Wurzel allen Übels	*the root of all evil*
Krieg führen, Frieden schließen	*wage war, conclude a peace*
die Ferne, die Nähe	*distance, closeness (vicinity)*
der Tag, die Nacht	*day, night*
die Gesundheit, die Krankheit	*health, sickness*
das Leben, der Tod	*life, death*
der Winter, der Sommer	*winter, summer*
vor Kälte zittern, bei solcher Hitze	*shiver with cold, in such heat*
die Länge, die Kürze	*length, shortness*

die Geschwindigkeit, die Langsamkeit	*speed, slowness*
die Intelligenz, die Dummheit	*intelligence, stupidity*
die Vernunft, der Wahnsinn	*reason, insanity*

Er ist zur Vernunft gekommen.	*He came to his senses.*
Er hat sie in den Wahnsinn getrieben.	*He drove her insane.*

By now it should be clear what contrasts are. The following examples illustrate contrasting nouns used in practical sentences:

Unser Haus blitzt jetzt vor Sauberkeit!	*Our house is sparkling clean now.*
Das wird viel Schmutz machen.	*That's going to make a big mess.*
Die Liebe ist stärker als der Hass.	*Love is stronger than hate.*
Damit kannst du keine Reichtümer erwerben.	*You won't get rich like that.*
Die Armut ist noch ein großes Problem.	*Poverty is still a big problem.*
Der Mann ist ein dreifacher Mörder!	*The man is a three-time murderer.*
Sie war die Retterin dieser politischen Bewegung.	*She was the savior of this political movement.*
Er führt eine Politik der Stärke.	*He's pursuing a policy of power.*
Meine Schwäche ist klassische Musik.	*I have a weakness for classical music.*
Seine Großzügigkeit ist berühmt.	*His generosity is famous.*
Alle kennen seine Geldgier.	*Everyone knows of his greed.*
Sie verwendet große Sorgfalt darauf.	*She puts a lot of care into it.*
Ich kann deine Nachlässigkeit nicht dulden.	*I can't stand your carelessness.*

Naturally, many of these nouns also have adjectival forms:

arm	*poor*
reich	*rich*
gut	*good*
böse	*evil*
friedlich	*peaceful*
kriegerisch	*warlike*
intelligent	*intelligent*
dumm	*stupid*
sorgfältig	*careful*
nachlässig	*careless*
sauber	*clean*
schmutzig	*dirty*
stark	*strong*
schwach	*weak*
großzügig	*generous*

The following word pairs and phrases contain adjectives that are contrasting or are true antonyms. Remember that many adjectives can also be used as adverbs.

alt, jung	*old, young*
besser, schlechter	*better, worse*
bestimmt, unbestimmt	*definite, indefinite*
dick, dünn	*fat, thin*
hoch, niedrig	*high, low*
hübsch, hässlich	*beautiful (handsome), ugly*
nüchtern, betrunken	*sober, drunk*
schnell, langsam	*fast, slow*

wahr, falsch	*true, false*
weltberühmt, unbekannt	*world-famous, unknown*
der erste Satz, der letzte Satz	*the first sentence, the last sentence*
ein trauriger Tag, ein komischer Witz	*a sad day, a funny joke*
ein kompliziertes Problem, eine einfache Idee	*a complicated problem, a simple idea*
Es ist langweilig. Es ist interessant.	*It's boring. It's interesting.*
Es ist wertvoll. Es ist wertlos.	*It's valuable. It's worthless.*
Das Radio ist zu laut.	*The radio is too loud.*
Sei doch mal ruhig!	*Be quiet!*
Er bewegt sich mit steifen Schritten.	*He moves stiffly (with stiff steps).*
Ist es biegsam genug?	*Is it flexible enough?*

ÜBUNG 19·2

Answer the following questions, based on your experience if possible. Sample answers are provided in the answer key.

1. Ist Ihr Vater jung oder alt? _____

2. Ist dieser Roman traurig oder komisch? _____

3. Ist Helga Schneider ein Kind? _____

4. Ist Ihr Schlafzimmer jetzt sauber? _____

5. Warum zittert die Frau so? _____

The following examples illustrate more adjectives used in contrasting sentences:

Der Himmel ist dunkel geworden.	*The sky has grown dark.*
Es ist schon heller Morgen.	*It's already broad daylight.*
Sind diese Tücher schon trocken?	*Are these towels already dry?*
Die Straßen sind naß.	*The streets are wet.*
Kathrin sieht sehr modisch aus.	*Kathrin looks very fashionable.*
So ein Kleid ist sehr altmodisch.	*That kind of dress is very old-fashioned.*
Bist du hungrig?	*Are you hungry?*
Nein, ich bin noch satt.	*No, I'm still full.*
Meine Tochter ist ziemlich faul.	*My daughter's rather lazy.*
Mein Sohn ist ein fleißiger Schüler.	*My son is a diligent student.*
Ich habe viel Geld und wenig Zeit.	*I have a lot of money and little time.*
Sind die Berge weit von hier?	*Are the mountains far from here?*
Die Bibliothek ist ganz nah.	*The library is quite close.*

Contrasts also occur as verbs. Many verbs, when formed as participles, can be used as adjectives. Let's look at some commonly used pairs of contrasting verbs and participles:

abfliegen, landen	*to take off, to land*
anfangen, enden	*to begin, to end*
arbeiten, (sich) ausruhen	*to work, to rest*
einschalten, ausschalten	*to turn on, to turn off*

einsteigen, aussteigen	to get on (board), to get off
finden, verlieren	to find, to lose
fragen, antworten	to ask, to answer
geben, nehmen	to give, to take
helfen, hindern	to help, to hinder
kaufen, verkaufen	to buy, to sell
lachen, weinen	to laugh, to cry
lieben, hassen	to love, to hate
stehen, sitzen	to stand, to sit
vergessen, (sich) erinnern	to forget, to remember
verlassen, mitnehmen	to leave, to take along
beliebt, verachtet	beloved, despised
gebrochen, repariert	broken, repaired
geöffnet, geschlossen	opened, closed

Place an X in the blanks that match each word listed on the left with a contrasting word at the top. Not all of the words on the left match a given contrasting word.

	schnell	Geldgier	Hitze	Wahnsinn	Ferne	kriegerisch
1. schwach	_____	_____	_____	_____	_____	_____
2. geschlossen	_____	_____	_____	_____	_____	_____
3. Kälte	_____	_____	_____	_____	_____	_____
4. Nähe	_____	_____	_____	_____	_____	_____
5. böse	_____	_____	_____	_____	_____	_____
6. langsam	_____	_____	_____	_____	_____	_____
7. verlieren	_____	_____	_____	_____	_____	_____
8. beliebt	_____	_____	_____	_____	_____	_____
9. Langsamkeit	_____	_____	_____	_____	_____	_____
10. Großzügigkeit	_____	_____	_____	_____	_____	_____
11. friedlich	_____	_____	_____	_____	_____	_____
12. Vernunft	_____	_____	_____	_____	_____	_____
13. abfliegen	_____	_____	_____	_____	_____	_____

Rewrite each of the following sentences in the past, present perfect, and future tenses.

1. Das Grau steht ihr nicht.

   PAST _____

   PRESENT PERFECT _____

   FUTURE _____

2. Das Flugzeug landet um 18 Uhr.

   PAST _____

   PRESENT PERFECT _____

   FUTURE _____

3. Sie treibt mich in den Wahnsinn.

   PAST _____

   PRESENT PERFECT _____

   FUTURE _____

4. Man kennt seine Geldgier.

   PAST _____

   PRESENT PERFECT _____

   FUTURE _____

5. Wir steigen am Marktplatz aus.

   PAST _____

   PRESENT PERFECT _____

   FUTURE _____

Fill in each blank with an appropriate word.

1. Wer hat das _____ gekauft?

2. Ist das Kleid rot oder grün? Ich bin _____.

3. Der neue Flügel ist schwarz wie _____.

4. Das Baby hat schöne _____ Augen.

5. Ist diese Bluse türkisblau oder _____?

6. Der arme Mann _____ vor Scham.

7. Dieses Buch ist nicht interessant, sondern _____.

8. Ich kann bei solcher _____ nicht schlafen.

9. Sie arbeitet langsam und _____.

10. Ist der Junge fleißig oder _____?

11. Wer hat das Radio eingeschaltet? Ich kann es nicht _____.

12. Ist es wirklich besser reich als _____ zu sein?

13. Wo ist die Lampe? Das Zimmer ist zu _____!

14. Das Kino ist ganz _____.

15. Sie war einmal weltberühmt. Jetzt ist sie _____.

ÜBUNG
19·6

Circle the letter of the word or phrase that best completes each sentence.

1. Man kann aus_____ nicht Weiß machen.
   a. den Farbton   b. Schwarz   c. die Ampel   d. das Blaue

2. „Willst du den brauen Gürtel?" „Nein, _____."
   a. die Braunen   b. ein Gelber   c. keine Rote   d. den Schwarzen

3. Die Wände sind _____ weiß gestrichen.
   a. gebrochen   b. viel   c. grün   d. türkisblau

4. Ist die junge Italienerin eine _____?
   a. Rote   b. gelbsüchtig   c. farblos   d. Grau

5. Sein neuer BMW ist _____.
   a. burgunderrot   b. lieber rot als tot   c. farblos   d. das Braun

6. Ihr Großvater ist _____ geworden.
   a. weiße Haare   b. blaue Augen   c. Braun   d. graubärtig

7. Sie hat ihm _____ vorgemacht.
   a. den Farbstoff   b. olivgrün   c. blauen Dunst   d. Farbigkeit

8. Das alte Auto hatte _____.
   a. Weißwandreifen   b. das Blaue   c. Schwarzfahrer   d. Rotkäppchen
                            vom Himmel

9. Die kleine Wohnung blitzte _____.
   a. schneller   b. Vernunft   c. ziemlich fleißig   d. vor Sauberkeit

10. Er ist immer betrunken. Ich habe ihn nicht einmal _____ gesehen.
    a. nachlässig   b. nüchtern   c. rotäugig   d. trocken

11. Ich bezahlte 100 Euro dafür, aber es ist _____.
    a. friedlich   b. verachtet   c. weltberühmt   d. wertlos

12. Die Erwachsenen sitzen im Wohnzimmer. _____ spielen im Garten.
    a. Die Blauäugigen   b. Die Kinder   c. Die Sorgfalt   d. Die Retterin

13. Sie war wegen _____ bekannt.
    a. ihrer Großzügigkeit b. Schwäche   c. die altmodischen   d. mit steifen Schritten
                                                     Röcke

14. Wo ist meine Tasche? Ich habe sie _____!
    a. eingestiegen   b. repariert   c. verloren   d. beliebt

15. Man soll nicht _____. Die Liebe ist stärker.
    a. langweilig sein   b. hassen   c. Sorgfalt   d. erinnern
                                                     verwenden

Special expressions

Developing a practical vocabulary in German goes beyond acquiring useful words. There are also many specialized expressions that combine words in such a way that the original meaning of the words is somewhat blurred, and often an entirely new meaning is derived. Some of these expressions are idioms. Others are part of the colloquial language or slang. Some expressions are sentence fragments that are pat responses to something just said. Consider the following English statement and the response to it:

> "Are you interested in accepting this offer?"
> "And how!"

The words *and* and *how* each have a specific function in English, but their combined use in the previous example illustrates an entirely new meaning for these words. German is no different.

Gar

The single word **gar** is a particle that generally translates as *at all*. But it functions in other ways as well. Let's look at how this tiny word affects meaning:

gar nicht	*not at all*
gar kein	*none at all*
gar keiner	*no one at all*
gar keines	*not a single thing whatsoever*
gar nicht so übel	*not so bad at all*

Sie wusste das gar nicht.	*She had no idea whatsoever.*
Er sagt, dass er gar keinen Hunger hat.	*He says that he's not hungry at all.*
Man kann gar nicht anders handeln.	*You can't do it any other way.*
Er hat gar kein Geld.	*He has no money at all.*
Ich wäre gar zu gern mitgegangen.	*I so would have liked to come along.*

Also

This is another tiny word that functions in a few different ways. Its basic meaning is *so* or *well*. Look at how it functions in the following phrases:

Also, gute Nacht.	*Well, good night.*
Also hast du genug Geld?	*So you have enough money, too?*
Also, wie ich schon sagte, das Problem lässt sich nicht lösen.	*Well, as I was saying, the problem can't be solved.*

Also, verstehst du jetzt oder nicht?	*So, do you understand now or not?*
Also schön!	*All right then!*
Na also!	*There you have it!*

Zwar

This little adverb means *admittedly* or *indeed* and alters the meaning of sentences in its own peculiar way:

Sie ist Richterin, und zwar eine strenge.	*She's a judge and indeed a strict one.*
Beherrsche dich, und zwar sofort!	*Get control of yourself, and I mean now!*
Ich wusste es zwar nicht genau.	*I have to admit I wasn't completely sure.*
Er kommt morgen, und zwar gegen Mittag.	*He's coming tomorrow and, indeed, toward noon.*
Sie war zwar auf der Party, aber hat nicht einmal getanzt.	*She was indeed at the party but didn't dance at all.*

Mal

This particle is a shorter version of **einmal** that particularly emphasizes a command:

Hör mal zu!	*Listen up.*
Steh mal auf!	*Get up.*
Komm mal her!	*Come here.*
Sei mal artig!	*Behave yourself.*

Doch

This adverb can mean *but* or *all the same*. But its use goes beyond those simple meanings and often colors the meaning of a sentence in a variety of ways. It can even stand alone as an emphatic response to an inquiry:

Hast du die Hunde nicht gefüttert?	*Didn't you feed the dogs?*
Doch!	*I did!*
Du bist noch nicht gesund!	*You're not well yet.*
Doch!	*Yes I am!*

Let's look at this word's usage in some other examples:

Ich habe das Buch doch gelesen.	*All the same, I read the book.*
Seine Rede war doch ganz langweilig.	*His speech was really quite boring.*
Das hätte sie doch nicht tun sollen.	*She really shouldn't have done that.*
Robert, sei doch ein bisschen artig!	*Robert, try to be a good boy.*
Sie hat doch selbst gefragt, ob er der Dieb wäre.	*She did ask herself if he was the thief.*
Das ist doch nicht zu glauben!	*That's quite unbelievable.*
Das ist doch ein Freund von mir!	*Hey, that's a friend of mine!*
Ich bin doch euer Vater.	*After all, I am your father.*

Now let's look at a variety of pat responses to certain statements or questions:

Wie bitte?	*What? I beg your pardon.*
Wieso denn?	*Why?*
Und wie!	*And how!*
Was ist los?	*What's the matter?*
Los doch!	*Go ahead! Go on!*

Das ist doch herrlich!	*That's really great!*
Das ist doch eine Lüge!	*That's a lie!*
Das ist nicht zu glauben.	*That's unbelievable!*
Das kommt darauf an.	*That depends.*
Ausgezeichnet!	*Excellent!*
Donnerwetter!	*For heaven's sake!*
Du spinnst!	*You're crazy! You're nuts!*
Erstaunlich!	*Astounding!*
Großartig!	*Great!*
Kaum!	*Hardly.*
Kaum zu glauben.	*It's hard to believe.*
Keine Ahnung.	*I have no idea.*
Keine Ursache.	*Don't mention it.*
Leider nicht.	*Unfortunately, not.*
Natürlich.	*Naturally.*
Offenbar.	*Obviously. Clearly.*
Offensichtlich.	*Obviously.*
Scheinbar.	*Apparently. So it seems.*
Selbstverständlich.	*Of course.*
Super!	*Super!*
Tatsächlich?	*Really?*
Toll!	*Terrific!*
Überhaupt nicht.	*Not at all.*
Unglaublich.	*Incredible.*
Unmöglich.	*Impossible.*
Wunderbar!	*Wonderful!*
Wundervoll!	*Wonderful!*

ÜBUNG
20·1

Respond to the following statements or questions. Choose your responses from the previous list. Sample answers are provided in the answer key.

1. Kannst du mir damit helfen? _____

2. Ich habe eine Fahrkarte gekauft, und muss sofort nach Berlin fahren. _____

_____

3. Wirst du das Wochenende im Harz verbringen? _____

4. Onkel Peter hat 500.000 Euro gewonnen! _____

5. Martin Keller ist verhaftet worden. Er ist Taschendieb! _____

_____

6. Willst du mit Marianne und mir zur Party gehen? _____

7. Danke für das schöne Hemd und den Schlips. _____

8. Weißt du, ob Gudrun wieder im Krankenhaus ist? _____

9. Musst du auch am Wochenende arbeiten? _____

10. Herr Benz sagt, dass du den Ring gestohlen hast. _____

Many useful expressions are idioms or colloquialisms. They are as varied in German as similar expressions are in English. Sometimes they even use the same vocabulary as their English counterparts. Let's look at some common examples:

Achtung!	*Attention! Watch out!*
Achtung, fertig, los!	*Get on your marks, get set, go!*
Alle Mann an Bord!	*All hands on deck!*
Armer Kerl.	*Poor guy.*
Bitten machen Sie es sich bequem!	*Please make yourself at home.*
Das ist doch reiner Quatsch!	*That's utter nonsense.*
Der junge Rechtsanwalt ist redegewandt.	*The young lawyer has the gift of gab.*
Die ganze Familie ist vor die Hunde gegangen.	*The whole family went to the dogs.*
Du musst den Kopf hoch tragen.	*You have to hold your head up high.*
Du nimmst mich auf den Arm.	*You're pulling my leg.*
Er freut sich aufs Wochenende.	*He's looking forward to the weekend.*
Er hat schon lange ins Gras gebissen.	*He kicked the bucket long ago.*
Er ist diese Woche nicht bei Kasse.	*He's short on cash this week.*
Er ist seinem Vater wie aus dem Gesicht geschnitten.	*He's a chip off the old block.*
Er war bis über beide Ohren in sie verliebt.	*He was head over heels in love with her.*
Es macht mir nichts aus.	*It doesn't matter to me.*
Frische dein Deutsch auf!	*Brush up your German.*
Gib Acht!	*Pay attention.*
Halt den Mund!	*Shut up!*
Hast du Lust ins Kino zu gehen?	*Do you feel like going to the movies?*
Hau ab!	*Knock it off! Get out!*
Ich bin gespannt diesen neuen Roman zu lesen.	*I'm anxious to read this new novel.*
Ich brach das Eis.	*I broke the ice.*
Ich freue mich sehr darüber.	*I'm really glad about it.*
Ich gebe dir eine Ohrfeige!	*I'll give you a good smack!*
Ich habe den Sommer im Ausland verbracht.	*I spent the summer abroad.*
Ich habe es satt.	*I'm sick of it.*
Ich habe klassische Musik gern.	*I like classical music.*
Ich habe mit dir ein Hühnchen zu rupfen.	*I've got a bone to pick with you.*
Ich kann den Mann nicht leiden.	*I can't stand the man.*
Ich kenne mich in der deutschen Literatur aus.	*I'm rather well versed in German literature.*
Ich war in der Klemme!	*I was in a real fix.*
im Namen aller Studenten	*in the name of all the students*
Kopf oder Zahl?	*Heads or tails?*
Mir war hundeelend.	*I was sick as a dog.*
Nimm dich zusammen!	*Get a grip.*
Seine Frau ist wieder in andern Umständen.	*His wife's in the family way again.*
Sie ist davon begeistert.	*She's enthralled with it.*
Sie können Gift darauf nehmen.	*You can bet your bottom dollar.*
Sie singt gern.	*She likes singing.*
Sie stimmt mit mir überein.	*She agrees with me.*
so viel ich weiß	*as far as I know*
trotz allem	*after all*
übrigens	*by the way*
um so besser	*all the better*

Verschwinde!	*Get out of here!*
von Kopf bis Fuß	*from head to toe*
Vorsicht!	*Careful! Caution!*
Wie immer schwatzt er.	*As usual he's talking a lot of hot air.*

Ich bin ...	*I'm ...*
... dankbar.	*... thankful.*
... aufgeregt.	*... excited.*
... eifersüchtig.	*... jealous.*
... enttäuscht.	*... disappointed.*
... ncugicrig.	*... curious.*
... wütend.	*... enraged.*

Certain German expressions require a reflexive verb. The following examples illustrate the use of reflexives in sentences and how the English translations do not necessarily contain a reflexive:

Beeile dich!	*Hurry up!*
Die Firma will sich von ihr trennen.	*The company wants to dispense with her services.*
Die Kinder fürchten sich vor ihm.	*The children are afraid of him.*
Er hat sich schlecht benommen.	*He behaved badly.*
Er versucht sich ruhig zu verhalten.	*He tries to keep quiet.*
Erinnerst du dich daran?	*Do you remember it?*
Ich kann mich nicht an die neue Wohnung gewöhnen.	*I can't get used to the new apartment.*
Martin hat sich zur Heirat entschlossen.	*Martin decided to get married.*
Sie hat sich gegen die Idee entschieden.	*She decided against the idea.*
Sie hat sich sehr bemüht.	*She really tried hard.*

ÜBUNG
20·2

Answer the following questions, based on your experience if possible. Sample answers are provided in the answer key.

1. Wer ist redegewandt? _____

2. Worüber haben Sie sich gefreut? _____

3. Worauf freuen sich die Kinder? _____

4. Warum war Robert in der Klemme? _____

5. War seine Aussage eine Lüge oder die Wahrheit? _____

_____

6. Was macht den Mann so froh? _____

7. Warum bist du böse auf mich? _____

8. War die Frau sehr krank? _____

9. Hast du Lust eine Radtour zu machen? _____

10. Ist der Sohn seinem Vater ähnlich? _____

Rewrite each of the following sentences in the past, present perfect, and future tenses.

1. Sie hat gar kein Geld.

   PAST _____

   PRESENT PERFECT _____

   FUTURE _____

2. Das sollst du doch nicht sagen.

   PAST _____

   PRESENT PERFECT _____

   FUTURE _____

3. Er glaubt es kaum.

   PAST _____

   PRESENT PERFECT _____

   FUTURE _____

4. Sie freut sich darüber.

   PAST _____

   PRESENT PERFECT _____

   FUTURE _____

5. Sie stimmen mit uns überein.

   PAST _____

   PRESENT PERFECT _____

   FUTURE _____

Fill in each blank with an appropriate word.

1. Das ist doch _____!

2. Seine Firma ist vor die _____ gegangen.

3. Du _____ mich auf den Arm!

4. Ihre Geschichte ist aber _____.

5. Das Publikum war von dem neuen Stück sehr _____.

6. Ich werde meinen _____ hoch tragen.

7. Der Roman war _____ ganz langweilig.

8. Wir entscheiden _____ gegen den Plan.

9. Sie will ihr _____ auffrischen.

10. Du kannst _____ darauf nehmen.

11. Wir haben den ganzen Winter in Goslar _____.

12. Das ist doch reiner _____!

13. _____, fertig, los!

14. Das ist doch eine _____!

15. _____! Ein Auto kommt um die Ecke!

ÜBUNG
20·5

Circle the letter of the word or phrase that best completes each sentence.

1. Das ist doch nicht zu _____.
   a. gar nicht   b. also   c. glauben   d. rupfen

2. Sie ist doch deine _____.
   a. Nacht   b. Mutter   c. Problem   d. Donnerwetter

3. Warum _____ du dich vor uns?
   a. machtest   b. gern   c. begeisterst   d. fürchtest

4. Wir freuen uns schon auf _____.
   a. die Reise   b. diesen   c. Kopf oder Zahl   d. Ausland
                            Geschenken

5. Der komische Mann ist wirklich _____.
   a. übrigens   b. leider   c. ausgemacht   d. redegewandt

6. Das ist eine Lüge! Du _____!
   a. spinnst   b. reiner Quatsch   c. verhieltst   d. verschwindest

7. Niemand spricht. Wie kann ich _____ brechen?
   a. die Ohrfeige   b. das Hühnchen   c. das Gesicht   d. das Eis

8. Das war _____ nicht so übel.
   a. mal   b. gar   c. hundeelend   d. satt

9. _____ haben Sie genug Zeit dafür.
   a. Also   b. Gar keine   c. Toll   d. Gespannt

10. _____ ich weiß, ist sie noch in Süddeutschland.
    a. Trotz allem   b. Übrigens   c. Zwar   d. So viel

11. _____ sieht sie wie eine Königin aus.
    a. Bemüht   b. Von Kopf bis Fuß   c. Gern   d. In der Klemme

12. _____! Warum lügst du wieder?
    a. Übrigens   b. Donnerwetter   c. Verliebt   d. Aufgeregt

13. Haben Sie _____ ins Theater zu gehen?
    a. Super   b. Vorsicht   c. Lust   d. Gift

14. _____ du dich mit Mathematik aus?
    a. Glaubst   b. Machst   c. Kennst   d. Nimmst

15. Die Kinder _____ sich sehr schlecht.
    a. achten   b. tragen   c. benehmen   d. verbrachten

Answer Key

1 Family and friends

1-1 *Sample answers are provided:* 1. Mein Urgroßvater ist neunundachtzig Jahre alt. 2. Der Mann meiner Tante ist mein Onkel. 3. Meine Geschwister sind meine Brüder und Schwestern. 4. Die Tochter meiner Stiefmutter ist meine Stiefschwester. 5. Mein Vetter und meine Kusine wohnen weit weg von mir.

1-2

	Vater	Tochter	Baby	Großmutter	Urgroßvater
1. alt	X	—	—	X	X
2. am ältesten	—	—	—	—	X
3. jung	—	X	X	—	—
4. am jüngsten	—	—	X	—	—
5. klein	—	X	X	—	—

1-3 *Sample answers are provided:* 1. Meine Großmutter sieht sehr alt aus. Sie hat graue Haare. 2. Mein Vater arbeitet bei der Eisenbahn. 3. Meine kleine Schwester ist krank geworden. 4. Mein Vater ist älter als meine Mutter.

1-4

	du	ihr	Sie
1. Tante und Onkel	—	X	—
2. Nachbar	X	—	X
3. Mieter	—	—	X
4. Wirtin	—	—	X
5. Zimmergenosse	X	—	—
6. Neffe	X	—	—
7. Freundin	X	—	—
8. Chef und Klubkamerad	—	—	X
9. Sohn	X	—	—

1-5 *Sample answers are provided:* 1. Mein bester Freund heißt Erik. 2. Meine Wirtin ist ungefähr vierzig Jahre alt. 3. Ich bin Mitglied in einem neuen Tennisklub. 4. Mein Chef wohnt in Heidelberg.

1-6 1. Geschwister 2. Großmutter 3. Vetter (Cousin) 4. Cousine (Kusine) 5. Urgroßmutter 6. Tochter 7. Schwager 8. Schwiegervater 9. Stieftochter 10. Tante 11. Enkelin 12. Onkel 13. Cousine (Kusine) 14. Schwiegermutter 15. Vetter (Cousin)

1-7 1. jung 2. schön (hübsch) 3. klug 4. klein 5. fleißig 6. alt 7. gesund 8. hässlich 9. glücklich 10. groß

1-8 1. Mannschaftskameraden 2. Wirtin 3. Landsmann 4. Mitbewohner 5. Klassenkameraden (Klassenkameradinnen) 6. Mieterin 7. Zimmergenosse

1-9 1. du 2. du 3. ihr 4. du 5. Sie 6. du 7. du 8. du 9. Sie 10. Sie 11. du 12. Sie 13. Sie 14. du 15. ihr

1-10 1. b 2. a 3. d 4. b 5. a 6. a 7. a 8. d 9. b 10. b

2 Occupations

2-1 *Sample answers are provided:* 1. Ich bin Rechtsanwalt. 2. Ein Onkel von mir ist Bauer. 3. Ich wohne in einer Wohnung. 4. Ein Makler kann mir eine neue Wohnung vermitteln. 5. Der Schaffner kontrolliert die Fahrkarten.

2-2

	Arzt	Bauer	Fotograf	Lehrer	Mechaniker	Sänger
1. Prüfung	—	—	—	X	—	—
2. Aufnahme	—	—	X	—	—	—
3. Musik	—	—	—	—	—	X
4. Hammer	—	—	—	—	X	—
5. Zange	—	—	—	—	X	—
6. Spritze	X	—	—	—	—	—
7. Forschung	X	—	—	X	—	—
8. Ernte	—	X	—	—	—	—

2-3 *Sample answers are provided:* 1. Nein. Aber mein Bruder arbeitet jetzt in einem Kaufhaus. 2. Ja, ein Schulkamerad spielt jetzt in Berlin auf einer Bühne. 3. Ein Mechaniker benutzt Hämmer, Schraubenzieher und Zangen.

2-4 1. die Sekretärin 2. die Präsidentin 3. die Beamtin 4. die Direktorin 5. die Leiterin 6. der Dirigent 7. der Chirurg 8. der Pfleger 9. der Koch 10. der Läufer

2-5 1. Arzt 2. Sängerin 3. Bauer 4. Bürgermeisterin 5. Kanzlerin 6. Briefträger 7. Fotografin 8. Taxifahrer 9. Richterin 10. Makler 11. Arbeiter 12. Mechaniker 13. Schaffnerin 14. Dolmetscherin 15. Schauspieler

2-6 1. der Verkäufer (die -in) 2. der Professor (die -in) 3. der Bürgermeister (die -in) 4. der Arbeiter (die -in) 5. der Arzt (die Ä-in) 6. der Bauer (die Bä-in) 7. der Briefträger (die -in) 8. der Schauspieler (die -in) 9. der Makler (die -in) 10. der Bauer (die Bä-in) 11. der Mechaniker (die -in) 12. der Arzt (die Ä-in) 13. der Richter (die -in) 14. der Lehrer (die -in) 15. der Bürgermeister (die -in)

2-7 1. b 2. a 3. d 4. b 5. b 6. d 7. a 8. d 9. b 10. a 11. d 12. c 13. a 14. b 15. c

3 Around the house

3-1 *Sample answers are provided:* 1. Wir haben drei Schlafzimmer in unserem Haus. 2. In unserem Keller gibt es eine Waschmaschine, aber keinen Trockner. 3. Der Bücherschrank ist im Wohnzimmer. 4. Im Esszimmer haben wir acht Stühle. 5. Im Badezimmer haben wir nur eine Badewanne.

3-2

	Badezimmer	Wohnzimmer	Küche	Schlafzimmer	Keller
1. Doppelbett	—	—	—	X	—
2. Sessel	—	X	—	X	—
3. WC	X	—	—	—	—
4. Herd	—	—	X	—	—
5. Dusche	X	—	—	—	—
6. Badewanne	X	—	—	—	—
7. Stehlampe	—	X	—	X	—
8. Kleiderschrank	—	—	—	X	—
9. Heizung	—	—	—	—	X
10. Schreibtisch	—	X	—	X	—

3-3 *Sample answers are provided:* 1. Ich bewahre meine Bücher im Bücherschrank in meinem Schlafzimmer auf. 2. Ich hänge meine Jacke und meinen Hut an der Garderobe auf. 3. Meine Familie frühstückt im Esszimmer. 4. Meine Familie sieht im Wohnzimmer fern. 5. Man kann im Schlafzimmer ein Nickerchen machen.

3-4 1. das Schlafzimmer 2. das Wohnzimmer 3. die Küche 4. das Esszimmer 5. der Flur 6. das Wohnzimmer 7. das Wohnzimmer *or* das Schlafzimmer 8. das Wohnzimmer *or* das Schlafzimmer 9. die Küche 10. der Keller 11. das Esszimmer 12. das Schlafzimmer 13. die Dachkammer 14. das Esszimmer 15. das Schlafzimmer *or* das Wohnzimmer 16. der Keller 17. das Badezimmer 18. der Keller 19. das Badezimmer *or* die Küche 20. die Dachkammer

3-5   1. Wo konnte man seinen Regenmantel aufhängen?

Wo hat man seinen Regenmantel aufhängen können?

Wo wird man seinen Regenmantel aufhängen können?

2. Wir frühstückten jeden Morgen in der Küche.

Wir haben jeden Morgen in der Küche gefrühstückt.

Wir werden jeden Morgen in der Küche frühstücken.

3. Wir empfingen Gäste in diesem großen Zimmer.

Wir haben Gäste in diesem großen Zimmer empfangen.

Wir werden Gäste in diesem großen Zimmer empfangen.

4. Musste Ihr Sohn auch kochen?

Hat Ihr Sohn auch kochen müssen?

Wird Ihr Sohn auch kochen müssen?

5. Mein Vater half meiner Mutter die Wäsche trocknen.

Mein Vater hat meiner Mutter die Wäsche trocknen geholfen.

Mein Vater wird meiner Mutter die Wäsche trocknen helfen.

6. Wer ging unter die Dusche?

Wer ist unter die Dusche gegangen?

Wer wird unter die Dusche gehen?

7. Im Wohnzimmer feierten wir Weihnachten.

Im Wohnzimmer haben wir Weihnachten gefeiert.

Im Wohnzimmer werden wir Weihnachten feiern.

8. Die Kinder wuschen sich die Hände.

Die Kinder haben sich die Hände gewaschen.

Die Kinder werden sich die Hände waschen.

3-6   1. Kleiderschrank   2. Garderobe   3. Waschbecken   4. Dachkammer   5. Lampe *or* Stehlampe   6. Esszimmer   7. Badewanne   8. Schreibtisch   9. Kühlschrank   10. Klavier   11. gekocht   12. Schlafzimmer   13. Aquarium   14. geräumig   15. Herd

3-7   1. b   2. d   3. b   4. c   5. b   6. c   7. c   8. b   9. d   10. b   11. a   12. a   13. b   14. a   15. d

4   Animals

4-1

	braun	gelb	grau	grün	rot	schwarz
1. Hund	X	—	X	—	—	X
2. Katze	X	—	X	—	—	X
3. Kaninchen	—	—	X	—	—	X
4. Maus	—	—	X	—	—	X
5. Ratte	—	—	X	—	—	X
6. Igel	X	—	—	—	—	—
7. Schlange	—	—	—	X	X	X
8. Kanarienvogel	—	X	—	—	—	—
9. Papagei	—	—	—	X	X	—

4-2   *Sample answers are provided:*   1. Igel sind braun.   2. Schlangen sind sehr lang und grün.   3. Hündchen sind sehr klein.   4. Kanarienvögel können singen.   5. Papageien können sprechen.

4-3   *Sample answers are provided:*   1. Der Bauer wohnt in einem Bauernhaus.   2. Die Scheune ist rot.   3. Nein, ein Esel ist kleiner als ein Pferd.   4. Das Vieh wird von dem Bauern gezüchtet.   5. Die Landwirtin milkt die Kühe.   6. Der Landwirt füttert die Enten und Gänse.   7. Die Pferde und Kühe sind auf der Weide.   8. Die Enten und Gänse schwimmen im Teich.   9. Der Schäfer hütet die Schafe.   10. Die Bäuerin hütet die Hühner.

	Haustier	Nutzvieh	wild	harmlos	gefährlich	giftig
1. Schmetterling	—	—	X	X	—	—
2. Schaf	—	X	X	X	—	—
3. Bär	—	—	X	—	X	—
4. Kätzchen	X	—	—	X	—	—
5. Kamel	—	X	X	X	—	—
6. Wal	—	—	X	X	—	—
7. Reh	—	—	X	X	—	—
8. Spinne	—	—	X	X	X	X
9. Henne	—	X	—	X	—	—

4-5   1. Schweine   2. Bauer *or* Landwirt   3. Schäfer   4. Pferde *or* Kühe   5. Esel   6. milkt   7. Kamel   8. kaltblütige   9. harmlos   10. Vogel *or* Schmetterling   11. giftig   12. Wal   13. Hennen   14. Papagei   15. Insekt

4-6   1. Der Schäfer hütete die Schafe.

Der Schäfer hat die Schafe gehütet.

Der Schäfer wird die Schafe hüten.

2. Einige Spinnen waren gefährlich.

Einige Spinnen sind gefährlich gewesen.

Einige Spinnen werden gefährlich sein.

3. Die Hennen legten wenige Eier.

Die Hennen haben wenige Eier gelegt.

Die Hennen werden wenige Eier legen.

4. Der Landwirt fütterte den Esel.

Der Landwirt hat den Esel gefüttert.

Der Landwirt wird den Esel füttern.

5. Die Bauern züchteten das Vieh.

Die Bauern haben das Vieh gezüchtet.

Die Bauern werden das Vieh züchten.

6. Die Katze wog 4 Kilo.

Die Katze hat 4 Kilo gewogen.

Die Katze wird 4 Kilo wiegen.

4-7   1. d   2. a   3. a   4. b   5. c   6. a   7. c   8. a   9. d   10. a   11. a   12. b   13. b   14. c   15. d   16. a   17. b   18. d   19. a   20. b

5   Fun, recreation, and sports

5-1   *Sample answers are provided:*   1. Ich sammle Briefmarken.   2. Ich spiele gern Schach.   3. Mein Freund jagt oder wandert gern.   4. Ich spiele mit meinen Kindern Karten.   5. Meine Schwester geht gerne kegeln.   6. Die Mädchen spielen Schach.   7. Mein Onkel geht oft angeln.

5-2   *Sample answers are provided:*   1. Ich spiele gern Tennis.   2. Man kann in den Bergen klettern.   3. Im Park kann man Fußball spielen, Rad fahren oder joggen.   4. Am Wochenende gehe ich surfen oder segeln.   5. Im Winter kann man Schlittschuh laufen oder Ski laufen.   6. Autorennen und Hockey können gefährlich sein.   7. Man kann die Muskeln durch Gewichtheben trainieren.

5-3

	im Sommer	im Winter	mit einem Ball	Mannschaft
1. Basketball	X	—	X	X
2. Fußball	X	—	X	X
3. Hockey	—	X	—	X
4. Langlauf	—	X	—	—
5. Leichtathletik	X	—	—	—
6. Radfahren	X	—	—	—

		X	—	—	—
7.	Reiten	X	—	—	—
8.	Schach	X	X	—	—
9.	Schlittschuhlaufen	—	X	—	—
10.	Schwimmen	X	—	—	—
11.	Skilaufen	—	X	—	—

5-4 1. Meine Kusine sammelte Briefmarken.

Meine Kusine hat Briefmarken gesammelt.

Meine Kusine wird Briefmarken sammeln.

2. Er erzählte gerne Witze.

Er hat gerne Witze erzählt

Er wird gerne Witze erzählen.

3. Die Jungen gingen rudern.

Die Jungen sind rudern gegangen.

Die Jungen werden rudern gehen.

4. Monika gewann eine Medaille.

Monika hat eine Medaille gewonnen.

Monika wird eine Medaille gewinnen.

5. Andreas fing den Ball nicht.

Andreas hat den Ball nicht gefangen.

Andreas wird den Ball nicht fangen.

6. Diese Mädchen trieben viel Sport.

Diese Mädchen haben viel Sport getrieben.

Diese Mädchen werden viel Sport treiben.

5-5 1. Schlittschuh laufen   2. Bergen   3. Schwimmbad   4. reiten   5. Spaß   6. gefährliche   7. Hanteln   8. läuft   9. fit   10. Rekord   11. Rad fahren   12. Ski laufen   13. segeln   14. Torwart   15. verlieren

5-6 1. c   2. a   3. a   4. a   5. b   6. d   7. b   8. c   9. b   10. d   11. b   12. b   13. c   14. d   15. a

6 Education

6-1 *Sample answers are provided:*   1. Mein Sohn besucht eine Grundschule.   2. Meine Tochter besucht eine Realschule.   3. Nein, mein Bruder ist Gymnasiast auf einem Gymnasium in der Nähe.   4. In der Grundschule lernt man lesen und schreiben.   5. Meine Schwester studiert Mathematik und Physik.   6. Ich gehe an die Universität Hamburg.   7. Nein, mein Sohn muss sitzen bleiben.   8. Ich studiere an der Universität Heidelberg.   9. Ich studiere Jura.   10. Nein, meine Tochter ist wieder durchgefallen.

6-2 *Sample answers are provided:*   1. Ich habe Schulbücher und einen Kuli in meiner Schultasche.   2. Chemie ist sehr schwierig.   3. Deutsch ist ziemlich leicht.   4. Nein, ich muss zu Hause bleiben und lernen.   5. Ich bekomme *gut* in allen Fächern.   6. Nein, die Lehrerin schreibt mit der Kreide.   7. Ich finde Geschichte sehr interessant.   8. *Mangelhaft* ist eine schlechte Note.   9. Ja, mein Sohn ist ein Genie.   10. Die neue Rechtschreibung ist wichtig zu lernen.

6-3 1. Was lerntest du in der Schule?

Was hast du in der Schule gelernt?

Was wirst du in der Schule lernen?

2. Erik studierte Jura.

Erik hat Jura studiert.

Erik wird Jura studieren.

3. Mein Neffe fiel wieder durch.

    Mein Neffe ist wieder durchgefallen.

    Mein Neffe wird wieder durchfallen.

4. Die Kinder besuchten eine neue Schule.

    Die Kinder haben eine neue Schule besucht.

    Die Kinder werden eine neue Schule besuchen.

5. Angela musste sitzen bleiben.

    Angela hat sitzen bleiben müssen.

    Angela wird sitzen bleiben müssen.

6. Die Hauptschule dauerte vier Jahre.

    Die Hauptschule hat vier Jahre gedauert.

    Die Hauptschule wird vier Jahre dauern.

7. Bekamt ihr nur gute Noten?

    Habt ihr nur gute Noten bekommen?

    Werdet ihr nur gute Noten bekommen?

8. Diese Schüler wollten ihre Schule wechseln.

    Diese Schüler haben ihre Schule wechseln wollen.

    Diese Schüler werden ihre Schule wechseln wollen.

9. Ich dankte ihm für das Geschenk.

    Ich habe ihm für das Geschenk gedankt.

    Ich werde ihm für das Geschenk danken.

10. Es tat mir leid.

    Es hat mir leid getan.

    Es wird mir leid tun.

6-4 *Sample answers are provided:* 1. Gymnasium 2. Studentin 3. leicht 4. Note 5. interessant 6. durchgefallen 7. Kuli 8. bedanken 9. Deutsch 10. Wiederhören 11. schreiben 12. schwierig 13. Tafel 14. leid 15. Bundesländer

6-5 1. c 2. a 3. a 4. d 5. b 6. d 7. b 8. b 9. a 10. a 11. b 12. b 13. d 14. b 15. d

7 Holidays

7-1 *Sample answers are provided:* 1. Man feiert in New Orleans Fasching. 2. Am Feierabend lese ich ein Buch oder sehe fern. 3. Der Bürgermeister hat eine lange Festansprache gehalten. 4. Mein Geburtstag ist am zehnten Mai. 5. Unser Hochzeitstag war am vierten Juni. 6. Seit ein paar Jahren feiern deutsche Kinder Halloween. 7. Neujahr ist am ersten Januar. 8. Die ganze Familie schmückt unseren Weihnachtsbaum. 9. Viele Leute tragen zum Fasching Kostüme. 10. Der Osterhase bringt den Kindern bunte Eier.

7-2

	gesetzlich	kirchlich	persönlich
1. Weihnachten	X	X	—
2. Ostern	X	X	—
3. Halloween	—	—	X
4. Hochzeit	—	X	X
5. Jubiläum	—	—	X
6. Tag der Deutschen Einheit	X	—	—
7. Fasching	X	—	X
8. Silvester	X	—	X
9. Geburtstag	—	—	X

10. Muttertag	—	—	X	
11. Feierabend	—	—	X	

7-3 *Sample answers are provided:*   1. Ich bin im August geboren.   2. Ich bin im Jahre 1990 geboren.
3. Ich habe viele Bücher bekommen.   4. Meine Mutter hat eine Geburtstagstorte gebacken.   5. Sein Großvater ist am achten Juli gestorben.   6. Er schämte sich zu Tode, weil er eine schlechte Note bekam.
7. Sie ist bei einem Unglück umgekommen.   8. Seine Beerdigung war am zweiten Dezember.

7-4   1. Wo feierten Sie Weihnachten?

Wo haben Sie Weihnachten gefeiert?

Wo werden Sie Weihnachten feiern?

2. Die Kinder trugen Kostüme.

Die Kinder haben Kostüme getragen.

Die Kinder werden Kostüme tragen.

3. Ich gratulierte ihr zum Geburtstag.

Ich habe ihr zum Geburtstag gratuliert.

Ich werde ihr zum Geburtstag gratulieren.

4. Heute schmückten sie den Weihnachtsbaum.

Heute haben sie den Weihnachtsbaum geschmückt.

Heute werden sie den Weihnachtsbaum schmücken.

5. Zu Ostern bekamen sie Besuch.

Zu Ostern haben sie Besuch bekommen.

Zu Ostern werden sie Besuch bekommen.

6. Die Familie sang Weihnachtslieder.

Die Familie hat Weihnachtslieder gesungen.

Die Familie wird Weihnachtslieder singen.

7. Der Mann kam um.

Der Mann ist umgekommen.

Der Mann wird umkommen.

8. Der Dieb tötete ihn.

Der Dieb hat ihn getötet.

Der Dieb wird ihn töten.

9. Er lebte sorgenfrei.

Er hat sorgenfrei gelebt.

Er wird sorgenfrei leben.

10. Sie schämte sich zu Tode.

Sie hat sich zu Tode geschämt.

Sie wird sich zu Tode schämen.

7-5   1. Neujahr   2. Geburtstag   3. Heiligabend   4. der Tag der Deutschen Einheit   5. Muttertag
6. Tod   7. Ostern   8. Halloween   9. Geburtstagkind   10. Fasching

7-6   1. d   2. c   3. a   4. a   5. b   6. d   7. b   8. a   9. b   10. a   11. b   12. d   13. c
14. b   15. b

8   Theater, music, radio, and television

8-1   *Sample answers are provided:*   1. Ja, ich gehe jeden Monat ins Theater.   2. Ich habe Dramen und Komödien gern.   3. Goethes „Faust" hat mir sehr gefallen.   4. Ich habe die Oper lieber.   5. Meine Lieblingsoper ist Beethovens „Fidelio."   6. Am Ende des Stücks klatscht das Publikum Beifall.   7. Der

Schauspieler in der Hauptrolle hat viel Applaus bekommen.   8. Die Kasse ist von 10 Uhr bis 21 Uhr offen.
9. Ja, sehr gute Plätze. Wir haben ein Abonnement.   10. Ich habe die Eintrittskarten leider verloren.

8-2 *Sample answers are provided:*   1. Wir gehen nur manchmal ins Konzert.   2. Ich habe klassische Musik gern. Mein Mann hat Jazz lieber.   3. Der Chor steht auf der Bühne.   4. Die Sopranistin und der Bariton haben gute Stimmen.   5. Das ist eine Sinfonie von Schumann.   6. Die Marschmusik ist zu laut.   7. Das Orchester spielt die Ouvertüre zu „Wilhelm Tell."   8. Bach hat Orgel gespielt.   9. Wenn der Dirigent erscheint, geht der Vorhang hoch.   10. Der Flügel ist am größten.

8-3 *Sample answers are provided:*   1. Nein, ich gehe morgen in die Oper.   2. Ja, die Filmzensur in Deutschland ist ziemlich streng.   3. Mein Neffe interessiert sich für die Filmkunst.   4. Im Kino läuft ein neuer amerikanischer Wildwestfilm.   5. Die nächste Vorstellung beginnt um 18 Uhr.   6. Dieser Filmstar ist nicht mehr als 30 Jahre alt.   7. Mein Lieblingsfilm ist ein alter Film—„Wir Wunderkinder"   8. Das neue Kinoprogramm ist ziemlich gut.   9. Ich schaue mir gerne Dokumentarfilme an.   10. Die Vorstellung fängt mit der Kinoreklame an.

8-4 *Sample answers are provided:*   1. Ich höre gern Rockmusik im Radio.   2. Nein, ich habe ein altes Radio.   3. Die Kindersendung beginnt um 18 Uhr.   4. Meine Familie sieht jeden Abend fern.   5. Wir haben sieben Fernsehkanäle.   6. Wir haben keine Fernsehantenne. Wir sind verkabelt.   7. Heute Abend wird eine Rede von der Kanzlerin übertragen.

8-5

	Theater	Kino	Konzert	Rundfunk	Fernsehen
1. Stück	X	—	—	—	—
2. Spielfilm	—	X	—	—	—
3. Chor	—	—	X	X	X
4. Sinfonie	—	—	X	X	X
5. Komödie	X	—	—	—	—
6. Nachrichten	—	—	—	X	X
7. Sportsendung	—	—	—	X	X
8. Oper	X	—	X	X	X
9. Dirigent	—	—	X	—	—
10. Ballett	X	—	—	—	X
11. Filmleinwand	—	X	—	—	—
12. Bühne	X	—	—	—	—
13. Flügel	—	—	X	—	—

8-6 1. Er sieht oft fern.

Er sah oft fern.

Er hat oft ferngesehen.

Er wird oft fernsehen.

2. Wir hören dem Lehrer zu.

Wir hörten dem Lehrer zu.

Wir haben dem Lehrer zugehört.

Wir werden dem Lehrer zuhören.

3. Ein Konzert wird übertragen.

Ein Konzert wurde übertragen.

Ein Konzert ist übertragen worden.

Ein Konzert wird übertragen werden.

4. Der Chor steht auf der Bühne.

Der Chor stand auf der Bühne.

Der Chor hat auf der Bühne gestanden.

Der Chor wird auf der Bühne stehen.

5. Ich schaue mir gerne Spielfilme an.

Ich schaute mir gerne Spielfilme an.

Ich habe mir gerne Spielfilme angesehen.

Ich werde mir gerne Spielfilme ansehen.

8-7 *Sample answers are provided:* 1. gerne   2. ins   3. Hauptrolle   4. Bühne   5. läuft   6. Vorstellung   7. Dirigent   8. Sendung   9. übertragen   10. Nachrichten   11. beginnt   12. Fernsehansager   13. hören   14. fern   15. Bildschirm

8-8 1. b   2. a   3. a   4. c   5. d   6. b   7. a   8. d   9. b   10. a   11. c   12. d   13. a   14. a   15. c

9 Transportation

9-1 *Sample answers are provided:* 1. Ich gehe oft zu Fuß zum Stadtpark.   2. Ein Fußgänger soll nicht auf der Autobahn spazieren gehen.   3. Man kann nur in eine Richtung auf einer Einbahnstraße fahren.   4. Ein Rennwagen ist schneller als ein Kombi.   5. Mein Freund fährt oft per Anhalter.   6. Der Taxifahrer wurde von der Polizei gestoppt.   7. Ich will mein Fahrrad reparieren lassen.   8. Wir fahren mit dem Sportwagen in die Stadt.   9. Ich warte auf den Bus.   10. Er hat es verkauft, weil er einen Unfall gehabt hatte.

9-2 *Sample answers are provided:* 1. Man soll auf die Straßenbahn an der Haltestelle warten.   2. Der InterCity kommt am schnellsten nach Freiburg.   3. Ich reise lieber erster Klasse.   4. Man soll vor der Fahrt einen Fahrschein lösen.   5. Ein Kajütboot ist größer als ein Paddelboot.   6. Ein Flugzeugträger trägt Düsenjäger.   7. Viele Matrosen sind noch nicht an Bord des Schiffes.   8. Ein großer Dampfer wird im Hafen anlegen.   9. Ich habe nur einmal einen Doppeldecker gesehen.   10. Alle fünf Minuten startet ein Flugzeug.

9-3   1. Er geht oft zu Fuß.

Er ging oft zu Fuß.

Er ist oft zu Fuß gegangen.

Er wird oft zu Fuß gehen.

2. Radfahren macht Spaß.

Radfahren machte Spaß.

Radfahren hat Spaß gemacht.

Radfahren wird Spaß machen.

3. Er will nicht per Anhalter fahren.

Er wollte nicht per Anhalter fahren.

Er hat nicht per Anhalter fahren wollen.

Er wird nicht per Anhalter fahren wollen.

4. Verpasst er den Bus?

Verpasste er den Bus?

Hat er den Bus verpasst?

Wird er den Bus verpassen?

5. Der Hubschrauber fliegt über der Stadt.

Der Hubschrauber flog über der Stadt.

Der Hubschrauber ist über der Stadt geflogen.

Der Hubschrauber wird über der Stadt fliegen.

9-4 *Sample answers are provided:* 1. gegangen   2. belegt   3. schneller   4. Straßenbahn   5. Autobahn   6. aussteigen   7. S-Bahn   8. Mittelmeer   9. lösen   10. schwarzfahren   11. verpasst   12. Doppeldecker   13. Flut   14. Bord   15. landen

9-5 1. b   2. a   3. d   4. a   5. a   6. a   7. c   8. a   9. b   10. d   11. b   12. c   13. b   14. c   15. a

10 Travel, vacation, and nationality

10-1 *Sample answers are provided:* 1. Ich reise gern in die Alpen.   2. Ich habe jedes Jahr zehn Ferientage.   3. Ich war als Kind in einem Ferienlager.   4. Meine Familie macht im Juli Urlaub.   5. Frau Schäfer ist noch nicht aus dem Urlaub zurück.   6. Mein Freund macht mit seinem Urlaubsgeld eine Afrikareise.   7. Man kann die Karten für eine Stadtrundfahrt im Reisebüro kaufen.   8. Die Reisebegleiterin begleitet die Schülergruppe im Museum.   9. An der Grenze werden Sie kontrolliert werden.   10. Ich suche ein kleines, billiges Hotel.

10-2

	Deutschland	Russland	Polen	Österreich	Norwegen	Schweiz
1. Moskau	—	X	—	—	—	—
2. die Alpen	X	—	—	X	—	X
3. die Elbe	X	—	—	—	—	—
4. Warschau	—	—	X	—	—	—
5. Bremen	X	—	—	—	—	—
6. Wien	—	—	—	X	—	—
7. Bern	—	—	—	—	—	X
8. Fjord	—	—	—	—	X	—
9. Wolga	—	X	—	—	—	—
10. Salzburg	—	—	—	X	—	—
11. Harzgebirge	X	—	—	—	—	—

10-3 *Sample answers are provided:*   1. Ich bin in Kanada geboren.   2. Ja, ich habe vor einer Woche ihre Geburtsurkunde bekommen.   3. Man braucht einen Führerschein, um ein Auto fahren zu dürfen.   4. Ja, mein bester Freund ist von Geburt Engländer.   5. Man braucht einen Reisepass, ein Visum und Passbilder.   6. Ich bin amerikanischer Staatsbürger.   7. Arnold Schwarzenegger ist von Geburt Österreicher.   8. Meine Familie stammt aus Indien.   9. In Belgien spricht man französisch.   10. Die Hauptstadt Norwegens ist Oslo.

10-4   1. Wir reisen nach Griechenland.

Wir reisten nach Griechenland.

Wir sind nach Griechenland gereist.

Wir werden nach Griechenland reisen.

2. Hier werden unsere Pässe kontrolliert.

Hier wurden unsere Pässe kontrolliert.

Hier sind unsere Pässe kontrolliert worden.

Hier werden unsere Pässe kontrolliert werden.

3. Er sucht ein gutes Hotel.

Er suchte ein gutes Hotel.

Er hat ein gutes Hotel gesucht.

Er wird ein gutes Hotel suchen.

4. Ist der Matrose auf Urlaub?

War der Matrose auf Urlaub?

Ist der Matrose auf Urlaub gewesen?

Wird der Matrose auf Urlaub sein?

5. Sie bekommt ihre Geburtsurkunde.

Sie bekam ihre Geburtsurkunde.

Sie hat ihre Geburtsurkunde bekommen.

Sie wird ihre Geburtsurkunde bekommen.

10-5 *Sample answers are provided:*   1. Führerschein   2. Ferien   3. Urlaub   4. Reisebüro   5. Grenze   6. Harz   7. Ansichtskarte   8. Geburtsort   9. Visum   10. deutscher   11. deutsch   12. Hauptstadt   13. aus   14. holländische   15. Französisch

10-6   1. b   2. a   3. d   4. c   5. d   6. b   7. a   8. d   9. a   10. b   11. c   12. d   13. b   14. a   15. b

11 Geography and history

11-1

	Afrika	Asien	Europa	Nordamerika	Südamerika
1. Ägypten	X	—	—	—	—
2. Brasilien	—	—	—	—	X
3. Großbritannien	—	—	X	—	—
4. Indien	—	X	—	—	—
5. Kalkutta	—	X	—	—	—
6. Leipzig	—	—	X	—	—
7. Manila	—	X	—	—	—
8. Mexiko	—	—	—	X	—
9. Minsk	—	—	X	—	—
10. Mongolien	—	X	—	—	—
11. Peru	—	—	—	—	X
12. Polen	—	—	X	—	—
13. Thailand	—	X	—	—	—
14. Toronto	—	—	—	X	—

11-2

Sample answers are provided: 1. Ich habe die amerikanische Staatsangehörigkeit.   2. Asien ist der größte Kontinent.   3. Europa ist der kleinste Kontinent.   4. Am 3. Oktober feiert Deutschland die politische Einheit.   5. Im Sonnensystem gibt es neun Planeten.   6. Morokko liegt in Afrika.   7. Der Panamakanal verbindet das Karibische Meer mit dem Pazifischen Ozean.   8. Portugal liegt an der Westküste Europas.   9. Irland ist eine Insel.   10. Tasmanien gehört zu Australien.

11-3

Sample answers are provided: 1. Es sind 20 Grad Celsius.   2. Hamburg liegt in Norddeutschland.   3. Los Angeles liegt im Westen der USA.   4. Bremerhaven ist an der Küste der Nordsee.   5. Ein großer Regenwald befindet sich in Brasilien.   6. Es ist heute kalt und regnerisch.   7. Ein heißer Wind kommt von Süden.   8. Man kann Gletscher im Norden finden.   9. Mongolien ist ein östliches Land.   10. Der Zug fährt nach Südwesten.

11-4

Sample answers are provided: 1. Ein Römer, Tacitus, hat „Germania" geschrieben.   2. Im Jahr 800 wurde Karl der Große zum Kaiser gekrönt.   3. Gutenberg hat die Druckpresse erfunden.   4. Das Zweite Deutsche Reich wurde 1871 gegründet.   5. Der Erste Weltkrieg endete 1918.   6. Die Deutsche Demokratische Republik wurde in der russischen Zone gegründet.   7. Im Jahr 1961 wurde die Mauer gebaut.   8. Deutschland feiert am 3. Oktober den Tag der Deutschen Einheit.   9. Deutschland gehört jetzt zur Europäischen Union.

11-5

1. Mittlere Geschichte   2. Alte Geschichte   3. Neue Geschichte   4. Neue Geschichte   5. Neue Geschichte   6. Mittlere Geschichte   7. Mittlere Geschichte   8. Neue Geschichte   9. Neue Geschichte   10. Neue Geschichte

11-6

1. Der Kanal verband zwei Seen.

   Der Kanal hat zwei Seen verbunden.

   Der Kanal wird zwei Seen verbinden.

2. Die Temperaturen stiegen.

   Die Temperaturen sind gestiegen.

   Die Temperaturen werden steigen.

3. Die Hauptstadt lag im Osten.

   Die Hauptstadt hat im Osten gelegen.

   Die Hauptstadt wird im Osten liegen.

4. Er erfand eine neue Maschine.

   Er hat eine neue Maschine erfunden.

   Er wird eine neue Maschine erfinden.

5. Hier wurde eine Mauer gebaut.

   Hier ist eine Mauer gebaut worden.

   Hier wird eine Mauer gebaut werden.

1. b   2. a   3. a   4. d   5. a   6. b   7. a   8. d   9. c   10. c   11. b   12. b   13. a   14. c   15. a

12 Farms and gardens

12-1 *Sample answers are provided:*   1. Auf diesem Bauernhof wird Hafer angebaut.   2. Man kann den Boden mit Chemikalien düngen.   3. In meinem Garten wachsen Erbsen und Möhren.   4. Mais soll im Frühling gesät werden.   5. Auf diesem Bauernhof werden Weizen und Gerste kultiviert.

12-2 *Sample answers are provided:*   1. In meinem Blumengarten wachsen nur Tulpen.   2. Er ist von Beruf Gärtner.   3. Ich gebe meiner Freundin einen Blumenstrauß.   4. Die Rosen blühen mitten im Sommer.   5. Die Kinder pflücken Weintrauben.   6. Die weiße Orchidee wächst in einem Topf.   7. Diese Gardenienblüten riechen so schön.   8. Ich jäte Unkraut.   9. Die Erdbeeren schmecken süß.   10. Ich habe Äpfel am liebsten.

12-3

	Bauernhof	Plantage	Gemüsegarten	Blumengarten
1. Rosenstrauch	—	—	—	X
2. Veilchen	—	—	—	X
3. Getreide	X	X	—	—
4. Kaffee	—	X	—	—
5. Blumenkohl	X	—	X	—
6. Kartoffeln	X	—	X	—
7. Schwertlilien	—	—	—	X
8. Fruchtfolge	X	X	—	—
9. Hafer	X	—	—	—
10. Tee	—	X	—	—
11. Obstbaum	X	—	—	—
12. Nelken	—	—	—	X

12-4   1. Was wurde hier angebaut?

   Was ist hier angebaut worden?

   Was wird hier angebaut werden?

   2. Die Bauern säten Weizen.

   Die Bauern haben Weizen gesät.

   Die Bauern werden Weizen säen.

   3. Der Mann fällte die alte Ulme.

   Der Mann hat die alte Ulme gefällt.

   Der Mann wird die alte Ulme fällen.

   4. Hier wuchs Gewürzkraut.

   Hier ist Gewürzkraut gewachsen.

   Hier wird Gewürzkraut wachsen.

   5. Diese Blumen blühten nur im Sommer.

   Diese Blumen haben nur im Sommer geblüht.

   Diese Blumen werden nur im Sommer blühen.

12-5 *Sample answers are provided:*   1. Plantage   2. Kiefern   3. Sommer   4. Birkenrinde   5. Gartenschlauch   6. riechen   7. trägt   8. gepflückt   9. Blumenstrauß   10. Gemüsegarten

12-6   1. b   2. b   3. d   4. d   5. a   6. a   7. b   8. c   9. a   10. a   11. b   12. d   13. a   14. a   15. d

13 The human body

13-1 *Sample answers are provided:*   1. Der Sportler hat einen guten Körperbau.   2. Die Krankenschwester misst mir den Blutdruck.   3. Der Fußballspieler hat sich den rechten Arm gebrochen.   4. Das Kind hat

Schnupfen.   5. Ich habe mir den Fuß verrenkt.   6. Sie hat ein Loch im Zahn.   7. Er kratzt sich den Kopf, weil er Schuppen hat.   8. Man sieht mit den Augen.

13-2   *Sample answers are provided:*   1. Er kämmt sich die Haare.   2. Mein Onkel trägt einen Bart und einen Schnurrbart.   3. Meine Augen sind braun.   4. Meine Großmutter hat Krähenfüße.   5. Der Sportler hat eine breite Brust.   6. Er hat sich den linken Fuß verrenkt.   7. Jeden Morgen waschen sie sich das Gesicht und putzen sich die Zähne.   8. Sie hat sich erbrochen, weil ihr der Magen weh tut.

13-3

	Bein	Blutdruck	Fuß	Haut	Knochen	Sportler
1. behaart	X	—	—	X	—	X
2. dünn	X	—	—	—	—	—
3. gebrochen	X	—	X	—	X	—
4. muskulös	X		—	—	—	X
5. normal	—	X	—	—	—	—
6. verrenkt	—	—	X	—	—	—
7. weich	—	—	—	X	—	—

13-4   1. Sie brach sich das Bein.

Sie hat sich das Bein gebrochen.

Sie wird sich das Bein brechen.

2. Mein Onkel trug einen Schnurrbart.

Mein Onkel hat einen Schnurrbart getragen.

Mein Onkel wird einen Schnurrbart tragen.

3. Die Kinder kämmten sich die Haare.

Die Kinder haben sich die Haare gekämmt.

Die Kinder werden sich die Haare kämmen.

4. Sie atmete durch die Nase.

Sie hat durch die Nase geatmet.

Sie wird durch die Nase atmen.

5. Es tat ihm weh.

Es hat ihm weh getan.

Es wird ihm weh tun.

13-5   *Sample answers are provided:*   1. verrenkt   2. Augen   3. Herz   4. Leber   5. Fingernägel   6. Zehen   7. atmet   8. Hände   9. Brust   10. Falten   11. hinkt   12. behaarte   13. schnarcht   14. Bart   15. Falten

13-6   1. b   2. a   3. d   4. a   5. b   6. d   7. b   8. d   9. a   10. a   11. b   12. c   13. b   14. d   15. d

14   Dining, foods, and beverages

14-1   *Sample answers are provided:*   1. Es gibt ein gutes Restaurant am Marktplatz.   2. Die Küche in diesem Gasthof ist ausgezeichnet.   3. Dieser Zug hat keinen Speisewagen.   4. Die Kinder frühstücken um halb 9.   5. Nein, ich esse lieber griechisch.   6. Der Wirt hat mir die Weinkarte gebracht.   7. Er hat die Suppe empfohlen.   8. Das Trinkgeld war eingeschlossen.   9. Ja, dieser ist schmutzig.   10. Ich trinke gern Mineralwasser.

14-2   *Sample answers are provided:*   1. Im Supermarkt habe ich Rindfleisch, Kartoffeln und Rotkohl gekauft.   2. Zum Frühstück esse ich gern Spiegeleier.   3. Mein Vater und meine Mutter kochen für meine Familie.   4. Im Restaurant bestelle ich Steak, Bratkartoffeln und Salat.   5. Zum Nachtisch esse ich gern Erdbeeren mit Schlagsahne.

14-3   *Sample answers are provided:*   1. Man kann ein Glas Wein an der Theke bestellen.   2. Ich trinke lieber Tee mit Sahne und Zucker.   3. In der Flasche gibt es Apfelsaft.   4. Nein, ich trinke lieber Pils.   5. Auf einer Party trinken die Gäste Sekt oder Weißwein.

	Frühstück	Mittagessen	Abendessen
1. Milch	X	X	X
2. Spargel	—	X	X
3. Blumenkohl	—	X	X
4. Wiener Schnitzel	—	—	X
5. Kompott	—	X	X
6. Sekt	—	—	X
7. Pils	—	—	X
8. Tee	X	X	X
9. Brot mit Butter	X	X	X
10. Apfelstrudel	—	X	X
11. Limonade	—	X	X
12. Orangensaft	X	—	—
13. Schweinefleisch	—	X	X
14. Suppe	—	X	X
15. Schokoladetorte	—	X	X

14-5

1. Sie frühstückten um halb 8.

   Sie haben um halb 8 gefrühstückt.

   Sie werden um halb 8 frühstücken.

2. Er aß keine Butter.

   Er hat keine Butter gegessen.

   Er wird keine Butter essen.

3. Ich trank gern Limonade.

   Ich habe gern Limonade getrunken.

   Ich werde gern Limonade trinken.

4. Mein Vater bestellte das Sauerkraut.

   Mein Vater hat das Sauerkraut bestellt.

   Mein Vater wird das Sauerkraut bestellen.

5. Sie kochte den Kohl 20 Minuten.

   Sie hat den Kohl 20 Minuten gekocht.

   Sie wird den Kohl 20 Minuten kochen.

14-6 *Sample answers are provided:* 1. italienisch 2. Gabel 3. Trinkgeld 4. Gasthaus 5. Mensa 6. Abendessen 7. Käse 8. Kakao 9. reserviert 10. Bier 11. Weißwein 12. eingeladen 13. Spiegeleier 14. Kaffee 15. Sekt

14-7 1. c 2. a 3. a 4. b 5. d 6. b 7. b 8. c 9. d 10. a 11. b 12. d 13. a 14. b 15. c

15 Days, months, and years

15-1 *Sample answers are provided:* 1. Im Frühling werden die Tage länger. 2. Japan ist im Morgenland. 3. Mein Vater arbeitet bis spät in der Nacht im Büro. 4. Heute ist Mittwoch. 5. Mein Geburtstag ist heute in einer Woche.

15-2 *Sample answers are provided:* 1. Meine Tochter ist im Oktober geboren. 2. Der alte Herr ist am zehnten Dezember gestorben. 3. Er blieb den ganzen Sommer zu Besuch. 4. Meine Frau ist Jahrgang 1985. 5. Am vierten Juli feiern sie ihre Unabhängigkeit. 6. Der neue Film beginnt am dreißigsten November. 7. Der Film spielt vom dreißigsten November bis zum elften Dezember. 8. Ich bezahle monatweise meine Miete. 9. Er kam (im Jahr) 2006 aus Irak zurück. 10. Ich bin am ersten August 1988 geboren.

15-3 *Sample answers are provided:* 1. Im 20. Jahrhundert betrat der erste Mensch den Mond. 2. George Washington wurde im 18. Jahrhundert geboren. 3. Ein Jahrhundert hat hundert Jahre.

15-4   1. Die Tage wurden länger.

Die Tage sind länger geworden.

Die Tage werden länger werden.

2. Sie kam am Freitag.

Sie ist am Freitag gekommen.

Sie wird am Freitag kommen.

3. Es geschah im Winter.

Es ist im Winter geschehen.

Es wird im Winter geschehen.

4. Wir feierten den Jahresbeginn.

Wir haben den Jahresbeginn gefeiert.

Wir werden den Jahresbeginn feiern.

5. Sie blieb den ganzen Winter zu Besuch.

Sie ist den ganzen Winter zu Besuch geblieben.

Sie wird den ganzen Winter zu Besuch bleiben.

15-5   *Sample answers are provided:*   1. Morgenland   2. Morgen   3. Abend   4. Sonntag   5. am   6. Woche   7. Geburtstag   8. Datum   9. am   10. Jahrgang   11. Schaltjahr   12. Jahr   13. Jahrhundert   14. Juli   15. Monat

15-6   1. c   2. a   3. d   4. d   5. c   6. a   7. a   8. a   9. c   10. b   11. c   12. d   13. a   14. d   15. b

16   Health

16-1   *Sample answers are provided:*   1. Ja, die beiden Kinder sind wieder gesund.   2. Meine Tante ist von zarter Gesundheit.   3. Meine Gesundheit ist ausgezeichnet.   4. Rauschgift kann Gesundheitsschäden bewirken.   5. Meine Tochter hat die Grippe gehabt.   6. Mein Mann leidet an Heuschnupfen.   7. Ich hatte eine Lungenentzündung.   8. Bei jüngeren Leuten wächst das Hautkrebsrisiko.   9. Ich habe sehr oft Kopfschmerzen.   10. Es tut mir am linken Fuß weh.

16-2   *Sample answers are provided:*   1. Mein Arzt hat seine Praxis in der Nähe des Rathauses.   2. Ja, Doktor Meier ist Onkologe.   3. Ich nehme das Medikament dreimal täglich.   4. Diese Drogen können sehr gefährlich sein.   5. Er hat empfohlen, dass ich meinen Sohn röntgen lasse.   6. Ja, sie wirkt gut und sehr schnell.   7. Der arme Mann leidet an Sodbrennen.   8. Er hat mich auf Diät gesetzt.   9. Nein, ich habe mich vollständig erholt.   10. Der alte Mann war unheilbar krank.

16-3   1. Es ging ihm viel besser.

Es ist ihm viel besser gegangen.

Es wird ihm viel besser gehen.

2. Der Junge erkältete sich.

Der Junge hat sich erkältet.

Der Junge wird sich erkälten.

3. Tat es weh?

Hat es weh getan?

Wird es weh tun?

4. Der Krankenpfleger impfte das Kind.

Der Krankenpfleger hat das Kind geimpft.

Der Krankenpfleger wird das Kind impfen.

5. Sie litt an Krebs.

Sie hat an Krebs gelitten.

Sie wird an Krebs leiden.

16-4   *Sample answers are provided:*   1. zarter   2. gesundheitlich   3. Mir   4. operiert   5. leidet
6. Rauschgift   7. Besserung   8. weh   9. Krankenversicherung   10. röntgen   11. plombiert
12. wirkt   13. Allergie   14. erholen   15. gestorben

16-5   1. c   2. a   3. d   4. a   5. d   6. b   7. a   8. c   9. c   10. a   11. b   12. d   13. b
14. a   15. c

17   Numbers, measurements, and dimensions

17-1   *Sample answers are provided:*   1. Sieben mal drei sind einundzwanzig.   2. Nein, ein Drittel ist größer
als ein Viertel.   3. Ein Sportler aus Deutschland hat den ersten Preis gewonnen.   4. Ich brauche nur ein
achtel Liter Milch.   5. Nein, heute ist der dritte Juli.

17-2   *Sample answers are provided:*   1. Mein Schlafzimmer ist 4 Meter breit.   2. Die Bank ist 2,5 Meter lang.
3. Meine neue Wohnung hat ungefähr 90 Quadratmeter.   4. Das Kind wiegt 7,5 Kilo.   5. Mein Sohn ist
1,75 Meter groß.   6. Ich brauche ein halbes Pfund Zucker.   7. Die Markise ist 2,5 Meter hoch.   8. Der
See ist mehr als 20 Meter tief.   9. München ist 350 Kilometer von hier entfernt.   10. Dieser Wagen
wiegt 2 Tonnen.

17-3   1. Er zählte bis zehn.

Er hat bis zehn gezählt.

Er wird bis zehn zählen.

2. Sie maß das Zimmer aus.

Sie hat das Zimmer ausgemessen.

Sie wird das Zimmer ausmessen.

3. Der dicke Mann nahm ab.

Der dicke Mann hat abgenommen.

Der dicke Mann wird abnehmen.

4. Sie wog mehr als 50 Kilo.

Sie hat mehr als 50 Kilo gewogen.

Sie wird mehr als 50 Kilo wiegen.

5. Der Junge konnte gut rechnen.

Der Junge hat gut rechnen können.

Der Junge wird gut rechnen können.

17-4   *Sample answers are provided:*   1. Zahlen   2. Billion   3. halbes   4. Rechnen   5. mal   6. durch
7. Kilometer   8. sieben   9. erste   10. Vierzehnte   11. wiegt   12. Zentimeter   13. tiefer
14. Kilo   15. Meter

17-5   1. b   2. b   3. b   4. d   5. c   6. a   7. b   8. c   9. b   10. a   11. c   12. d   13. c
14. b   15. d

18   Clothing and fashion

18-1   *Sample answers are provided:*   1. Meine Frau zieht die Kinder am Morgen an.   2. Ich ziehe ein neues
Hemd an.   3. Ich habe einen komischen Hut auf.   4. Die alte Dame trägt eine Brille.   5. Das neue
Schultertuch ist sehr kleidsam.   6. Wenn der Tag sonnig ist, trage ich oft eine Schirmmütze.

18-2   *Sample answers are provided:*   1. Heute trage ich eine weiße Bluse und einen blauen Rock.   2. Der neue
Büstenhalter ist weiß.   3. Nein, ich schlafe in einem Schlafanzug.   4. Nein, sie hat einen Badeanzug
gekauft.   5. Mein Freund hat ein T-Shirt und Jeans an.   6. Nein, im Sommer tragen sie Sandalen.
7. Nein, er trägt eine Krawatte, nur wenn er einen Anzug trägt.   8. Mein Nachbar trägt ein kariertes
Hemd.   9. Sein Pullover ist gestreift.   10. Heute wasche ich die Unterwäsche.

18-3   1. Ich zog mir die Hose an.

Ich habe mir die Hose angezogen.

Ich werde mir die Hose anziehen.

2. Er trug neue Turnschuhe.

  Er hat neue Turnschuhe getragen.

  Er wird neue Turnschuhe tragen.

3. Sie hatte einen Pelzmantel an.

  Sie hat einen Pelzmantel angehabt.

  Sie wird einen Pelzmantel anhaben.

4. Der Schauspieler zog sich um.

  Der Schauspieler hat sich umgezogen.

  Der Schauspieler wird sich umziehen.

5. Diese Sachen mussten gewaschen werden.

  Diese Sachen haben gewaschen werden müssen.

  Diese Sachen werden gewaschen werden müssen.

18-4 *Sample answers are provided:* 1. ausziehen 2. Mütze 3. getragen 4. dich 5. kleidsam 6. trägt 7. um 8. Unterhosen 9. Schlafanzug 10. Mode 11. Damenschneider 12. anprobieren 13. Krawatte 14. Juweliergeschäft 15. stehen

18-5 1. c 2. a 3. b 4. d 5. d 6. b 7. a 8. d 9. b 10. c 11. b 12. b 13. a 14. b 15. c

19 Colors and contrasts

19-1

	Großvater	Auto	Augen	Hemd	See	Himmel
1. blauäugig	X	—	—	—	—	—
2. burgunderrot	—	X	—	X	—	—
3. errötet	X	—	—	—	—	—
4. gelb	—	X	—	X	—	—
5. gelbsüchtig	X	—	X	—	—	—
6. grau	—	X	X	X	X	X
7. grün	—	X	X	X	X	—
8. rot	—	X	—	X	—	X
9. schwarz	—	X	X	X	—	X
10. türkisblau	—	X	—	X	X	X
11. weißhaarig	X	—	—	—	—	—

19-2 *Sample answers are provided:* 1. Mein Vater ist alt. 2. Dieser Roman ist sehr komisch. 3. Nein, Helga Schneider ist eine Erwachsene. 4. Nein, mein Schlafzimmer ist leider ziemlich schmutzig. 5. Sie zittert vor Kälte.

19-3

	schnell	Geldgier	Hitze	Wahnsinn	Ferne	kriegerisch
1. schwach	—	—	—	—	—	—
2. geschlossen	—	—	—	—	—	—
3. Kälte	—	—	X	—	—	—
4. Nähe	—	—	—	—	X	—
5. böse	—	—	—	—	—	—
6. langsam	X	—	—	—	—	—
7. verlieren	—	—	—	—	—	—
8. beliebt	—	—	—	—	—	—
9. Langsamkeit	—	—	—	—	—	—
10. Großzügigkeit	—	X	—	—	—	—
11. friedlich	—	—	—	—	—	X
12. Vernunft	—	—	—	X	—	—
13. abfliegen	—	—	—	—	—	—

19-4 1. Das Grau stand ihr nicht.

  Das Grau hat ihr nicht gestanden.

  Das Grau wird ihr nicht stehen.

2. Das Flugzeug landete um 18 Uhr.

　　Das Flugzeug ist um 18 Uhr gelandet.

　　Das Flugzeug wird um 18 Uhr landen.

3. Sie trieb mich in den Wahnsinn.

　　Sie hat mich in den Wahnsinn getrieben.

　　Sie wird mich in den Wahnsinn treiben.

4. Man kannte seine Geldgier.

　　Man hat seine Geldgier gekannt.

　　Man wird seine Geldgier kennen.

5. Wir stiegen am Marktplatz aus.

　　Wir sind am Marktplatz ausgestiegen.

　　Wir werden am Marktplatz aussteigen.

19-5 *Sample answers are provided:* 1. Kleid 2. farbenblind 3. Ebenholz 4. braune 5. türkisgrün 6. errötete 7. langweilig 8. Hitze 9. sorgfältig 10. faul 11. ausschalten 12. arm 13. dunkel 14. nah 15. unbekannt

19-6 1. b 2. d 3. a 4. a 5. a 6. d 7. c 8. a 9. d 10. b 11. d 12. b 13. a 14. c 15. b

20 Special expressions

20-1 *Sample answers are provided:* 1. Leider nicht. 2. Wieso denn? 3. Das kommt darauf an. 4. Großartig! 5. Das ist doch nicht zu glauben! 6. Und wie! 7. Keine Ursache. 8. Keine Ahnung. 9. Selbstverständlich. 10. Das ist doch eine Lüge!

20-2 *Sample answers are provided:* 1. Der Schauspieler ist redegewandt. 2. Ich habe mich über die vielen Geschenke gefreut. 3. Die Kinder freuen sich auf Weihnachten. 4. Er hat seinen Pass und seinen Koffer verloren. 5. Seine Aussage war doch reiner Quatsch. 6. Seine Frau ist in andern Umständen. 7. Ich habe ein Hühnchen mit dir zu rupfen. 8. Und wie! Ihr war hundeelend! 9. Ich kann leider nicht. 10. Ja, er ist ihm wie aus dem Gesicht geschnitten.

20-3 1. Sie hatte gar kein Geld.

　　Sie hat gar kein Geld gehabt.

　　Sie wird gar kein Geld haben.

2. Das solltest du doch nicht sagen.

　　Das hast du doch nicht sagen sollen.

　　Das wirst du doch nicht sagen sollen.

3. Er glaubte es kaum.

　　Er hat es kaum geglaubt.

　　Er wird es kaum glauben.

4. Sie freute sich darüber.

　　Sie hat sich darüber gefreut.

　　Sie wird sich darüber freuen.

5. Sie stimmten mit uns überein.

　　Sie haben mit uns übereingestimmt.

　　Sie werden mit uns übereinstimmen.

20-4 *Sample answers are provided:* 1. wunderbar 2. Hunde 3. nimmst 4. unglaublich 5. begeistert 6. Kopf 7. doch 8. uns 9. Englisch 10. Gift 11. verbracht 12. Quatsch 13. Achtung 14. Lüge 15. Vorsicht

20-5 1. c 2. b 3. d 4. a 5. d 6. a 7. d 8. b 9. a 10. d 11. b 12. b 13. c 14. c 15. c